PROGRESS IN EDUCATION

PROGRESS IN EDUCATION

VOLUME 55

PROGRESS IN EDUCATION

Additional books and e-books in this series can be found on Nova's website under the Series tab.

PROGRESS IN EDUCATION

VOLUME 55

ROBERTA V. NATA
EDITOR

Copyright © 2019 by Nova Science Publishers, Inc.

All rights reserved. No part of this book may be reproduced, stored in a retrieval system or transmitted in any form or by any means: electronic, electrostatic, magnetic, tape, mechanical photocopying, recording or otherwise without the written permission of the Publisher.

We have partnered with Copyright Clearance Center to make it easy for you to obtain permissions to reuse content from this publication. Simply navigate to this publication's page on Nova's website and locate the "Get Permission" button below the title description. This button is linked directly to the title's permission page on copyright.com. Alternatively, you can visit copyright.com and search by title, ISBN, or ISSN.

For further questions about using the service on copyright.com, please contact:
Copyright Clearance Center
Phone: +1-(978) 750-8400   Fax: +1-(978) 750-4470   E-mail: info@copyright.com.

NOTICE TO THE READER

The Publisher has taken reasonable care in the preparation of this book, but makes no expressed or implied warranty of any kind and assumes no responsibility for any errors or omissions. No liability is assumed for incidental or consequential damages in connection with or arising out of information contained in this book. The Publisher shall not be liable for any special, consequential, or exemplary damages resulting, in whole or in part, from the readers' use of, or reliance upon, this material. Any parts of this book based on government reports are so indicated and copyright is claimed for those parts to the extent applicable to compilations of such works.

Independent verification should be sought for any data, advice or recommendations contained in this book. In addition, no responsibility is assumed by the publisher for any injury and/or damage to persons or property arising from any methods, products, instructions, ideas or otherwise contained in this publication.

This publication is designed to provide accurate and authoritative information with regard to the subject matter covered herein. It is sold with the clear understanding that the Publisher is not engaged in rendering legal or any other professional services. If legal or any other expert assistance is required, the services of a competent person should be sought. FROM A DECLARATION OF PARTICIPANTS JOINTLY ADOPTED BY A COMMITTEE OF THE AMERICAN BAR ASSOCIATION AND A COMMITTEE OF PUBLISHERS.

Additional color graphics may be available in the e-book version of this book.

Library of Congress Cataloging-in-Publication Data

ISBN: 978-1-53614-551-9
ISSN: 1535-4806

Published by Nova Science Publishers, Inc. † New York

Contents

Preface		vii
Chapter 1	Addressing the Crisis in Education: External Threats, Embracing Cognitive Science, and the Need for a More Engaged Citizenry *Joshua Cuevas*	1
Chapter 2	Improving Teaching Practice and Student Learning through Collaborative Action Research: A Case Study of an Effective Partnership Programme Involving Teacher-Educators and Four Middle School Teachers *Alaster R. Gibson and Janette M. Blake*	39
Chapter 3	Best Practice in Mathematics Learning: A Theoretical-Conceptual Discussion for Consideration *Bing H. Ngu, Huy P. Phan, Hui-Wen Wang, Jen-Hwa Shih, Sheng-Ying Shi and Ruey-Yih Lin*	79

Chapter 4	Virtual Educational Guidance Tools for Preventing University Drop-Out Ana B. Bernardo, Antonio Cervero, Constanza López, María Esteban and Ellián Tuero	**113**
Chapter 5	Influences of Cultural Capital on Junior Secondary School Students' Musical Preferences in Hong Kong, China Siu-Hang Kong	**143**
Chapter 6	Digitally Enhanced Spaces: A New Innovation? Damian Maher 167	**167**
Chapter 7	Element Interactivity as a Construct for the Analysis of Science Problem-Solving Processes Munirah Shaik Kadir, Alexander Seeshing Yeung and Anne Forbes	**185**
Chapter 8	Objectivity and Subjectivity in Research Martin Spurin and Paul Stansbie	**205**
Contents of Earlier Volumes		**221**
Index		**229**

PREFACE

Progress in Education. Volume 55 opens with an examination of current issues in education that may impede progress in the field. A variety of external threats are analyzed, including k-12 and university funding and ideological threats in the form of political forces that may attempt to dictate k-12 curriculum.

The research underpinning the following chapter is derived from the authors' personal involvement as teacher-educators in leading a Collaborative Action Research project in a New Zealand suburban Christian school. The overarching research question was, "How might the Collaborative Action Research process affect teachers' professional practice and student learning?"

The authors explore the concept of optimal best practice situated within the context of secondary school mathematics learning. In particular, they provide a complex methodological conceptualization for the understanding of optimal best practice, which takes into account cognitive load imposition.

As new computer and web-based tools present an opportunity to motivate students and improve educational guidance services, this collection describes an online guidance project for secondary school students. The results of this project seem promising for improving the quality of guidance and students' decision-making processes regarding their academic futures.

The relationship between individuals' possession of cultural capital and their musical preferences has been extensively examined in Western society; however, little attention has been given to it in contemporary Chinese contexts. As such, the next study focuses on junior secondary school students' preferred musical listening styles, and their perception of how their cultural capital has shaped their musical preferences in contemporary Hong Kong society.

Many contemporary classrooms are currently designed to be flexible and open. Such designs reflect those that were trialed in classrooms during the mid-1960s to the late 70s when the open plan classroom became popular. The authors explore this initial open plan movement in the 60s and 70s, investigating some of the changes that influence classrooms today.

Following this, the authors illustrate how element interactivity gives rise to different types of cognitive load (intrinsic, extraneous, and germane) when middle school students solve a complex science problem. Analyzing learning tasks in terms of element interactivity assesses their suitability for targeted students, thus lowering the chances of cognitive overload.

The final chapter is directed at scholars thinking of undertaking a research project, particularly at post-graduate level, and discusses the concepts of objectivity and subjectivity in educational research. The authors suggest that true objectivity is challenging due to researchers' familiarity with the subject matter, however research may still be valid providing researchers accept and acknowledge that this plays its part in their interpretation of the findings.

Chapter 1 - This chapter examines current issues in education that may impede progress in the field. A variety of external threats are analyzed, including k-12 and university funding and ideological threats in the form of political forces that may attempt to dictate k-12 curriculum. Business and political forces seek to influence university curriculum through monetary gifts and undermine the credibility of education at the university level through sensationalized media coverage and social media attacks. One avenue to address positive change within the field of education is with an increased emphasis on cognitive science. Myths regarding cognition common among educators are examined along with less well-known approaches that are supported by research on cognition. While the field of education can make internal refinements to strengthen students' outcomes from k-12 through the university level, ultimately the citizens of the United States must make the choice to once again value education as an essential public resource, demand that states fully support it, and protect it from those who would seek to undermine it.

Chapter 2 - This chapter will be of interest to school leaders and teachers desiring to facilitate beneficial and transformational professional development. It is also relevant to teacher-educators working in partnership with schools to foster teacher inquiry leading to improved student outcomes. The research underpinning the chapter is derived from the authors' personal involvement as teacher-educators in leading a Collaborative Action Research (CAR) project involving four middle school (Year 7-10) teachers from a New Zealand, suburban Christian school. The overarching research question was, 'How might the Collaborative Action Research process affect teachers' professional practice and student learning?' The project extended across two consecutive, ten-week school terms during 2017 and included fortnightly, half-day release times to ensure the volunteer teacher participants could effectively and sustainably inquire into their professional practice. During the release times, participants met with the teacher-educators on their neighbouring campus, and engaged in a range of intentional professional activities such as community building, Critical Friends Group discussions, sharing of research literature, reflective journaling and action planning. The meetings allowed the teacher-educators to mentor and motivate the participants through the process of developing and exploring their self-selected inquiries. Time was also set aside to gather triangulated, qualitative data on the efficacy of the programme via semi-formal interviews, focus group sessions and several naturalistic class observations of the teachers *in* action. The four female teacher participants brought a rich, diverse range of professional experiences, qualifications, and leadership responsibilities to the project. Their chosen research topics included; helping students understand and effectively use success criteria and give formative peer feedback; exploring the pedagogical strategy of co-operative group dynamics to strengthen student relationships and improve learning outcomes; developing students' critical thinking skills through interpreting and applying biblical scripture to everyday life with the assistance of digital study tools, and lastly, wrestling with ways to authentically model and integrate virtues into lessons to increase student well-being. The findings affirm the value of Collaborative Action Research as a tool to enable teachers to inquire into their practice leading to improved pedagogy and student achievement.

Chapter 3 - The concept of optimal best practice, reflecting the paradigm of positive psychology, gained extensive research interests from scholars in the fields of Psychology and Education. Optimal best practice, from the perspective of academia, is concerned with the maximization of a person's cognitive competence in a specific domain of academic learning. Achieving optimal best practice, in this sense, requires the 'activation and enactment' of the process of optimization. In recent years, with the emergence of the study of positive psychology, educators and researchers have explored and focused on the development of different theoretical and methodological conceptualizations that could explain a person's experience of optimal best. The authors' significant theoretical and empirical contributions, which consisted of research development in Australia, Malaysia, and Taiwan, have involved the proposition of the Framework of Achievement Bests. The Framework of Achievement Bests (Ngu & Phan, 2018), recently introduced, emphasizes a person's optimal best practice in daily settings. Best practice encompasses three major components: acquired knowledge, personal experience, and personal functioning. The coining of this term 'best practice,' in particular, focuses on different levels of best practice that may exist on a continuum, for example: realistic achievement best and optimal achievement best. This book chapter, in line with the scope of progressive education, explores in detail the concept of optimal best practice, situated within the context of secondary school mathematics learning. In particular, reflecting the authors' recent research development, the authors provide a complex methodological conceptualization for understanding of optimal best practice, which takes into account cognitive load imposition.

Chapter 4 - Educational guidance is a counselling process that addresses students' personal and academic development, although traditionally it has mainly focused on students' academic and vocational decisions. Despite education legislation attempting to ensure the effectiveness of this service, there are many difficulties when it comes to practice, from a lack of teacher training, to a lack of material resources and economic support. However, new computer and web-based tools and programs present an opportunity to increase the motivation of students and improve educational guidance services. The authors describe an on-line guidance project for secondary school students, the results of which seem promising for improving the quality of guidance and the students' decision-making processes about their academic futures, something which may in turn influence a reduction in drop-out rates, especially from university courses.

Chapter 5 - The relationship between individuals' possession of cultural capital and their musical preferences has been extensively examined in Western society; however, little attention has been given to it in contemporary Chinese contexts. Based on Bourdieu's (1973, 1986) concept of cultural capital, this study focuses on junior secondary school students' (Grades Seven to Nine) preferred musical listening styles, and their perception of how their parents' and their own cultural capital have shaped their musical preferences in contemporary Hong Kong society. Two research questions are addressed: (1) How does parental cultural capital influence students' cultural capital? (2) To what extent does students' cultural capital shape their musical preferences in contemporary Hong Kong society? A survey questionnaire was distributed to nine Hong Kong secondary schools in the summer of 2015, followed by an interview survey conducted in the spring of 2016. Based on a synthesis of the 1,614 completed questionnaires and 28 in-depth individual interviews, the quantitative and qualitative findings provide nuanced insights into students' perceptions of their musical preferences, and how one's cultural capital shapes one's musical preferences, in a Hong Kong context. This study finds that the students' music listening not only served as an aesthetic and leisure activity, but also as a means of inculcating cultural capital—proficiency of English—that is legitimate in Hong Kong and deemed an influential factor in school performance. The study also shows that through technological advancements, more specifically a readily-available platform for accessing comprehensive musical resource databases, a new factor has emerged that weakens the relationship between familial social status and students' musical preferences and leads to more autonomous music listening behaviour. In addition, students' musical cultural capital, which is transformed from their parents' cultural capital, may directly and explicitly inform their musical listening behaviour. Further supplementing and revisiting Bourdieu's cultural capital by considering technological invention and conceptualising cultural capital in Hong Kong society, this study offers a new insight on how cultural capital influences one's musical preferences and contributes to students' academic success in contemporary Chinese societies. Given the extensive penetration of technology in all sectors, the study also offers recommendations on how music educators could assist students' music listening by using technological devices to develop their music learning in a more enriched and complete manner.

Chapter 6 - Many contemporary classrooms are now being designed to be flexible and open. Such designs reflect designs that were trialed in classrooms during the mid 1960s to the late seventies when the open plan classroom became popular. Many of these spaces reverted back to closed traditional classrooms with the experiment failing. Starting in the early 2000s such open plan flexible learning spaces again came into vogue. This time around technology played a big part in the use of such spaces. The underlying pedagogical approaches to teaching and learning have also developed from a teacher-centred to a more student-centred approach. This chapter explores the initial open plan movement in the sixties and seventies and then investigates some of the changes that now shape the practices within contemporary learning spaces.

Chapter 7 - Element interactivity is a construct used by cognitive load theory researchers to explain the complexity in learning tasks. Despite advances in cognitive load research, element interactivity in science problem solving has not been vastly studied. In this book chapter, the authors illustrate how element interactivity gives rise to different types of cognitive load (intrinsic, extraneous, and germane) when middle school students solve a complex science problem. Analyzing learning tasks in terms of element interactivity assesses their suitability for targeted students, thus lowering the chances of cognitive overload, and therefore facilitating the cognitive processes for effective learning.

Chapter 8 - The quantitative and qualitative methods used in social science research are founded on different ontological and epistemological understandings and generally associate themselves with contrasting concepts and methods. Traditionally, quantitative approaches tend to focus on objective, statistical descriptions of reality whereas qualitative methods often reject the notion of non-subjective knowledge. This chapter considers these two methods through a critical consideration of the notions of objectivity and subjectivity involved in the research process with particular reference to educational research. Furthermore, it evaluates the value of both and questions whether objectivity is truly achievable leading to criticisms of both objective and subjective research and the debate of value-free and value-laden investigation. This chapter further posits that researchers cannot help but bring with them connections to their subject and that this is part of the investigation process and an integral element of a researcher's understanding of the subject matter. It concludes by emphasising the need to recognise and be aware of the influences the researcher brings to their academic work in the pursuit of objectivity.

In: Progress in Education. Volume 55
Editor: Roberta V. Nata

ISBN: 978-1-53614-551-9
© 2019 Nova Science Publishers, Inc.

Chapter 1

ADDRESSING THE CRISIS IN EDUCATION: EXTERNAL THREATS, EMBRACING COGNITIVE SCIENCE, AND THE NEED FOR A MORE ENGAGED CITIZENRY

Joshua Cuevas[*], PhD
University of North Georgia, Dahlonega, Georgia, US

ABSTRACT

This chapter examines current issues in education that may impede progress in the field. A variety of external threats are analyzed, including k-12 and university funding and ideological threats in the form of political forces that may attempt to dictate k-12 curriculum. Business and political forces seek to influence university curriculum through monetary gifts and undermine the credibility of education at the university level through sensationalized media coverage and social media attacks. One avenue to address positive change within the field of education is with an increased emphasis on cognitive science. Myths regarding cognition common among educators are examined along with less well-known approaches that are

---
[*] Corresponding Author Email: josh.cuevas@ung.edu.

supported by research on cognition. While the field of education can make internal refinements to strengthen students' outcomes from k-12 through the university level, ultimately the citizens of the United States must make the choice to once again value education as an essential public resource, demand that states fully support it, and protect it from those who would seek to undermine it.

INTRODUCTION: CRISIS IN EDUCATION

The focus of this book is progress in education. That would be an outcome all citizens would ostensibly profess support for, even those who have done the most to damage education by defunding k-12 schools and state universities and funneling money and resources towards private and for-profit institutions. But therein lies the issue- exactly how do we achieve progress in education? Here I will argue that the surest way to do that is through citizens making the decision to once again value education and by those in the field creating an increased emphasis on educational research and in particular cognitive science. But first we must look at how we got here and the current threats to education.

There should be little doubt that education in the United States is at a point of crisis. But, contrary to popular belief, that crisis does not stem from the classroom, it does not radiate from the teachers or students, and is not a result of students failing to learn, though that is where progress, if it comes, will happen. Instead, the root of the greatest crises facing education comes from outside education, from political forces, ideological entities, from sources of dark money eager to make their stamp on the future of the country, and from a disengaged populace that does not value education and is largely ambivalent to those forces that may work to undermine it. And if left to their devices, these forces will indeed do great harm to students, their development, and ultimately, the progress this nation makes in science, medicine, business, and most importantly, the human condition.

The threats to education currently encroach upon the field at a variety of levels. K-12 education has been undermined through changes to curriculum and funding being directed away from public schools and towards private entities. Likewise, universities have lost funding in recent decades and turned to part-time faculty at an alarming rate, which disadvantages both students and those professors tasked with teaching them. At the same time, professors across the spectrum have become targets of harassment and attacks due in large part to ideological forces attempting to weaken the influence of higher education on society. And colleges of education in particular have become the focus of intense criticism which has the potential to bring the threats full circle as the preparation of future K-12 teachers is destabilized. We will briefly examine recent developments on all of those fronts before positing possible solutions.

K-12 FUNDING

The number of low income students in the U.S. has increased greatly since the turn of the century, with more than half of all k-12 students now coming from low income households and being eligible for free or reduced lunch (Suitts, 2016). During that time state expenditures per-student have stagnated, and over the last 30 years the achievement gap for low income students has remained unchanged while the proportion of low income students has increased by approximately 20%. The lack of state funding for k-12 education led to an unprecedented wave of teacher strikes in 2018 in the deeply conservative states of West Virginia, Oklahoma, Kentucky, and Arizona. The strikes were the result of a host of issues related to a lack of funding for public education- low teacher salaries, reduction of teacher salaries in comparison to inflation, and reductions in per-pupil spending (Hansen, 2018). While the national and state economies have largely recovered from the recession that began near the end of the G. W. Bush administration in 2007, teachers and students across the country continue to feel the detrimental effects. Funding has returned at a pace that is not on par with inflation, and at the same time political forces have sought to channel more funds towards alternative forms of education shown to have questionable benefits for students.

Meanwhile the federal government has continued the push to privatize education under the auspices of school "choice" and parents' rights by proposing voucher systems that would allow parents to direct money that originally would have been allocated to public schools to instead go to private schools and unregulated charter schools. Recent research evidence has suggested that the privatization of education is likely to have the detrimental effects on the nation's educational system that one of the earliest and most prominent advocates of school choice, Milton Friedman, worried might unfold (Laitsch, 2016). Of the 47 states that have charter or voucher programs that ultimately siphon funds from public schools, the majority have little to no regulations on how those schools function. The charter and private schools can operate under such poor conditions that basic standards are not met, to the extent that in most states teachers are not required to be certified, students with disabilities are not accommodated, and some do not provide for English language learners or require the schools to be registered or accredited (Schott Foundation, 2018).

Yet these policies have gained traction despite the fact that researchers have begun to conclude that, when controlling for confounding variables, public school students outperform their counterparts who attend private and charter schools (Crawford, 2013; Lubienski & Lubienski, 2006; Lubienski, Lubienski, & Crane, 2008). Essentially, when factors such as income and race are controlled for, it becomes clear that private and charter schools have actually done a worse job of educating students, with charter schools doing the most poorly. Indeed, in Michigan, the home state of U.S. Secretary of Education Betsy DeVos, the movement towards school choice and charter schools championed by DeVos herself has had a devastating effect, with the state ranking near the bottom in several critical areas and charter school students performing worse than their public-school counterparts (Emma, Wermund, & Hefling, 2016).

One reason for the apparent disparity in performance is that public schools are under pressure to ensure their students perform well as a result of mandated curricular standards and extensive testing, and thus have been more likely to incorporate new research-based methods (Crawford, 2013). In contrast, the options available to private and charter schools actually allow them to continue to utilize outdated and ineffective methods or to direct resources from the classroom to marketing or sports. And in the case of Michigan, students from the poorest areas have been subjected to the whims and ineffectiveness of for-profit schools that have been characterized by fraud and waste (Emma, Wermund, & Hefling, 2016). Public schools, on the other hand, have been forced to attempt new reforms, which may explain their relative effectiveness compared to those schools defined by "choice." Yet it is the choice model that has become a favorite of federal policymakers such as DeVos.

In this case business interests have teamed with political forces to initiate policies that are not supported by research. If implemented correctly, a shift towards charter schools may ultimately have a beneficial impact, but research would have to be conducted to determine exactly what the characteristics of a successful charter environment would be. Instead of conducting the research and then implementing policy based on the outcomes of those experiments, as the process should unfold, currently business and political entities have enacted changes prior to gathering the evidence of their effectiveness, and a generation of students are becoming unknowing subjects of these experiments. With clever marketing and ballot phrasing on the part of school choice proponents, it has not been difficult to convince voters to support school "choice" that allows them the "freedom" to "reform failing schools." But unfortunately, because politics have superseded research in this case, the issue appears to have halted the progress of education in many districts across the country as funds that could go to making public schools more effective are channeled to less effective private and charter schools.

At a time when the nation's economy has largely recovered from the Bush Recession of 2007, these school funding issues are not so much a matter of money but one of public will (Suitts, 2016). The public has not demanded adequate funding of the public education system, and too often public education is not seen as the investment in human capital that it once was. Absent a citizenry that demands better conditions for students, teachers, and professors, state and federal governments have little incentive to make education a higher financial priority and change funding formulas. As you will see, such issues do not only plague k-12 education but also threaten the viability of higher education as well.

UNIVERSITY FUNDING

In higher education, for more than a decade, funding for public colleges and universities has been declining while enrollment has simultaneously increased (Sav, 2017). During this time student debt in the U.S. has climbed to $1.4 trillion with many students borrowing the maximum and their parents' debt also increasing significantly as they attempt to make up for the shortfall for their children who cannot cover the full costs of college (Bernard & Russell, 2018). Whereas in 1989-1990, half of all seniors had taken out student loans, by 2011-12, that number had risen to 68% (Velez, Woo, National Center for Education Statistics, & RTI, 2017). Despite the increasing costs of college attendance, students feel compelled to enroll regardless of the debt they might incur because statistics show that those who complete college earn substantially more over their lifetime than those who do not. Yet graduates with high levels of student debt have lower rates of graduate school attendance, home ownership, savings, and investments. This suggests an unhealthy spiral leading to greater income inequality with non-college graduates at the bottom, a large portion of college graduates in the middle swimming in debt and unable to afford the middle-class lifestyle of previous generations, and a small portion of those free from debt at the top who are able to purchase homes and comfortably participate in what for them is a thriving economy.

Recently, Webber, a professor of economics at Temple University, examined the reasons for rising tuition costs across the country (2016; 2017). It is no secret that state governments have been cutting funding for universities over the past several decades, with per-student funding dropping more than 30% over the last 30 years (Webber, 2017). Specifically, states have been reducing per-student appropriations that supplement students' tuition which had previously been a large part of meeting operating costs at universities. The result is that tuition has increased dramatically as those funds must be replaced, a burden that falls upon students, thereby inflating the debt that most students are left with. Webber found that bloated administrative budgets (largely via an expansion of those in administrator roles) and new facilities have driven some of the increased costs, but the deficits caused by declining state funding have been by far the biggest factor in the rising cost of college, estimated as being responsible for 75% of the tuition increases. Below in Figure 1 you will see a state-by-state breakdown of changes in tuition and higher education funding from 2000–2014.

State	Current Tuition	Increase in Tuition	State Funding Per Student	Share of Tuition Increase Due to Cuts
Colorado	$15.8k	+$7.7k	-$7.8k	101.3%
Arizona	10.8	+5.4	-6.0	111.3
California	9.0	+4.6	-5.6	123.2
Florida	7.0	+3.7	-5.6	153.1
Iowa	10.0	+5.0	-5.5	110.9
South Carolina	11.5	+6.4	-5.3	83.0
Georgia	7.2	+3.5	-5.1	147.9
Washington	9.6	+4.2	-4.8	114.3
Mississippi	5.8	+2.1	-4.4	211.2
Michigan	11.3	+4.7	-4.0	85.4
Rhode Island	11.5	+5.1	-3.9	76.4
Texas	7.5	+3.2	-3.9	121.2
Oregon	8.5	+3.5	-3.9	111.2
New Mexico	5.2	+2.6	-3.7	142.5
Ohio	10.6	+3.9	-3.6	91.2
Wisconsin	7.1	+2.7	-3.4	123.3
Hawaii	9.2	+4.0	-3.3	84.1
Massachusetts	9.0	+4.1	-3.3	79.9
Missouri	6.3	+2.2	-3.3	151.3
Pennsylvania	11.0	+3.4	-3.2	92.9
Indiana	8.1	+3.0	-3.2	106.7
Minnesota	8.0	+3.7	-3.2	86.0
Tennessee	8.3	+3.7	-3.1	84.6
Idaho	7.2	+3.1	-3.1	101.2
New Jersey	12.5	+5.5	-3.0	54.8
Connecticut	8.0	+2.4	-2.8	119.1
Kansas	6.6	+2.8	-2.8	98.1
Delaware	14.1	+4.9	-2.6	54.0

Figure 1. (Continued)

State	Current Tuition	Increase in Tuition	State Funding Per Student	Share of Tuition Increase Due to Cuts
Nevada	6.0	+2.5	-2.6	106.0
New Hampshire	13.7	+4.7	-2.6	55.2
Kentucky	8.0	+4.2	-2.5	60.1
Virginia	9.4	+4.2	-2.4	56.6
Alabama	8.6	+4.0	-2.0	49.3
Utah	6.1	+2.9	-1.9	66.6
Maine	8.3	+3.2	-1.6	50.1
North Carolina	7.1	+3.9	-1.6	41.5
Louisiana	5.9	+2.5	-1.5	57.8
Oklahoma	5.4	+3.1	-1.5	47.5
South Dakota	6.7	+2.8	-1.4	50.5
Arkansas	5.1	+2.3	-1.2	52.4
West Virginia	5.6	+2.2	-1.1	49.7
Vermont	12.1	+4.7	-0.9	19.0
Nebraska	4.8	+1.8	-0.8	48.3
Maryland	8.3	+2.0	-0.8	37.9
Illinois	9.0	+4.5	-0.4	8.5
New York	6.7	+1.2	-0.4	30.9
Montana	7.0	+2.9	-0.2	8.3
North Dakota	7.2	+3.3	+1.1	—
Alaska	6.3	+2.6	+3.4	—
Wyoming	5.1	+0.7	+7.6	—

Source: Department Of Education (per Webber and FiveThirtyEight, 2016)

Figure 1. Change in Tuition and Funding in Higher Education from 2000–2014.

Clearly, students have carried the burden of the declining funding in higher education. Tuition has increased in all 50 states while tuition funding per student has decreased in 47 of those states. Of those 47 states, the tuition increase is partially attributable to decreases in per-student funding in each one, and the decrease in student funding accounts for the majority of tuition increases in 37 of them with substantial effects in another 8 more. There should be little doubt that such a dynamic is a main factor in the growing student debt crisis.

In addition to inflating tuition costs and driving up student debt, the reductions in the amount of funding universities have received have negatively impacted faculty, and thus, will likely lead to detrimental outcomes in student learning. Over the last several decades there has been a

Addressing the Crisis in Education

sharp increase in adjunct faculty and a sharp decrease in tenured faculty. One report indicates that in 1969, 80% of college faculty were tenured or in tenure track positions while today only 17% of faculty are tenured (Greteman, 2017). Data compiled by the American Association of University Professors shows that part-time faculty increased from 24% in 1975 to 41% in 2011, while tenured and tenure track faculty have declined from 45% to just 24% over that same time frame.

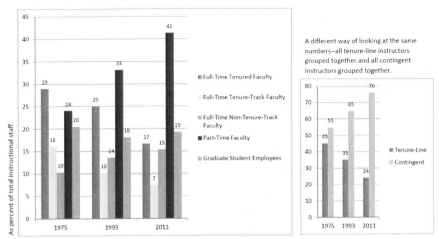

Notes: All institutions, national totals. Figures for 2011 are estimated. Figures are for degree-granting institutions only, but the precise category of institutions included has changed over time. Graduate student employee figure for 1975 is from 1976. Percentages may not add up to 100 due to rounding.

Source: US Department of Education, National Center for Education Statistics, IPEDS Fall Staff Survey; published tabulations only.

Compiled by: AAUP Research Office, Washington, DC; John W. Curtis, Director of Research and Public Policy (3/20/13).

Figure 2. Trends in Instructional Staff Employment Status, 1975-2011.

Adjunct faculty, who make up an increasing portion of university faculty today, earn far less than tenure track faculty and are often paid $3000 or less per course, which equates to roughly $30,000 per year for a full, year-long teaching load, including summer. This is below the individual median income in the United States and roughly half the median household income in the country (U.S. Bureau of the Census, 2018). Adjunct professors also typically do not receive benefits, so they are ineligible for defined retirement accounts or health insurance.

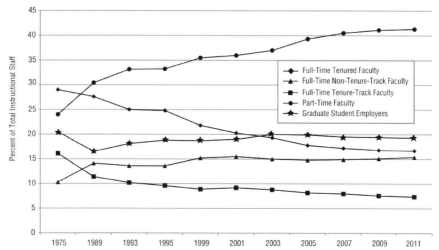

Notes: Figures for 2011 are estimated. Figures from 2005 have been corrected from those published in 2012. Figures are for degree-granting institutions only, but the precise category of institutions included has changed over time. Graduate student employee figure for 1975 is from 1976. Percentages may not add to 100 due to rounding.
Source: US Department of Education, IPEDS Fall Staff Survey.

Figure 3. Trends in Instructional Staff Employment 1975 -2011. All Institutions, National Totals.

Due to these circumstances, colleges cut costs by expanding their use of adjuncts and decreasing the number of tenure track faculty. Yet there is no doubt a cost to students. Adjunct professors often must work multiple jobs, sometimes teaching at several different colleges simultaneously, to compensate for the poor pay and lack of benefits and thus are spread much thinner in their attention to individual courses and students. Certainly, their ability to conduct research, the main hallmark of academic expertise and current knowledge in the field, is diminished to nothing in these circumstances. And adjunct professors tend to have lesser academic qualifications in terms of advanced degrees (often adjuncts are eligible to teach with only a master's degree), high level training at research universities, and research publications that would keep them and their students abreast of the newest knowledge in the field. So while such cost cutting measures may help universities balance their budgets in the face of decreased funding, they negatively impact the adjunct professors who might otherwise have tenure track positions and the students who receive instruction that may be of lesser quality than they would receive from professors with more extensive expertise and a more reasonable workload.

IDEOLOGICAL THREATS

At the same time both k-12 education and higher education have been hampered by inadequate funding that disadvantages students, teachers, and professors, ideological entities have been working to manipulate the curriculum at both levels to conform to their subjective beliefs. Yet those beliefs and the content advocated by those groups are not supported by research and scholarship. If they were, those topics would already be included in the curriculum and there would be no need for political and business interests to attempt to exert their influence upon school districts and universities to force what is taught in the classroom.

K-12 IDEOLOGICAL THREATS

In the modern era, outside forces, whether political or religious, that have attempted to control curriculum in public schools have usually focused their efforts on the science classroom. This goes as far back as the Scopes trial in 1925 when a test case took place and a teacher was charged with violating Tennessee's law that forbade the teaching of evolution in public schools (Larson, 1997). John Scopes, the teacher, was defended by the American Civil Liberties Union and was convicted in a show trial that captured the nation's attention. But while he, and the ACLU, lost the case, science prevailed in the court of public opinion, and the science curriculum was more or less left to experts in the field of science across the country for the next several decades.

Then in the 1980's the states of Alabama, Arkansas, and Louisiana all passed laws that required schools to teach creationism in public schools, giving it equal time in comparison to the Theory of Evolution (Andersen, 2017). The U.S. Supreme Court declared such laws unconstitutional in 1987 as a violation of the Establishment Clause that prevents the government from establishing a state religion, and proponents subsequently began using the more ambiguous (and no more scientifically valid) term "intelligent design" as a way to introduce creationism into the curriculum. This culminated in a landmark trial in Dover, Pennsylvania in 2005 when parents objected to the school board's decision to inject intelligent design into the science curriculum, and the case went to federal court (Andersen, 2017; Boston, 2008). Just as the court did nearly 20 years earlier, the judge in the case ruled that intelligent design was inherently religious in nature and that the teaching of it was unconstitutional and violated the Establishment Clause.

But within several years precedent on the issue was again being tested across the country. Five states introduced "academic freedom" bills in 2008, though the term as used in the bills did not resemble its meaning at the university level (Boston, 2008). Instead, the purpose was to allow educators the "freedom" to introduce supplemental materials that would undermine the information on evolution that students were supposed to be taught according to science standards. In 2009, legislators in the state of Texas voted on whether to include creationism in science standards (New Scientist, 2009). In the same year a school board in North Carolina attempted to add creationism to its science curriculum (Mates, 2009). Similarly, in 2012 a bill in Indiana to allow the integration of creationism into science curriculum in public schools was scheduled for a vote in the state House but was pulled at the last minute due to numerous lawsuits filed against public schools because of it (Church & State, 2012). And in 2018, rather than attempt to inject creationism under the guise of intelligent design or academic freedom, the Arizona school board instead made a move to delete the term "evolution" from the k-12 curriculum and have the theory presented as conjecture (Castle, 2018).

Interestingly, researchers recently examined data from a large sample of 2,000 individuals to ascertain the variables associated with extreme anti-evolution perspectives and found that the strongest predictor of a person's advocacy for a creationism-only curriculum was low educational attainment (Lac, Hemovich, & Himelfarb, 2010). But lest one think that such ideological intrusions on k-12 education are relegated to the subject of evolution, science curriculum has also been infringed upon regarding topics such as the age of the Earth and climate change (Andersen, 2017; Boston, 2008).

One should not make the mistake of believing that interference in science curriculum by outside forces is harmless. Evolution, for example, is the foundational tenet of biology and underlies all concepts in the field, tying all evidence together under a confirmed, well-supported scientific theory. (Here it might be good to point out that contrary to the layman's version of the term "theory," which means a guess or hypothesis, a scientific theory is an explanation for a natural phenomenon that has been *confirmed* by extensive testing and is supported by a myriad of facts and often laws.) If students do not sufficiently learn the principles of biology in high school, they will struggle with the subject at the college level, as that will be their first exposure to it at a time when they are already expected to have a basic grasp of its concepts. This could eventually disqualify those students from careers in fields steeped in biology such as medicine, bioengineering, environmental science, and a host of other related areas. The same can be said for students who are denied instruction in geology (due to its dating of the Earth) and climate science.

It is no small thing that potential doctors, scientists, and researchers may not attain those positions because they lack the prerequisite knowledge and skills coming out of high school due to subjective political and religious factions that object to scientific findings. Thus, it is essential that curriculum, especially science curriculum, be constructed by actual experts in the field who have studied the content for decades- professors, researchers, and teachers. There is a real danger that students, education, and the future of the nation could be put at risk if what students learn in k-12 classrooms is dictated by ideological forces who have the least expertise in the subject matter rather than those who have devoted their lives to studying these issues.

IDEOLOGICAL THREATS TO HIGHER EDUCATION

Historically, universities have been completely independent in their ability to dictate curriculum. Because the vast majority of research compiled through the years has emerged from universities, the expectation has long been that teaching and research would be intricately intertwined at the college level. As professors made new discoveries, experimented, and developed new lines of scholarship, this new knowledge would be brought to the classroom, and students would participate in and learn from this expansion of human knowledge. The university curriculum was supposed to be outside the purview of political and ideological forces seeking to dictate what was taught. Instead, professors were expected to teach from the latest and strongest information their respective fields had to offer without the threat of being imposed upon and having their livelihood challenged if that new knowledge was not popular or politically expedient. Indeed, this academic freedom was at the core of every public university's mission and is the very purpose of tenure.

However, recent events have begun to call that independence and academic freedom into question. As universities struggle to function in the face of declining state funding, some have been tempted to trade that independence and devotion to scholarship by allowing outside groups to have influence in dictating curriculum in exchange for monetary "gifts." In one egregious example, through donations of approximately $48 million to George Mason University, the Koch brothers, wealthy businessmen known for their support for extreme political causes, were able to influence the hiring and work of economics professors, thereby injecting their political ideology into the college classroom (Gluckman, 2018a). They bought influence, and affected students were taught material that was essentially promoted at the behest of the highest bidder rather than because it was academically valid. After inquiries and the protests of both faculty and students, George Mason began an internal investigation into the inappropriate influence of the donors of cash "gifts."

A similar scenario recently played out at Arizona State University (Strauss, 2018). Wealthy donors essentially used their financial gifts to tamper with curriculum and dictate the hiring of professors to fit their ideological mold. After the donation of cash gifts to the university, a department was created that operated like a think tank, espousing particular ideological stances, and the professors who were hired to teach in that department were hired because of their political affiliations and not their academic qualifications. Faculty objected, and there were protests over their assertion that those professors brought in at exorbitant salaries actually lacked the qualifications for the positions they filled. At least one prominent professor resigned in protest.

Faculty at both universities have pushed back, and the presidents at both universities have come under scrutiny for what some view as accepting bribes from these wealthy donors in return for allowing their political and economic ideologies to be taught at the universities under the guise of academic course work. Despite heightened ethical scrutiny of the university presidents involved, backtracking on the part of the universities that have accepted the questionable gifts, protests from faculty and students, and a flood of negative press, the Koch Foundation has actually continued to increase the amount it has given to universities (Gluckman, 2018b) and with it continued its attempt to expand its influence.

SOCIAL MEDIA ATTACKS ON HIGHER EDUCATION

At the same time universities are being starved of funding and outside entities make attempts to buy influence and interject their ideology into curriculum, there is also a loosely organized campaign being mounted against professors to undermine their influence and stifle their teaching. While there has been a long history in the United States of outside influences attacking professors due to unpopular positions or statements, as well as a strong defense of professors' free speech and academic freedom from organizations such as the American Association of University Professors, the advent of social media has allowed for unprecedented levels of vitriol to be directed at professors and the universities that employ them (Scott, 2018).

As a result, professors have become frequent targets of harassment. In some cases that harassment has been a response to situations that took place on campus when students whose ideological stances contrasted with topics covered in class sought out media attention which in turn became an onslaught of personal online attacks against the professors (Quintana, 2017a; Quintana, 2017b; Schmidt, 2017; Vasquez, 2018a). In other cases, professors became targets due to circumstances that were entirely unrelated to classroom, course, or university issues when their political leanings were revealed on social media, and harassment campaigns, including threats of violence and attacks on family members, were undertaken by internet trolls (Cuevas, 2018; Kolowich, 2017). In most of these instances the allegations against the professors were either entirely fabricated or distorted in order to misrepresent the professors' words and actions.

The common mechanism for such attacks is convoluted, with loose ties between the various entities so that when the attacks do cross the line to become criminal harassment and threats of violence, it is difficult for authorities to trace responsibility back to those involved. The ideological motivation and funding are thought to emanate from far-right organizations such as the Bradley Foundation, the Goldwater Institute, and once again, the Koch family foundations (Scott, 2018). Muckraking organizations such as Turning Point USA and CampusReform.com distort, fabricate, and distribute inflammatory information. This falsified information is picked up by anonymous internet users on forums often known for racism, nationalism, White supremacy, misogyny, and hate speech who then launch attacks on the professors from afar through social media and university websites.

Indeed, the Anti-Defamation League's research wing, the Center on Extremism, has noted that during the 2017-2018 academic year, White supremacist intrusions on campuses across the country have increased 77% over the previous academic year in attempts to simultaneously recruit students and undermine faculty and the university (Zahneis, 2018). Recently the Koch Institute attempted to distance itself publicly from the most heinous aspects of the attacks on higher education when a spokesperson for the organization denounced Turning Point USA and the Professor Watchlist and spoke in support of academic freedom (Vasquez, 2018b). Time will tell whether this development indicates a long-term shift in their approach or is simply a superficial attempt to save face publicly as the organization continues to undermine and ideologically influence higher education behind the scenes.

At a time when universities are being starved of funding and simultaneously attempting to maintain enrollment, university presidents may struggle to know how to deal with such attacks. A handful of anonymous users with multiple accounts each may appear to be a large public outcry. Gullible local residents and even politicians may fall prey to the ruses and join the fray (Cuevas, 2018) and thus political pressure may mount. In an effort to suppress the negative publicity, some university presidents have chosen to act prematurely, submit to the pressure, and sanction the professors, thereby violating the educators' rights and giving more power and credence to those outside forces who would seek to undermine the very fabric of higher education (Quintana, 2017b; Scott, 2018; Vasquez, 2018a).

QUESTIONS ABOUT COLLEGES OF EDUCATION AS CENTERS OF INDOCTRINATION

Recently, a professor (Asher, 2018) from a private college leveled harsh criticism specifically at colleges of education in a widely read position piece. While the subject matter fell well outside his field of expertise as an English professor whose academic work has been in the area of fiction, Asher's criticisms are worth examining, particularly because his views seem to represent a wider public perception of education, if not a scholarly one. His central claim seemed to be that higher education is being compromised because most administrators at the college level earn their credentials in schools of education, in fields such as leadership, educational administration, and policy. The issues with this, according to Asher, are that colleges of education have low levels of rigor, are sources of indoctrination, and result in a type of groupthink where their graduates employ similar terminology to proliferate baseless ideological policies.

However, in his argument Asher never takes into account the varied subfields that are common in most colleges of education- preparation programs for elementary, middle, and secondary teachers which comprise by far the greatest number of students in colleges of education; early childhood education; special education; health and physical education; curriculum and instruction; reading specialist majors; human development; counseling; behavior analysis; educational psychology; and others in addition to the aforementioned leadership, administration, and policy. Each of these program areas are quite different.

While there are indeed valid questions about the rigor of educational leadership programs that offer popular, easily earned degrees, often at fly-by-night for-profit colleges, they have little resemblance to other education programs. And those leadership programs tend to encompass only a small percentage of education students at most universities. In contrast, undergraduates in teacher preparation programs that make up the largest proportion of students in education spend a great deal of their time completing coursework in content areas (English, math, science, or social studies) with some coursework devoted to practitioner-oriented topics in education such as classroom management, curriculum, and assessment, and a great deal of time in clinical internships. As seniors, they generally spend 40 – 50 hours each week on these endeavors, which surpasses the amount of time students in most other majors spend on course work. They then undergo a fairly rigorous certification process when they have to pass state and national assessments of content knowledge and pedagogical skills. Programs such as reading, counseling, and special education attempt to bridge the gap between research and practice. And the fields of behavioral analysis and educational psychology are science-oriented in their approach with the majority of knowledge in the areas being derived from university professors conducting and publishing empirical, peer reviewed studies with human subjects. Needless to say, while it may be reasonable to question the rigor of some educational leadership, administration, and policy programs, these areas make up only a small segment of the field of education at the university level and are certainly not representative of the whole.

Asher's (2018) claim that colleges of education are centers of indoctrination as opposed to education is a more insidious one, a charge that has become popular among the broader public and on social media in regard to the general university experience. But the assertion that universities indoctrinate students most often belies a lack of understanding of what "indoctrination" means in psychological terms. Indoctrination occurs when one person convinces another person in the absolute truth of some premise when the first person (the one doing the convincing) has no evidence whatsoever of what he or she is convincing the other person of (Cuevas, 2008). So, if one person was to convince another that he had an invisible magic centaur living in his basement that only he could detect, and the other person was to believe this premise with absolute certainty, obviously in lieu of evidence of any sort, then the second person would be said to have been indoctrinated.

Yet this is very much the opposite of what occurs at universities. Professors are tasked with teaching the most up-to-date, research-based content known to mankind. This is why they are expected to conduct and publish research on a consistent basis, so that they are at the cutting edge of current human knowledge. In short, their instruction is meant to be steeped in the strongest current evidence. Chemistry professors teach from a foundation of the latest studies in the field. Professors of biology, psychology, math, history, and all other fields are expected to teach content based on the best evidence in their respective fields. Even in more subjective areas such as literature and art, professors are expected to have their students come to an understanding of the current scholarly consensus on a topic before pursuing their own creative paths. While no body of knowledge is ever complete and all fields are subject to corrections, new discoveries, and paradigm shifts, the expectation is that university professors will pass along information derived from the soundest evidence to date. Thus, education is literally the antithesis of indoctrination, even if we must adjust our perspectives on an issue from time to time, which is actually a hallmark of science.

While those in the general public will often mistakenly characterize higher education due to a lack of understanding of what indoctrination would actually entail, Asher (2018) unwittingly uses the term correctly even if his conclusions are without merit. By making the claim that colleges of education are machines for indoctrination, he is asserting that they teach content from an ideological perspective and persuade students of that perspective without a basis in evidence. Because ideologies are subjective by nature and are not necessarily dictated by evidence, if indeed students were exposed to them in the absence of evidence and convinced of the infallible truth of that perspective, then this would fit the psychological definition of indoctrination. And if this was the case, then it would likely result in the type of hollow, baseless groupthink Asher suggests.

EMBRACING COGNITIVE SCIENCE

While Asher's (2018) criticisms are themselves ideological in nature and largely echo uninformed opinions parroted on social media, we may use such criticisms to reflect upon the field and attempt to make internal improvements. Too often, in my opinion, the field of education does focus on subjective sociological perspectives that may overemphasize demographic differences and veer towards cultural relativism. Let me be clear in saying that demographic differences such as socio-economic status and racial inequities absolutely do have an impact on students' learning outcomes and are greatly important. And there are many strands of research evidence to support this. However, there is a legitimate question regarding how much colleges of education should focus on such issues when an overemphasis on them may detract from a focus on cognitive science- how the individual may learn beyond broader cultural influences and how the mind processes and stores information.

If one was to thumb through the catalog for the 2018 American Educational Research Association conference, the premier association devoted to educational research with over 25,000 members, you would find an overwhelming number of academic presentation sessions devoted to socio-cultural aspects of education that are often subjective in nature. These made up by far the largest proportion of presentations at this research conference and in the recent past. Such presentations most often focus on what have come to be known as identity issues- gender, race, cultural background, etc. Again, these are certainly important in education and worthy of study. Yet studies based on cognitive science with implications for individual learning were practically nonexistent at the conference. This conference is just one example, but as the primary educational research association in the country, if not the world, it is highly illustrative of the field of education in the U.S. because it represents the faculty and researchers who train or have trained hundreds of thousands of teachers across the nation. Thus, it is indicative of where the focus of the field of education currently is.

While a great deal of the college-level curriculum in education is currently mired in an overemphasis on socio-cultural issues in my opinion, the same types of issues that Asher and so many outside of education criticize the field for, an abundance of myths exist regarding cognitive science and how individuals learn, myths often propagated in those very colleges of education where they should be dispelled. I would argue that if those training to be teachers consistently leave their time in higher education harboring misconceptions about learning, then the current focus in the field is not a productive one and that progress is not being served by the current direction.

COMMON MYTHS ABOUT LEARNING AND COGNITION

Probably the most common and egregious example of a myth regarding learning and cognition that is ubiquitous across the field of education is the concept of learning styles. A majority of practicing teachers believe that students have learning styles and that students will learn more effectively if the teacher tailors instruction to their preferred style. They believe this in spite of the fact that numerous systematic reviews over the last decade have examined the research on the issue and found the premise to be incorrect (Bishka, 2010; Cuevas 2015, 2016, 2017; Fridley & Fridley, 2010; Kirschner & van Merriënboer, 2013; Pashler, McDaniel, Rohrer, & Bjork, 2009; Scott, 2010). In addition to those reviews that analyzed the body of research on the subject, a wave of well-designed empirical studies have tested and consistently disproven the hypothesis and shown that learning styles either do not exist or have no impact on actual learning (Allcock & Hulme, 2010; Cuevas & Dawson, 2018; Husmann & O'Loughlin, 2018; Kozub, 2010; Martin, 2010; Rogowsky, Calhoun, & Tallal, 2015). Yet learning styles-based instruction persists at the k-12 and university levels, which is likely due to a failure of universities to adequately educate students in the cognitive science underlying their field.

While learning styles may be the most widespread and high-profile example, other common myths also persevere. Kirschner and van Merriënboer (2013) have identified a number of misconceptions about learning that permeate education. One is that students today are "digital natives" who have a natural capacity and affinity for learning through technology that previous generations did not possess. But in reality, this is not the case. Unless students become involved in a STEM-oriented educational program, their use of technology may be constant but is likely to be limited to superficial uses of social media and is unlikely to result in deep learning without the purposeful guidance of teachers or programs specifically designed with learning outcomes in mind. Thus, it is important for teachers to understand that technology alone is no panacea for education and will not automatically lead to learning. The technological platform should be carefully designed to assist with scaffolding and help students meet precise learning outcomes. Yet too often teachers have the erroneous assumption that because students "are" digital natives, the inclusion of any technology will result in increased learning and students will automatically use it to expand their knowledge and skills in meaningful ways.

Another myth identified by Kirschner and van Merriënboer (2013) is the ability of students to multi-task during the learning process. Multitasking has long been a valued "skill" in the business world, and often students are encouraged to develop multi-tasking ability in educational environments.

But research in cognitive science has consistently found that splitting attention between any complex tasks greatly decreases performance on all the tasks, whether it be in a business or school environment. This research has been conducted in the sub-fields of attention theory, information processing, and cognitive load theory with results that have been replicated across a variety of experiments. Simply put, when an individual attempts to split his or her focus between different complex tasks, the level of concentration is diminished on each task and less information from each task is devoted to long term memory.

In addition, Kirschner and van Merriënboer (2013) point to the myth of what they call "learners as self-educators," a misconception also highlighted by Clark, Kirschner, and Sweller (2012). The idea that students will learn successfully when they direct and propel their own instruction has become very popular in education, and in practice has resulted in methods such as discovery learning, inquiry-based learning, the democratic classroom, and a variety of other similarly named strategies. However, there are a number of problems with these approaches. First, they tend to be inefficient, and students spend a great deal of class time randomly manipulating variables without making progress, often without discovering the underlying principles they were tasked with finding. Research has shown that this type of instruction can actually *increase* students' misconceptions because they tend to focus their attention on the wrong aspects of a problem, and students remember those incorrect aspects that they spent the most time focusing on instead of the correct principles that are only revealed to them at the end of the lesson.

But unlike the example of learning styles, which research has concluded do not exist as commonly portrayed, the answers to incorporating student-driven learning are much more nuanced. Certainly, we want students to be active in their learning and show high levels of interest and engagement. Research on procedural knowledge (knowledge of how to do things) has shown that it is the most durable form of memory, suggesting great benefits of high levels of student involvement. We do not want classrooms where students are passive receptacles expected to simply memorize static and isolated facts. So in this case the question becomes, what is the correct level of teacher guidance? Research is clear that students do not learn well when left entirely to their own devices but also that the "cram and dump" methods associated with passive learning do not lead to student success. There is not yet a clear consensus on where the optimal point on the continuum of teacher guidance lies, though it appears to lean towards more structured and assertive guidance. But without an understanding of the established cognitive science on the issue and the subtleties involved, teachers will often err on the side of too much random, self-directed student learning that results in outcomes that are less than ideal.

Research has identified many other myths regarding learning and cognition that are commonly-held beliefs of educators, such as the claim that humans only use 10% of their brains, that students' learning is influenced by whether they are "left-brained" or "right-brained," about the causes and signs of dyslexia, and that ingesting sugar causes students to have lower levels of attention, among others (MacDonald, et al., 2017). But my purpose here is not to detail every instance of the numerous misconceptions about learning held by educators. Instead it is to illustrate that despite training in the field, these types of beliefs are still highly prevalent. When professionals in the field hold such widespread misunderstandings about learning, it suggests that the field of education is not adequately focused on cognitive science. One could argue that beyond specific content knowledge in language arts, math, science, and social studies, knowledge regarding how humans learn is the most important trait for educators.

Promising Avenues for Cognitive Science and Classroom Learning

While cognitive myths abound and both teachers and students spend an inordinate amount of time on classroom activities structured upon questionable approaches, there are methods that are less well known among educators that have the potential to improve student outcomes, but only if teachers know about them and purposely incorporate them into instruction. Rohrer and Pashler (2010) have identified several of these. One is retrieval practice, which in its most common form surfaces in the classroom as quizzing. Yet teachers most often view retrieval practice as an assessment technique, to be used to gauge what students know and as a way to produce minor grades, rather than an instructional technique to promote learning. Research has shown consistently that when students make the effort to retrieve previously covered information from memory, those memories and the information gained become more enduring. Moreover, when students retrieve the information in response to an open-ended prompt, drawing upon recall (whether in writing or verbally), as opposed to a closed-ended prompt such as multiple choice that draws upon recognition, more mistakes are made during practice, but students are more likely to retain the correct information long term. This may be incorporated as simply as pairing students and having them quiz each other on recent material using open ended prompts that require students to recall information and elaborate briefly on it.

Another strategy noted by Rohrer and Pashler (2010) is interleaving, which has great potential for math instruction, though the benefits have been revealed across a number of different educational environments. Often, teachers and textbooks present information to students in blocked form (the opposite of interleaving), where students solve a set of problems that all require the same equation. Students simply plug different numbers into the same type of equation and go down the list, repeating the same process over and over. In this scenario students appear on the surface to learn quickly and make few mistakes, but the learning is superficial and based on short term repetition. Research has shown that after blocked instruction students subsequently perform poorly on major tests when they have to choose the correct equation to use out of a variety of options they have practiced with.

In contrast, when material is interleaved during individual problem-solving instructional time, the types of problems are mixed and cannot be solved in a mechanical fashion using the same process for each one. For instance, there may be a variety of problems requiring multiplication, division, fractions, algebra, geometry, etc., presented in a random order, which may require not only different operations, but also for the student to identify which operation is applicable for each particular problem. In this scenario students make more mistakes during practice, likely leading them and teachers to believe it is less effective, but they show stronger performance on major tests when the same types of skills are necessary. And importantly, their problem-solving skills, the central purpose of math instruction, increase to a greater degree.

Rohrer and Pashler also identified temporal spacing as a beneficial learning strategy (2010). It has long been known that cramming just prior to a test is a poor approach and leads to the vast majority of the information being lost from memory soon afterward. Yet this remains a common strategy for students, and the way teachers implement curriculum unintentionally encourages it. We know with reasonable certainty that if students are to retain information long term, then that information must be revisited sporadically, which causes them to cognitively "rehearse" their understanding of it, solidifying it in their memories. Researchers have examined how long the ideal gap should be between the introduction of new information and the time when it is revisited, from a gap of a day or two, to weeks or months. While the findings of such studies have not provided a consensus as to the optimal spacing for long term retention, there is little doubt that some gap is necessary.

But importantly, temporal spacing is not a component of most schools' curricular maps. Instead, due to what teachers view as the constraints imposed upon them by pacing guidelines and standardized testing, they feel that they do not have the time to devote to revisiting information on a regular basis and must constantly move on to the next topic. This most commonly results in a scenario where students are exposed to new material over the course of several days before moving on and then moving on again, only to see that material again for a day or two of review just before the end-of-course test that may be months removed from when they initially covered it. This allows for too much time for them to have forgotten it completely by then. But temporal spacing could easily be incorporated with only a bit of planning for it in mind. For instance, every three weeks, instead of planning for 5 days of instruction before moving on to the next topic, a teacher could plan only 4 days of instruction, which would leave 3 extra days every 3 weeks to revisit information that has been previously covered, thereby promoting long term retention.

One cognitive theory that offers substantial promise is dual coding, but it is rarely addressed in teacher preparation training and thus rarely purposely applied by educators in the classroom environment. Dual coding posits that there are two distinct pathways for processing and encoding information, one linguistic and one visual (Cuevas, 2016; 2017). These two pathways, when activated simultaneously, provide additive cognitive processing power. For example, students can easily be thrown into cognitive overload if they are asked to process too much linguistic information at once, as that one "pathway" gets saturated and any information beyond that point is lost. Since almost all academic information is communicated linguistically (either verbally or in writing) this pathway is used in almost every circumstance, and students are often pushed into cognitive overload. A common scenario for this would be when a teacher displays a PowerPoint on the board with many written explanations in the form of sentences that students are supposed to read while they simultaneously listen to the teacher's lecture and take notes. The overwhelming amount of linguistic information- reading, listening, writing done at the same time- creates cognitive overload and ensures the students will retain little from the lesson. There is simply too much language for them to process at one time without allowing it to sufficiently transition to long term memory.

If instead the PowerPoint is used not for written explanations, but for visuals that will supplement the words the teacher is saying, then that second pathway, the visual one, is engaged and the visual information can be processed and devoted to memory without interfering with the linguistic information they are also processing. It essentially activates another component of students' cognition, as if another storage unit is added, thereby expanding capacity for what can be learned. In contrast to learning styles, which posits (incorrectly) that students have a preferred mode of sensory perception and that learning will increase if teachers provide instruction in that mode, dual coding predicts that all learners should benefit from incorporating both linguistic and visual stimuli simultaneously. Importantly, is not necessary for students to actually see the information, and the benefit can occur when students simply use imagery to visualize the information.

Recent research has shown this to be the case. In one study, students who were asked to process information both linguistically and visually by using imagery retained twice the amount of information as those who were asked to process the information using linguistic means alone (Cuevas & Dawson, 2018). And with the preponderance of technology currently available in the classroom, the options for using visuals to supplement the ubiquitous linguistic instruction are nearly endless. I will note that teachers *do* indeed often use visual prompts in the classroom, but seldom do they use them in such a way that the principles of dual coding are purposefully planned and incorporated into the lesson; more often the visuals are designed to add interest rather than supplement memory.

There are scores of other concepts from the field of cognitive science that have the potential to refine education. The related strategies of backward fading and concrete fading are interesting avenues for teaching and educational research (Fyfe, McNeil, & Borjas, 2015; Goldstone & Son, 2005). In concrete-to-representational-to-abstract sequence of instruction (CRA), students are first provided with prompts that are concrete in nature, then provided with ones that are analogous to the initial ones and represent the ideas (yet not so literally), before moving on to fully abstract depictions of the concepts. In this way scaffolding occurs as the previous, more basic, more literal prompt is removed (or faded) as the student learns the material.

There is also now a rich and abundant line of research on metacognition, a recognition and focus on one's own thought processes, and how it may enhance reading, writing, and learning in general (Anderson & Thiede, 2008; Dunlosky, Rawson, & Middleton 2005; Rawson & Dunlosky, 2007; Thiede, Anderson, & Therriault, 2003). Teachers have begun to implement another instructional strategy, the use of manipulatives, in many classrooms, a method that has the potential to improve student learning in math. However, similar to inquiry-based approaches, research on manipulatives has not consistently shown positive results and can lead to poorer learning outcomes in certain conditions (Willingham, 2017). In instances such as this, it is important for teachers to have been exposed to research on the subject so that they are aware of the nuances that can and do make a difference between enhancing student learning and limiting it.

As in the previous section on cognitive myths, my purpose here is not to detail every potential avenue that cognitive science has to offer to the field of education but instead provide examples of some interesting and worthwhile possibilities. But perhaps the question is not what cognitive science can offer the field of education. Perhaps it's a matter of the two being one in the same, with cognitive science being an essential aspect of the field of education, one that should be the focus of education rather than the curious, tangential offshoot that it is too often regarded as now. Because of the widespread existence of cognitive myths among educators and the lack of attention to well supported cognitive science, both at the university and k-12 levels, it suggests that a stronger focus on cognitive science may allow for progress in the field of education that we desperately crave. It would improve the knowledge and skills teacher-candidates develop in university teacher education programs, and with that they may transfer those benefits to future students in the k-12 classroom. A focus on cognitive science would also inevitably lessen the overemphasis on certain ideological socio-cultural perspectives that can be viewed as political in nature. In essence, it would allow us to treat education more as a science that is above subjective ideological criticisms from outside and less of an active player in the culture wars.

CONCLUSION: MAKING PROGRESS IN THE FIELD OF EDUCATION; WHAT ARE THE SOLUTIONS?

I would like to able to propose that the field of education can generate large scale improvements to itself unilaterally, but because so many of the most egregious threats it faces come from external forces, it is unlikely that will happen. A shift towards cognitive science is likely to improve and refine education rather than transform it. Teachers often unwittingly use some of strategies discussed here that research has shown to be effective. Most teachers may not be aware of the research, nor plan for or incorporate those instructional approaches in a purposeful or deliberate manner, and thus students are unlikely to get the full benefit from them. But those methods are neither completely foreign to educational practice, nor are they magic-bullet panaceas. And while teachers may believe many myths about human learning, when they act on those myths the outcome is likely to be that instructional time is used less efficiently than it could be and students' intellectual growth proceeds at slower increments than is ultimately possible. This is certainly not something we would desire, but less-than-efficient practices will usually not cause students outright harm. Students in this country are still learning, progressing, going on to college and succeeding in the workforce, and the vast majority of teachers are doing their best to benefit those students, even if their approaches may be somewhat misguided at times.

So while I advocate for a greater emphasis on cognitive science and believe that such a shift will improve student outcomes, as I noted at the beginning of this chapter, the greatest threats to the advancement of education come from outside the classroom. There must be a shift in the values of the citizens of this country. Education must once again be viewed as a cherished public resource that holds the key to children's long-term success and the success of the nation. Citizens must demand that states allocate sufficient funds to k-12 schools and to public universities, both of which have been grossly underfunded over the last decade. They must demand that teachers are paid adequate salaries on par with similar professions that require employees to earn bachelors and graduate degrees. If politicians refuse to support education, then citizens have a right to protest and teachers may feel the need to strike, as tens of thousands of teachers did in 2018. And all citizens can, and must, make their voices heard at the ballot box.

Education is a public entity meant for the public good. As such, the value the public places on it will dictate its effectiveness. Issues with funding and ideological attacks must be addressed through a more engaged populace that puts renewed emphasis on education. When we allow outside forces to damage and diminish education, we ultimately damage and diminish the nation. Certainly, educating the nation's citizens, whether they be younger generations through k-12 schooling or adults at the university level, will always be a costly endeavor. But unless we once again begin to view education as an investment in our nation and our people, the political impetus will not be present to ensure that the citizens of this country continue to benefit from the vast stores of human knowledge built over the millennia.

Education is not an entity separate from the people, to be embraced or rejected at the whims of politicians or extremist factions. Education is a part of us, as citizens of this nation. We can choose to continue to have the greatest, most inclusive education system in the world, one that has allowed the United States to be the world's leader in advancement and the only remaining super power, however tenuous that status remains. We can choose to continue to support an education system that has enabled citizens from all walks of life, all backgrounds, and all races to thrive and achieve successes and levels of well-being unknown to previous generations. Or we can continue to allow our education system to stagnate, to fall behind the rest of the world, and with it our citizens and our nation would become less exceptional as other nations embrace the knowledge and discovery that we reject. The quality of our educational system is our choice. Over the last several decades we have allowed one of our greatest resources to wither on the vine. But that does not have to be the case, and if we choose to value public education as the root of our democracy as we once did, we will continue to be at the forefront of human progress. That is the choice we must make.

REFERENCES

Allcock, S. J., & Hulme, J. A. (2010). Learning styles in the classroom: Educational benefit or planning exercise? *Psychology Teaching Review*, *16*(2), 67-79.

American Association of University Professors (2012a). [Graph illustration source: US Department of Education, IPEDS Fall Staff Survey]. *Trends in Instructional Staff Employment Status, 1975–2011*. Retrieved from https://www.aaup.org/sites/default/files/files/2013%20Salary%20Surv ey%20Tables%20and%20Figures/Figure%201.pdf .

American Association of University Professors (2012b). [Graph illustration source: US Department of Education, National Center for Education Statistics, IPEDS Fall Staff Survey]. *Trends in Instructional Staff Employment Status, 1975–2011.* Retrieved from https://www.aaup.org/ file/Instructional_Staff_Trends.pdf .

Andersen, K. (2017). *Fantasyland: How America went haywire. A 500-year history.* New York: Random House.

Anderson, M. C., & Thiede, K. W. (2008). Why do delayed summaries improve metacomprehension accuracy? *Acta psychologica, 128,* 110-118.

Asher, L. (2018, April 8). How ed schools became a menace: They trained an army of bureaucrats who are pushing the academy toward ideological fundamentalism. *The Chronicle of Higher Education.* Retrieved from https://www.chronicle.com/article/How-Ed-Schools-Became-a-Menac e/243062 .

Bernard, T. S., & Russell, K. (2018, July 11). The new toll of student debt in 3 charts. *New York Times.* Retrieved from https://www.nytimes.com/ 2018/07/11/your-money/student-loan-debt-parents.html?smid=fb-nyti mes&smtyp=cur .

Bishka, A. (2010). Learning styles fray: Brilliant or batty? *Performance Improvement, 49*(10), 9-13. DOI: 10.1002/pfi.20181.

Boston, R. (2008). Evolving strategy: Creationists promote "academic freedom" bills. *Humanist, 68*(5), 36-37.

Castle. L. (2018, May 22). Evolution wording removed from draft of Arizona school science standards. *The Republic.* Retrieved from https://www.azcentral.com/story/news/local/arizona-education/2018/0 5/22/arizona-draft-school-science-standards-removes-evolution-diane- douglas-intelligent-design/628941002/.

Church & State. (2012). Bill advocating creationism dies In Indiana house due to lawsuit concern. *65*(4), 18-19.

Clark, R. E., Kirschner, P. A., Sweller, J. (2012). Putting students on the path to learning: The case for fully guided instruction. *American Educator*, 36(1), 6-11.

Crawford, A. (2013, December 15). Public schools beat private schools. *Boston Globe*. Retrieved from https://www.bostonglobe.com/ideas/ 2013/12/15/public-schools-beat-private-schools/hWLzdKv1x7wwupcj k5zonI/story.html .

Cuevas, J. A. (2008). The psychological processes and consequences of fundamentalist indoctrination. *Essays in the Philosophy of Humanism*, *16*(2), 57-70.

Cuevas, J. A. (2015). Is learning styles-based instruction effective? A comprehensive analysis of recent research on learning styles. *Theory and Research in Education*, *13*(3), 308-333. doi: 10.1177/147787 8515606621.

Cuevas, J. A. (2016). An analysis of current evidence supporting two alternate learning models: Learning styles and dual coding. *Journal of Educational Sciences & Psychology*, *6*(1), 1-13.

Cuevas, J. A. (2017). Visual and auditory learning: Differentiating instruction via sensory modality and its effects on memory. In *Student Achievement: Perspectives, Assessment and Improvement Strategies* (pp. 29-54) New York: Nova Science Publishers. ISBN-13: 978-1536102055.

Cuevas, J. A. (2018, January/February). A new reality: The far right's use of cyber-harassment against academics. *Academe* (American Association of University Professors), *104*(1). https://www.aaup.org/ article/new-reality-far-rights-use-cyberharassment-against-academics#. WmDcYHanHIU.

Cuevas, J. A., & Dawson, B. L. (2018). A test of two alternative cognitive processing models: Learning styles and dual coding. *Theory and Research in Education*, *16*(1), 40-64. DOI: 10.1177/1477878517 731450.

Dunlosky, J., Rawson, K. A., & Middleton, E. L. (2005). What constrains the accuracy of metacomprehension judgments? Testing the transfer-appropriate-monitoring and accessibility hypotheses. *Journal of Memory and Language, 52*, 551-565.

Emma, C., Wermund, B., & Hefling, K. (2016, December 9). DeVos' Michigan schools experiment gets poor grades. *Politico*. Retrieved from https://www.politico.com/story/2016/12/betsy-devos-michigan-school-experiment-232399?cmpid=sf.

Fridley, W. L., & Fridley, C. A. (2010). Some problems & peculiarities with the learning styles rhetoric and practice. *Journal of Philosophy & History of Education, 60*, 21-27.

Fyfe, E. R., McNeil, N. M., & Borjas, S. (2015). Benefits of "concreteness fading" for children's mathematics understanding. *Learning and Instruction, 35*, 104-120.

Gluckman, N. (2018a, April 30). George Mason's president says some donor agreements fell 'short' of academic standards. *The Chronicle of Higher Education*. Retrieved from https://www.chronicle.com/article/George-Mason-s-President/243285.

Gluckman, N. (2018b, May 29). Undeterred by criticism, Koch Foundation increases spending in higher education. *The Chronicle of Higher Education*. Retrieved from https://www.chronicle.com/article/Undeterred-by-Criticism-Koch/243528 .

Goldstone, R. L., & Son, J. Y. (2005). The transfer of scientific principles using concrete and idealized simulations. *Journal of the Learning Sciences, 14*, 69-110.

Greteman, B. (2017, February 22). Don't blame tenured academics for the adjunct crisis. *The Chronicle of Higher Education*. Retrieved from https://www.chronicle.com/article/don-t-blame-tenured/239268.

Hansen, M. (2018, April 13). Which states might experience the next wave of teacher strikes? *The Brookings Institute*. Retrieved from https://www.brookings.edu/blog/brown-center-chalkboard/2018/04/13/which-states-might-experience-the-next-wave-of-teacher-strikes/ .

Husmann, P. R., & O'Loughlin, V. D. (2018). Another nail in the coffin for learning styles? Disparities among undergraduate anatomy students' study strategies, class performance, and reported VARK learning styles. *Anatomical Sciences Education* doi: 10.1002/ase.1777.

Kirschner, P. A., & van Merriënboer, J. J. G. (2013). Do learners really know best? Urban legends in education. *Educational Psychologist, 48*(3), 169-183, DOI: 10.1080/00461520.2013.804395.

Kolowich, S. (2017, July 26). Who's left to defend Tommy Curry? *The Chronicle of Higher Education.* Retrieved from https://www.chronicle.com/article/Who-s-Left-to-Defend-Tommy/240757.

Kozub, R. M. (2010). An ANOVA analysis of the relationships between business students' learning styles and effectiveness of web based instruction. *American Journal of Business Education, 3*(3), 89-98.

Lac, A., Hemovich, V., & Himelfarb, I. (2010). Predicting position on teaching creationism (instead of evolution) in public schools. *Journal of Educational Research, 103*(4), 253-261.

Laitsch, D. (2016). After 60 years, do the arguments for K-12 vouchers still hold? *Global Education Review, 3*(2), 23-32.

Larson, E. J. (1997). *Summer for the gods.* New York: Basic Books.

Lubienski, C., & Lubienski, S. T. (2006). Charter schools, academic achievement and NCLB. *Journal of School Choice, 1*(3), 55. doi: 10.1300/J467v01n03•07.

Lubienski, S. T., Lubienski, C., & Crane, C. C. (2008). Achievement differences and school type: The role of school climate, teacher certification, and instruction. *American Journal of Education, 115*(1), 97-138.

Macdonald, K., Germine, L., Anderson, A., Christodoulou, J., McGrath, L. (2017). Dispelling the myth: Training in education or neuroscience decreases but does not eliminate beliefs in neuromyths. *Frontiers in Psychology,* 8:1314. doi: 10.3389/fpsyg.2017.01314.

Martin, S. (2010). Teachers using learning styles: Torn between research and accountability? *Teaching and Teacher Education, 26*(8), 1583-1591.

Mates, A. (2009). Creationism in Brunswick County. *Reports of the National Center for Science Education, 29*(2), 4-5.

New Scientist (2009). Texas creation vote. *201*(2701), 4.

Pashler, H., McDaniel, M., Rohrer, D., & Bjork, R. (2009). Learning styles: Concepts and evidence. *Psychological Science in the Public Interest, 9*, 105-119.

Quintana, P. (2017a, June 16). For one scholar, an online stoning tests the limits of public scholarship. *The Chronicle of Higher Education.* Retrieved from https://www.chronicle.com/article/For-One-Scholar-an-Online/240384.

Quintana, P. (2017b, June 28). Under fire, these professors were criticized by their colleges. *The Chronicle of Higher Education.* Retrieved from https://www.chronicle.com/article/Under-Fire-These-Professors/240457?cid=wcontentlist_hp_latest.

Rawson, K. A., & Dunlosky, J. (2007). Improving students' self-evaluation of learning for key concepts in textbook materials. *European Journal of Cognitive Psychology, 19*, 559-579.

Rogowsky, B. A., Calhoun, B. M., & Tallal, P. (2015). Matching learning style to instructional method: Effects on comprehension. *Journal of Educational Psychology, 107*(1), 64-78. doi: 10.1037/a0037478.

Rohrer, D., & Pashler, H. (2010). Recent research on human learning challenges conventional instructional strategies. *Educational Researcher, 39*(5), 406 – 412. https://journals.sagepub.com/doi/10.3102/0013189X10374770.

Sav, G. T. (2017). Efficiency evaluations of U.S. public higher education and effects of state funding and Pell grants: Panel data estimates using two stage data envelope analysis, 2004 – 2013 academic years. *Journal of Education Finance, 42*(4), 357 – 385.

Schmidt, P. (2017, June 22). Professors' growing risk: Harassment for things they never really said. *The Chronicle of Higher Education.* Retrieved from https://www.chronicle.com/article/Professors-Growing-Risk-/240424.

Schott Foundation for Public Education. (2018). *Grading the states: A report card on our nation's commitment to public schools.* Retrieved from http://schottfoundation.org/report/grading-the-states.

Scott, C. (2010). The enduring appeal of "learning styles." *Australian Journal of Education, 54*(1), 5-17. (EJ889818).

Scott, J. W. (2018). Targeted harassment of faculty: What higher education administrators can do. *Liberal Education, Association of American Colleges and Universities, 104*(2). Retrieved from https://www.aacu.org/liberaleducation/2018/spring/scott .

Strauss, V. (2018, April 22). Professor: A disturbing story about the influence of the Koch network in higher education. *Washington Post.* Retrieved from https://www.washingtonpost.com/news/answer-sheet/wp/2018/04/22/professor-a-disturbing-story-about-the-influence-of-the-koch-network-in-higher-education/?noredirect=on&utm_term=.cf190f6fe3bc.

Suitts, S. (2016). Students facing poverty: The new majority. *Educational Leadership, 74*(3), 36-40.

Thiede, K. W., Anderson, M., & Therriault, D. (2003). Accuracy of metacognitive monitoring affects learning of texts. *Journal of Educational Psychology, 95,* 66-73.

U.S. Bureau of the Census. *Real Median Personal Income in the United States* [MEPAINUSA672N]. Retrieved from FRED, Federal Reserve Bank of St. Louis; https://fred.stlouisfed.org/series/MEPAINUSA672N, June 4, 2018.

Vasquez, M. (2018a, May 31). How a student got kicked out of class- And became a conservative hero. *The Chronicle of Higher Education.* Retrieved from https://www.chronicle.com/article/How-a-Student-Got-Kicked-Out/243549.

Vasquez, M. (2018b, Aug 7). The Koch Institute is worried about free speech on campus. But not in a way you might think. *The Chronicle of Higher Education.* Retrieved from https://www.chronicle.com/article/The-Koch-Institute-Is-Worried/244184 .

Velez, E. D., Woo, J. H., National Center for Education Statistics, & RTI. (2017). *The Debt Burden of Bachelor's Degree Recipients. Stats in Brief.* NCES 2017-436. Retrieved from https://files.eric.ed.gov/fulltext/ED573698.pdf .

Webber, D. (2016, September 13). Fancy dorms aren't the main reason tuition is skyrocketing. *FiveThirtyEight.* Retrieved from https://

fivethirtyeight.com/features/fancy-dorms-arent-the-main-reason-tuition-is-skyrocketing/?ex_cid=538fb .

Webber, D. A. (2017). State divestment and tuition at public institutions. *Economics of Education Review, 60*, 1-4. https://doi.org/10.1016/j.econedurev.2017.07.007.

Willingham, D. T. (2017, Fall). Ask the cognitive scientist: Do manipulatives help students learn? *American Educator,* 25-40. Retrieved from https://www.aft.org/sites/default/files/periodicals/ae_fall2017_willingham.pdf .

Zahneis, M. (2018, June 28). White-supremacist propaganda on campuses rose 77% last year. *The Chronicle of Higher Education.* Retrieved from https://www.chronicle.com/article/White-Supremacist-Propaganda/243786.

In: Progress in Education. Volume 55
Editor: Roberta V. Nata
ISBN: 978-1-53614-551-9
© 2019 Nova Science Publishers, Inc.

Chapter 2

IMPROVING TEACHING PRACTICE AND STUDENT LEARNING THROUGH COLLABORATIVE ACTION RESEARCH: A CASE STUDY OF AN EFFECTIVE PARTNERSHIP PROGRAMME INVOLVING TEACHER-EDUCATORS AND FOUR MIDDLE SCHOOL TEACHERS

Alaster R. Gibson[*], PhD and Janette M. Blake
Bethlehem Tertiary Institute (BTI), Tauranga, New Zealand

ABSTRACT

This chapter will be of interest to school leaders and teachers desiring to facilitate beneficial and transformational professional development. It is also relevant to teacher-educators working in partnership with schools to foster teacher inquiry leading to improved student outcomes. The research

---

[*] Corresponding Author Email: a.gibson@bti.ac.nz.

underpinning the chapter is derived from the authors' personal involvement as teacher-educators in leading a Collaborative Action Research (CAR) project involving four middle school (Year 7-10) teachers from a New Zealand, suburban Christian school. The overarching research question was, 'How might the Collaborative Action Research process affect teachers' professional practice and student learning?'

The project extended across two consecutive, ten-week school terms during 2017 and included fortnightly, half-day release times to ensure the volunteer teacher participants could effectively and sustainably inquire into their professional practice. During the release times, participants met with the teacher-educators on their neighbouring campus, and engaged in a range of intentional professional activities such as community building, Critical Friends Group discussions, sharing of research literature, reflective journaling and action planning. The meetings allowed the teacher-educators to mentor and motivate the participants through the process of developing and exploring their self-selected inquiries. Time was also set aside to gather triangulated, qualitative data on the efficacy of the programme via semi-formal interviews, focus group sessions and several naturalistic class observations of the teachers *in* action.

The four female teacher participants brought a rich, diverse range of professional experiences, qualifications, and leadership responsibilities to the project. Their chosen research topics included; helping students understand and effectively use success criteria and give formative peer feedback; exploring the pedagogical strategy of co-operative group dynamics to strengthen student relationships and improve learning outcomes; developing students' critical thinking skills through interpreting and applying biblical scripture to everyday life with the assistance of digital study tools, and lastly, wrestling with ways to authentically model and integrate virtues into lessons to increase student well-being. The findings affirm the value of Collaborative Action Research as a tool to enable teachers to inquire into their practice leading to improved pedagogy and student achievement.

Keywords: Collaborative Action Research, teacher inquiry, Critical Friends Group discussions, reflective practice, mentoring, professional development.

INTRODUCTION

This chapter begins by reviewing literature related to Action Research (AR); providing a robust foundation to its meaningfulness and effectiveness in supporting teacher inquiry. Secondly, the chapter provides an overview of the Collaborative Action Research project undertaken with four middle school teachers. It includes ethical considerations, participant recruitment processes, and participant demographics. This section also provides insight into the structure of the programme, the underlying research questions, and how data was gathered and subsequently analysed. The third section identifies the participants' inquiry topics and discusses the findings. The final section of the chapter highlights a range of implications, limitations and recommendations for readers to consider.

LITERATURE REVIEW

Paradigmatic and Methodological Foundations

Action Research (AR) is a form of participatory action inquiry (Tripp, 2005), and relates to a relativist, interpretive, and constructivist perspective on reality (Mills, 2013; Somekh & Zeichner, 2009). AR may also fit within a unique paradigm of 'praxis' (O'Brien, 2001), based on the premise that it, 'goes beyond the notion that theory can inform practice, to a recognition that theory can and should be generated through practice' (Brydon-Miller, Greenwood, & Maguire, 2003, p. 15).

Action Research is also a form of 'insider' research associated with qualitative methodological approaches such as classroom ethnography and autobiographical case-study (Zeni, 2009); well suited for individual and collaborative, professional endeavours in school-based communities (ERO, 2016a; Whitehead & McNiff, 2006). Ontologically and epistemologically, AR recognises the value of teachers being actively involved in researching their own life-world contexts; constructing knowledge through their own interpretive perspectives (Kemmis & McTaggart, 2005). Meanings, action and change are understood as non-linear, complex and subjective, reflecting unique, socio-cultural, interpersonal, and organizational factors (Lathouris, Piliouras, Plakitsi, & Stylianou, 2015; Ponce & Pagan-Maldonado, 2015). Collaborative Action Research affirms socio-cultural learning theory and recognises the importance of engaging with others within a broader construct of a community of practice (Rogoff, 2003; Wennergren & Rönnerman, 2006).

Relevance of Collaborative Action Research in Educational Contexts

Action Research is widely used in educational contexts today, particularly because of its relevance and responsiveness to people's immediate professional life-world contexts (Coghlan & Brannick, 2014; Edwards-Groves, Grootenboer, & Ronnerman, 2016; McNiff, 2010). AR has developed and diversified gradually over the past 75 years, being influenced by people such as John Dewey, Kurt Lewin, Paulo Freire, William Barry, and Jack Whitehead (Carson & Sumara, 1997; Maksimović, 2010). The aims and processes of Collaborative Action Research when applied to school learning communities are for groups of teachers to constructively inquire into their professional praxis; to explore and strengthen effective teaching and to enhance students' engagement and learning (Piggot-Irvine, 2006; Stoll & Louis, 2007). These aims and processes are similar to those associated with Professional Learning Communities and Professional Learning Groups (PLC and PLG); popular in-service programmes within schools, internationally and within New Zealand (Huffman & Jacobson, 2003).

Du Four (2004, p. 6) asserts, 'The rise or fall of the Professional Learning Community concept depends not on the merits of the concept itself, but on the most important element in the improvement of any school - the commitment and persistence of the educators within it.' A recent quantitative study on PLCs in the United States by Ratts, Pate, Archibald, Andrews, Ballard, and Lowney (2015, p. 51), showed, 'PLC members who observed peers, provided feedback on instructional practices, worked with colleagues to judge student work quality, and collaboratively reviewed student work to improve instructional analysis were more likely to improve their quality of teaching.' Du Four (2004) also acknowledges the importance of the collaborative nature of effective Professional Learning Community activities saying,

> The powerful collaboration that characterizes professional learning communities is a systematic process in which teachers work together to analyse and improve their classroom practice. Teachers work in teams, engaging in an ongoing cycle of questions that promote deep team learning. This process, in turn, leads to higher levels of student achievement. (p. 6)

Collaborative Action Research has the capacity to embody the characteristics of PLCs emphasized by Du Four (2004). For example within the New Zealand context, Piggot-Irvine (2006, p. 483) says in the context of Action Research, 'effective professional development programmes cannot be quick-fix, or surface or skills translation (training) focused,... programmes need to be deep in orientation.' The notion of deep learning involves data-informed planning and evaluation, as well as teachers generating professional knowledge and insights through self and collegial reflexive practice that then feed back into their teaching. Piggot-Irvine (2006) also emphasizes the research component, that participant decision-making is not impromptu but informed and carefully planned. More recently, the New Zealand Education Review Office report, School Evaluation Indicators (ERO, 2016a, p. 25), affirms the need for 'Teacher professional learning and development that is focused and deep, rather than fragmented and shallow' and that 'teachers will learn how to improve their teaching by engaging in collective inquiry into the effectiveness of current practice.'

Non-Technicist Action Research Method

As a practitioner-led, field-based method or technique for inquiry, AR is essentially focused on personal and professional improvement. The topics and approaches participants select to achieve professional improvement will influence the mode of action research used. For example Tripp (2005), differentiates between technical (implementing initiatives from somewhere else), practical (developing and implementing own initiatives) and socially critical modes of action research (exploring ways to change the status quo of the social-political culture of the organisation). Tripp (2005) also discusses how practitioner researchers may engage with a range of these modes in the process of working through successive action research cycles.

AR can be autobiographical or collaborative. An autobiographical approach might be more manageable and allow a teacher participant to be less vulnerable. In contrast, Collaborative Action Research in school contexts recognizes there are reciprocal benefits for teacher participants when they include others such as colleagues, students, and external researchers in the process (Evans, Lomax, & Morgan, 2000; Nelson & Bishop, 2013). Such collaboration may include peer coaching and critical friend conversations, collegial observations of teaching practice, and critique of action plans and outcomes. Teachers actively collaborating with whole classes or groups of students often find mutual benefits and fresh perspectives from including and valuing student voice in the pursuit of more effective ways to teach and learn (Brydon-Miller & Maguire, 2009; Keegan, 2016; Lundy, McEvoy, & Byrne, 2011). Reciprocal benefits from working alongside external researchers allows for professional support for busy teachers while at the same time providing a case-study for the researchers to develop their own skills.

Linked to the virtues of collaboration is the notion that Action Research is not an objective or apolitical process (Brydon-Miller & Maguire, 2009). Gathering information, developing and enacting action plans, and critically reflecting on teaching praxis will inevitably be influenced by social-cultural, organisational and personal contexts (Freire, 1998). Brydon-Miller and Maguire (2009, p. 83), affirm that 'research can never be neutral.' Differences in power and privilege exist between teachers and students, and between students and students. Collaborative Action Research affords opportunities to model democratic values and examine issues of inclusion and social-justice. For example, teachers exploring students' perspectives, allowing them to shape some of the research questions and to share in the responsibilities for strengthening teaching and learning can be reciprocally empowering and transformative. Valuing students as co-researchers invites students to be active 'catalytic agents of change' (ibid., p. 86). AR therefore, is ideal for those teachers and teacher-leaders who reject the notion of a technicist approach to teaching, who are looking for a more dynamic, professional development opportunity than those typically offered via external workshop presenters (Goodnough, 2011; Pellerin, 2011). It is insider research as action, on action and in action with people, rather than research by an outsider merely 'on' people (Gustavsen, 2001; Tripp, 2005). It values the notion that people have the innate capacity to engage with their own life-world challenges and be instrumental in bringing about improvement. Reason and Bradbury describe action research as,

> a participatory, democratic process concerned with developing practical knowing in the pursuit of worthwhile human purposes... It seeks to bring together action and reflection, theory and practice, in participation with others, in the pursuit of practical solutions to issues of pressing concern to people, and more generally the flourishing of individual persons and their communities. (2001, p. 1)

Data Informed Cyclical Inquiry to Improve Professional Practice

Action Research within educational contexts has traditionally engaged with textual information derived from reflective journaling, small sets of statistical data derived from, for example, in-class surveys, and test scores (Zeni, 2009). This is not to be confused with a mixed methods research approach, and is quite different from a quantitative, experimental research design, based on the analysis of entirely numeric data (Ponce & Pagan-Maldonado, 2015). Increasingly popular over the past decade, is the inclusion of visual methods in school-based AR to encourage and elicit student data (Mengwasser & Walton, 2011; Woolner, Clark, Hall, Tiplady, Thomas, & Wall, 2008).

It is important that Action Research is a reflective (examining actions) and reflexive (examining attitudes and assumptions) process in order to critically examine practice, in pursuit of tangible beneficial outcomes. Simply described, AR involves practitioners 'in self-contained cycles that involve planning a change, implementing the change, observing the outcomes of the change, and reflecting on the outcomes of the change' (Goodnough, 2011, p. 75). AR invites participants to interrogate and improve the status quo of their practice (Coghlan & Brannick, 2014). Outcomes from AR in educational contexts can therefore positively influence teacher identity and agency, organizational culture, and social values such as equity and justice (Brydon-Miller, Greenwood, & Maguire, 2003; Goodnough, 2011). AR has also been shown to assist teachers to develop sustainable inquiry mind-sets (Seidre & Lemma, 2004).

However, educational research has also shown that teachers can struggle to apply sufficient reconnaissance and rigour to their Action Research projects (Tripp, 2005). They can feel intimidated and frustrated with the non-linear processes of AR; especially if there is a lack of support (particularly release time), and if participation is mandated and overly prescriptive (Seider & Lemma, 2004; Sheridan-Thomas, 2006; Tripp, 2005; Zeichner, 2003). Furthermore, although the research literature affirms the capacity for AR to have a systematic and positive effect on student learning outcomes (Hargreaves, 2007), achieving and sustaining these effects, is seldom easy or straightforward (Talbert, 2010). This is particularly so because; it involves the teacher in what Eriksson, Romar, and Dyson, (2017, p. 53) refer to as, 'the messy classroom work,' and that 'educational change is often overwhelmed by ambiguity, conflict and uncertainty' (ibid., p. 63).

COLLABORATIVE ACTION RESEARCH PROJECT

Methodology and Methods

Consistent with the literature reviewed, the research from which this chapter is derived was based on a relativist, interpretivist, constructivist paradigm, and a qualitative methodology (Denzin & Lincoln, 2003). In addition, because of the faith-based school context and the shared spirituality of the participants, the research was inclusive of applied phenomenological and theistic epistemological perspectives on reality (Gibson, 2014a, 2014b, 2016; Sarantakos, 2005; Shepherd, 2012). This stance allowed authentic, descriptive analyses of the textural data as presented by participants. The importance of spiritual wellbeing and spirituality is broadly acknowledged in educational literature (e.g., Fraser, 2007; Fry, 2005; Gibson, 2014b). In the current New Zealand secular context, the Education Review Office report, Wellbeing for success: A resource for schools (ERO 2016b, p. 10), says school leaders will, 'ensure school values are actioned in the school's partnerships, curriculum and operations including celebrating of different religions, spirituality...' In this document spiritual wellbeing is acknowledged as an integral component of holistic well-being within the Maori cultural concepts of manaakitanga and hauora (ERO 2016b, p. 7 and 26).

Two research methods were employed concurrently throughout this project. Firstly, Collaborative Action Research cycles were pursued across two terms (twenty weeks) with four teachers inquiring into their professional practice. Concomitantly a singular case-study method was applied by the two teacher-educators facilitating the research project. Not only were the teacher-educators involved in mentoring the teacher participants and facilitating the release sessions, but they also gathered rich, descriptive qualitative data through a range of strategies. This data was used to understand the effects of the Collaborative Action Research process on the teachers, their teaching and their students.

Research Questions

The teacher-educators' case-study, focused on one overarching question: 'How might the Collaborative Action Research process affect teachers' professional practice and student learning?' There were a further six subsidiary questions. 1. 'What personal, professional and contextual factors influence teacher-participants' choice of topic to explore through the Collaborative Action Research processes?' 2. 'How do the participant teachers develop, implement and refine their action plans.' 3. 'How might the Collaborative Action Research processes influence teacher-participants' professional practice?' 4. 'How might the teacher-participants' action plans impact student engagement and learning?' 5. 'What challenges or hindrances did participants experience when enacting their plans?' 6. 'What aspects of the half-day fortnightly release sessions were believed to be effective and how might the sessions be strengthened?'

Each teacher participant focused on five inquiry questions, repeated across two consecutive school terms. 1. What particular aspect of my professional practice or learning needs of the students do I want to inquire into and why? 2. What data might I gather data on the issue that I am interested in strengthening? 3. How might I develop an informed and robust action plan to make improvements to my professional practice and the students' learning? 4. How might I implement and evaluate my action plan? 5. Upon reflection, what have I learned and what needs further refinement?

Ethical Considerations, Participant Recruitment and Demographics

Ethical approval to conduct the project was obtained via the authors' institutional Research Ethics Committee in February, 2017. Following negotiations and permission from the leadership of a local faith-based, integrated, Area School (Y1-13), the researchers presented the concept of the project to approximately 25 teaching staff involved in the middle school (Years 7-10). Written invitations for teachers to volunteer to participate in the project were provided. Within a week, four teachers had given consent to volunteer.

Crucial to the project was the school's leadership supporting the funding of relief-teachers so participant-teachers could attend fortnightly, half-day release meetings across two consecutive school terms. The venue for these meetings was intentionally set off-site from the school at the neighbouring teacher-education institution where the researchers worked. This facility afforded less distraction and easy access to library and online resources. These decisions were informed by educational literature (Barkhuizen, 2009; Borg, 2009; Firkins & Wong, 2005), and designed to enable participants' to sustainably engage with the aims and processes of AR.

For ethical reasons, and to encourage participants to openly inquire into their practice, participation was not linked to the in-school performance appraisal system. However commitment and accountability to the programme was emphasized, along with the right to withdraw at any time without adverse consequences. The demographics of the four female participant-teachers varied in terms of areas of responsibility, professional experience, ethnicity, qualifications and age. They shared a similar theistic, Christian world-view perspective. Care was taken to build collegial trust and respect among participants while at the same time encouraging them to be open and vulnerable to inquire into and share areas of concern in their professional practice.

Table 1. Participant-teacher demographics for Collaborative Action Research project

Teacher participant	Current teaching profile	Teaching experience	Ethnicity	Educational qualifications
P1	Y8 experienced senior teacher with a leadership role with Y8 teachers.	15 years	Māori	Master's degree
P2	Y7 class teacher with lead role in a performing arts group.	3 years	Māori	Bachelor's degree
P3	Y8 class teacher with a leadership role in English and E-learning within Junior Secondary School.	13 years	European	Master's degree
P4	Y9 class teacher (English, Social Sciences, Christian Living) with a leadership role in Physical Education Y7-Y11, Health Science Y13, volley ball coaching and peer support.	5 years	European	Bachelor's degree & graduate diploma

Inviting participant teachers to self-select an aspect of professional practice that they wanted to explore and strengthen was designed to be intrinsically motivating and maximize relevance to each teacher within their unique situated contexts (Korthagen, 2010). Prior to formal commencement of the programme, participants met with one of the teacher-educators and a senior school leader to discuss the expectations of the project. This meeting at the end of term one provided participants with the opportunity to begin to think about what aspect of their teaching they might like to inquire into during the second school term. The focus of the teachers' two term CAR was linked to their school's strategic plan to strengthen effective pedagogy within their faith-based school context.

Descriptive, Triangulated Data, and Inductive Analysis

To strengthen the credibility and trustworthiness of the research findings (Bryman, 2004; Creswell, 2003), the research design was triangulated by recruiting four participants from diverse teaching roles and experiences, and engaging these participants in five data gathering activities. Most of this data was obtained via the fortnightly half-day release sessions (ten in total, across two school terms).

Firstly, there were two 45 minute, semi-formal interviews, conducted, one per term (Houston, Ross, Robinson & Malcolm, 2010). Interview questions were provided to participants in advance. Secondly, participants were required to engage in several 20 minute reflective journal writing activities. Guiding questions were provided to help participants introspectively and reflexively critique their action plans, their praxis and beliefs (Luttenburg, Meijer, & Oolbekkink-Marchand, 2017; Stingu, 2012). Thirdly, two focus group sessions were convened at the end of each term whereby the researchers were able to review each teacher's evidence of progress and invite participant feedback (Joubert & Hocking, 2015). Fourthly, the researchers conducted two naturalistic, in-class observations of the participants outworking their action plans in their respective classes (Jordan, 2015; Meadowcroft & Moxley, 2009). These appointments were arranged at mutually agreeable times and provided rich opportunities for the researchers to understand more clearly each participant's unique context.

They involved the researchers taking notes and where appropriate, sitting alongside and communicating with students about what they were doing in a natural manner, without disrupting the normal flow of the class. They were also designed to equip the researchers to serve more effectively as mentors and critical friends (Kapachtsi & Kakana, 2012) during subsequent half-day release sessions. Fifthly, and finally, each participant submitted an end of term evaluative report addressing questions such as, why they were motivated to pursue their topic, analysis of the data from reconnaissance within their class contexts, and descriptions of their planning and intervention initiatives. These reports also invited participants to recall any pedagogically critical incidents or 'aha moments', and their perceptions of influence on student learning. These five diverse techniques ensured a holistic, rich set of descriptive, qualitative data was obtained in each of the two cycles of the project.

To enable a credible and trustworthy set of findings to be extrapolated from the data, the authors employed an iterative, non-linear, recursive and inductive analysis of the transcribed interviews, focus group and in-class naturalistic observation notes. The observation data in particular was considered through abductive reasoning, a kind of logical inferencing (Reichertz, 2010) which recognises the incompleteness of the observer's understanding of the context and subject observed. The critical journal entries and summative evaluations were similarly analysed for key statements and themes. These approaches were consistent with Creswell's (1998, p. 143), 'cyclical, inductive and interpretive' analysis process of qualitative data in which meanings, themes, relationships and differences, rather than frequency and statistical significance, are looked for.

Strategies to Engage Participants in the CAR Process

There were a range of strategies and conditions used by the researchers to promote the teachers' engagement in the CAR processes. For example, each fortnightly meeting commenced with team building activities and refreshments. Other activities involved action planning, sharing ideas, mentoring, and discussing literature pertaining to Action Research and their chosen inquiries. Mentoring involved sitting alongside the teachers, and interactively discussing their ideas, needs, resources, intentions, and learning activities. Additionally, the concept of Critical Friends Group (CFG) discussions was applied on four occasions (Bambino, 2002; Curry, 2008; National School Reform Faculty, 2018). These group sessions followed established protocols and were highly regarded by participants. CFG discussions provided invaluable opportunities for the teachers to present issues that they were grappling with and to invite non-judgmental, constructive feedback from their colleagues. Another activity used on several occasions in the second term cycle, involved discussing links between each participant's project and the New Zealand Education Review Office report (ERO, 2016a), 'School Evaluation Indicators' pertaining to effective pedagogy. This was designed to ensure each teacher was making sound professional decisions that supported improved student learning outcomes. Considered together these various planned activities provided a variety of enriching professional learning opportunities.

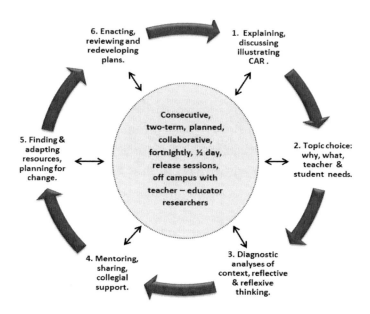

Figure 1. Conceptual diagram of the first phase of the Collaborative Action Research design.

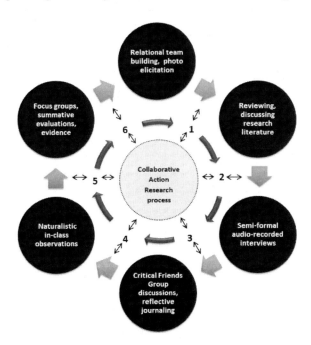

Figure 2. Conceptual diagram of the Case Study components integrated with the CAR design (Refer to Figure 1 for details of the inner circle).

DISCUSSION OF THE FINDINGS

Facilitating Timely Professional Inquiry through Relational, Collegial Support

The findings of this report, coupled with the literature reviewed, affirm Collaborative Action Research as a flexible, meaningful, and robust strategy to support collegial work-related professional learning and development. The findings affirm that the CAR model can be effectively sustained across two consecutive school terms. However, the findings also show that CAR was not a quick, linear process; quality teacher-led inquiry, inclusive of data gathering, planning, implementing initiatives, and reflecting critically on the outcomes, took time, perseverance and professional capacity. Supportive mentoring and release sessions were vital for the sustainability of the process and the well-being of participants.

In this case study, the two term process was assisted by quality, regular, well-planned fortnightly release times for participants. The agenda of these off-site sessions was always communicated in advance and provided for a range of affective, social-spiritual, cognitive and practical professional needs. Fostering relational trust, team building, sharing, discussion, professional reading, reflection, collegial critique, individual planning and mentoring were regularly on the menu. Mutually agreed upon naturalistic in-class professional observations, end of term focus group sessions and evaluative summaries were found to be vital to the success of this project. By doing so, reciprocal clarity and accountability between teacher participants and researchers was achieved.

The findings showed the importance of the four teacher participants being active agents in selecting areas of professional inquiry that were important to them. The findings also highlighted the value of encouraging the teachers to articulate why they'd chosen their respective topics. In common, they shared concerns over the learning and social/behavioural needs of their students. The findings affirm that the CAR project provided a timely opportunity for them to examine these needs and try out some interventions to improve the situation. The teacher participants found the input of mentoring, collegial critique, and personal reflective thinking helpful in refining and extending their interventions. Of note was the progression from an initial focus by the teachers on their teaching, to a more comprehensive focus including the students; their learning experiences and outcomes.

Empowering Students to Understand and Apply Assessment Criteria and Feedback

P1 had recently become aware, via student feedback, that many children in her class did not understand the wording of the assessment criteria as stated in the school's well-established oral language unit plan. As a result, students were not able to give effective assessment feedback to their peers following the presentation of their speeches. This current problem was chosen by P1 to be the initial focus of her CAR project. She embarked on learning about success criteria, and how to explain and use them within rubrics. In commenting on the practical ways that participation in the CAR project influenced her professional practice she said,

> It's provided an opportunity for me to look at assessment criteria for the units we teach in Year 8 and the student response to that criteria… it's made a way for me to be able to sit down and explore what they understand it to be and to make changes. (Semi-formal interview #2, p. 1)

This reflection highlights how the teacher was able to respond to a significant, current pedagogical issue through the provision of quality time within the project. Additionally, P1 wanted to support the school's strategic goal of promoting student agency. So she decided to re-develop the success criteria in collaboration with her students, ensuring they understood and had ownership of the process. Not only was the participant's practice influenced but she noticed a positive change in the way students talked about assessment.

> The language of our classroom is slowly changing when we're talking to each other about our work or what success means in relation to a piece of work… and I hear it more of that assessment language and feedback and encouragement coming through when we're looking at each other's work. (Semi-formal interview #2, p. 1)

The following quote highlights several additional findings; the participant's enhanced well-being and sense of efficacy, as well as collegial influence within her team leadership role.

> It makes me feel like I'm making some ground,… it makes me feel satisfied that I'm starting to understand something that I really didn't have time to… or focus to do before… I want to share some of the findings with my peers, just talking to the team about what I'm finding with the children

and asking them what's it like in your class... and some collegial conversations have opened up because of it. And I think that's powerful... slowly people drift in to have conversations, 'Oh what did you do about that? Where's your criteria?' It's really been helpful in that regard... and been beneficial to us as a team. (Semi-formal interview #2, p. 1)

Although P1 found the first CAR cycle challenging at times, once she had completed the initial process and seen tangible results, she was able to apply her learning into a second context more efficiently, this time a written language unit on narrative writing. The results of this second phase of the project are expressed as follows.

Recently we've been writing narratives and we've discussed the success criteria for narrative and how we might express that and how we might feed that back to other students. So we've created a success rubric, and then I've put posters up on the wall, to help students start sentences to enable them to bring the success criteria into their feedback. And just to read the feedback on the bottom of the draft of their narratives was so exciting, because I thought oh my ___ they're really thinking about ... they're seeing deeper features, they're really looking into the stuff that says what a successful piece of narrative looks like, and that is so exciting to me. (Semi-formal interview #2, p. 2)

The conclusion to the project did not mean an end to this teacher's application of the learning achieved. While she recognised progress had been made with using success criteria and feedback, she felt further progress was required to equip students to give specific feedforward to their peers. The quote below concludes with an indication that the CAR project had ignited in the students a desire to continue learning about and applying peer feedback.

When we first started feedback was basically, 'This is good work, I liked it.' 'It was good because you used a lot of describing words.' But there was no real indication that they were able to say, 'But you could work on...' So they couldn't feedforward, they couldn't get to the next step and I think in that sense we've now provided the scaffold or we're developing a scaffold together that will enable us to do that. Because I think moving forward, we need to focus on the next steps, how to we identify those from the information we have... And I think they're excited about it, 'Oh OK I can do this for my friend or for myself... (Semi-formal interview #2, p. 2)

P1 was also able to describe her own professional goals beyond the completion of the project. In the excerpt following she indicates the research has opened up her understanding to a wider issue across the middle school of the College: That being, to revisit established units of work, to see if they can be made more relevant to students and more authentically connected to the espoused aims of the school's special character. This was an unexpected finding of this CAR project.

I think for me it will mean going back over all that I'm teaching and really examine them and see if they are student friendly, that the purpose that we describe in the unit, the children actually see as relevant and that the content asserts that. Because I've found doing this research that I've looked at one of our units and it could be so much more than what it is. We took it at surface value but we kind of really missed the essence biblically as it being a tool to equip our children to love their neighbours... so professionally as a Christian educator I want to explore that across our units in Y8- I think it's vital that we are actually meeting the biblical standards that we say we are. (Semi-formal interview #2, p. 2)

Developing a Relational and Collaborative Class Culture

P2, a young, early career teacher working with Y7 students had only recently become fully registered. She had been informed by previous teachers of the historical social-behavioural problems of a range of students in her class. Experiencing first-hand these problems and social cliques between the students, she proactively *worked hard* on *modelling* and *building* a more relational and supportive class culture linked to the Māori concept of whanaungatanga (Ministry of Education, 2011). The CAR project affirmed P2s locus of control, inviting her to inquire into a topic of immediate relevance rather than having a topic imposed upon her by an external agency.

> I did get straight into it because I found that it was such an issue to me because I didn't like the culture that had first formed in the class. Because that was something that was uncomfortable to me; and something I didn't like, I found that it was something that I really worked hard at to kick off right at the start. (Focus group session #2, p. 2)

Consistent with the New Zealand Curriculum (2007) and her school's strategic goals, she was aware of the value of nurturing a safe, inclusive, learning environment that empowered students to self-manage and take responsibility for their learning. However, achieving this aspiration with socially dysfunctional students was not an easy undertaking. The teacher wrote that she 'struggled at first in knowing how to build whanaungatanga' (P2, End of term two report, p. 1). She got the students to take the Gallup Youth Strength Finders test. She noted, 'Students loved knowing their strengths but when it came to implementation they had no idea what to do' (ibid. p. 1). Her breakthrough came, as expressed, 'Through reflection upon my research and critical discussions I came to the second idea... developing the concept of whanaungatanga in the classroom through cooperative learning' (Ibid. p. 1). As facilitators and mentors we shared readings and resources on co-operative learning with her.

> After reading about these benefits, I knew cooperative learning should be my focus... so far my students have adopted this form of learning very well. After a few minor issues with personality clashes, students are now developing the understanding and knowledge of how to work well together, how to learn from others and how to contribute to the class and their group. (ibid. p. 1)

Due to extra-curricular teaching responsibilities, the teacher was required to intermittently spend time out of her regular classroom for several weeks which resulted in the students having a number of relieving teachers. However, she wrote,

Every time I have had a reliever they have all commented on how amazing my students are and how well they work together. This has been very encouraging to me… the fruits of this labour are definitely beginning to show and now more than ever it helps me to realise just how important this research is. (ibid., p. 1)

Her initial strategy used mixed ability, co-operative group learning processes within a Social Science inquiry unit. This led on, in the second term cycle, to exploring collaborative group narrative writing with *different* mixed ability groups of students. The benefits of these endeavours were noticeable in the interactive life and emotional security of the class as well as specific students' learning achievements. For example in the second interview P2 said,

The a-ha moment was yesterday, I was able to read some of the narrative assessments, and I had one boy in particular who is dyslexic and he just really dislikes writing. His assessment was just amazing. It was structured so well, and he knew how to use dialogue and I was just so proud of him and I knew that he probably wouldn't have had that standard of work if he wasn't working with others and learning from those people. So I thought that was really cool to see. I kind of knew it was to do with the work you've been doing [teacher-educators] with this group. (Semi-formal interview #2, p. 1)

In summing up her experiences with the CAR project, P2 perceived she had experienced transformation in her own teaching and in the culture of the class whereby collaboration was now normative, and not something that needed to be forced. She affirmed the fruit of her Action Research was more readily apparent in this second cycle.

I think that this term has been more encouraging to me because I found that the kids are just naturally collaborating in their groups. And it's just like the overall classroom culture it's more of a natural thing than a forced thing. And so I think, in regards to it being effective, I think it's been really good this term and really pleasing to see. I think it's definitely changed me as a teacher in the way I talk to the kids and how I decided to do a certain topic or teach a certain lesson. (Focus group session #2, p. 1)

It is noteworthy that P2 has commenced her Masters of Professional Practice this year, 2018, being influenced in part as a result of the experiences during the CAR project.

Modelling and Facilitating Innovative Inquiry via Digital Applications

P3, a middle school teacher, with leadership responsibilities in English and E-learning identified two persistent challenges she needed to overcome during the project. 'Time, would be the big one… also self-doubt in my ability to be able to do this well for the students.' These findings highlight that even with the release time this participant was still very busy with everything on her workload, not to mention her out of school role as a mother to young children. Even though she was a successful teacher with a Masters' degree, she still felt a lack of confidence to effectively support students' learning achievement in the topic of her choice. Notwithstanding, she did persevere and with collegial support, her Action Research was successfully implemented around scaffolding students to interpret and apply scripture with the aid of digital device applications.

> The highlight would be seeing the effect it's had on the students, when their eyes light up and they want to know more about scripture; when they're actually motivated to investigate it for themselves; what scripture says and how they can apply to their lives and how certain topics are relevant to them, they can turn to the bible to get wisdom and understanding from it. They are motivated to do it, rather than just choosing the first verse that comes to them and doing what they think it says. (Focus group session #2, p. 1)

P3 described how participation in the CAR project helped her to interrogate *why* she taught the way she did; a significant issue, distinct from how and what she taught. The following quote also reveals a shift from imparting knowledge to empowering students with not only the tools for biblical inquiry but also a passion to want to learn from scripture.

> I think it has motivated me as a teacher to critique why I teach scripture to my students and the importance of digging deep, especially with the Y8 students ... they're at that stage where they want to know more and they are questioning quite a bit. So in terms of my professional practice for me it's not good enough to impart knowledge; it's to enable students to have a passion to want to learn from scripture at a more deep level and I think that's what's changed in how it's influenced my professional practice. (Semi-formal interview #2, p. 1)

In describing an a-ha moment in her CAR experience, P3 shared how impacting it had been for the students when they realised a popular verse from the Bible was being misapplied and taken out of context. The verse referred to in the following interview excerpt is, 'For I know the thoughts I think toward you says the LORD, thoughts of peace, and not of evil, to give you an expected end' (Jeremiah 29:11 KJV). This was a verse often heard by P3 in the culture of the school.

> I think a big moment for the students was when they realised that Jeremiah 29:11 wasn't about them, and along the way their understanding that scripture has been interpreted differently through history, and the importance of studying scripture and not just going with what is read at face value. (Semi-formal interview #2, p. 1)

At the outset of the CAR project P3 had a concern that although students could memorise scripture they did not know how to interpret scripture or apply it to their lives. Initially, she wanted to learn about biblical hermeneutics, so *she could teach* her students better. But as we engaged in collegial critique, her focus expanded to developing pedagogical strategies to empower her 12-13 year old students with a method and tools to interpret scripture collaboratively. She then facilitated lessons involving the students inquiring into topics that were meaningful to them. For example the students wanted to explore the controversial and popular topic of tattoos. P3 described that experience as follows.

> When they started to look at tattoos… and some of them had already decided that tattoos were sinful and God didn't like tattoos and so when we studied the scriptures, when we collaboratively came together and discussed it in class and said, so what is your view of tattoos and they said, well God doesn't mind tattoos if … and they were able to talk about if they were done not to worship another god or not in the form of vanity, if they were done tastefully, then it would possibly be OK. And so that for them, understanding that and applying it to real-life situations, was huge, I feel. (Semi-formal interview #2, p. 1)

This comprehensive approach to the CAR project meant the students were no longer passive learners, but actively involved, having choice in the topics for inquiry, within a well-scaffolded and safe learning environment.

> I think the benefits for students and their learning is the questioning, not being willing to sit back and be given the knowledge but to take an active role in their own learning, … dig deeper, things that are applicable to them, that they want to know about and enabling them to have the tools to then search through the Bible and get the answers that they so readily want. So I feel that for me was hugely beneficial. And now we're going on with 'bullying' and we're all studying scriptures. Each student has a specific scripture in the context of bullying. And they're studying it and going to come together. (Semi-formal interview #2, p. 2)

Consistent with the findings from the other participants, P3 also found that it was during the second cycle of the project where the effects of the action research gained momentum. And like the others, P3 also felt motivated to pursue her topic beyond the conclusion of the CAR project.

> I feel I was more effective this term than last term because it finally got going… it was a mixture of group discussions, presentations, investigations and student individual assignment work. In terms of

effectiveness, I think it needs to be ongoing, redeveloped more, in order for it to be overall effective. (Semi-formal interview #2, p.2)

Encouraging Virtues through Authentic Care, Teaching Activities and Curriculum Integration

P4 an experienced teacher-leader, was passionate about nurturing virtues in her students, such as care and respect for each other. Known in Māori culture as manaakitanga, this theme also links with the biblical concept of, the 'Fruit of the Spirit'. At first the teacher wanted to outwork the CAR with two student groups; her Y9 Home Room/English Class and a separate girls-only Year 10 group, with whom she met voluntarily during lunchtimes on a weekly basis. The teacher gathered diagnostic data from both student groups regarding their perceptions of the degree to which virtues were evident in her own teaching and personality. She wanted to grow in these virtues and to be an authentic role model. She then surveyed the student groups for their feedback on the virtues that were absent or lacking in their own interactions with one another. The findings from these two surveys helped P4 to prioritise her action planning. Her interest was further motivated by a genuine concern for the well-being of her students.

> We've got a lot of mental health challenges and also bullying within the classroom that is quite underlying – you wouldn't pick it out unless you knew about it, cause they're quite devious in the way they do it… and then the mental health issues, you wouldn't know but I only know because parents tell me that their kids, what's going in their kids' lives…some of these kids are very good at hiding how they're truly feeling. (Semi-formal interview #2, p. 2)

However, P4's intentions for the project were too broad and abstract; her initial, transformational goals too ambitious, overly complex, and difficult to implement. This created a slow start for P4 and was complicated by additional pressures within and outside of school. When asked to describe her action planning, progress and challenges at the beginning of the second cycle of the project she said,

It's been quite vague, I think it's been a hard thing... because it's not like a set classroom activity or challenge. It's kind of changing who people are. So I found it's been really hard, it's not been clear, it's applying this abstract like concept almost of changing who you are through the classroom activities that you do which has been really, really challenging. So I'm trying to think of practical ways that we can actually apply, show and reflect on the fruit of the Spirit constantly so it's ... constantly reflecting on what it does look like and examples of in the Bible or in people, or examples when it's not those things, and through creative writing which we're about to do, we haven't got to the activity I want to. (Semi-formal interview #2, p. 3)

Furthermore, when asked in this interview to clarify her role in the process, P4 said,

It's like showing it myself, through loving them I think, like all of those goals will be achieved through love, God's greatest commandment was love, and I think when you love them those other fruits come off naturally. So if I show those things... I'm not sure. (Semi-formal interview #2, p. 3)

In time, through collegial critique and mentoring, her plans were narrowed down to just the students in her Y9 Home Room/English Class and involved a combination of role modelling strategies, songs, activities, a story book, posters, as well as integrating the virtues of the fruit of the Spirit into a series of English lessons. The first set of these lessons was observed by one of the researchers by mutual agreement. The time commenced with the teacher warmly welcoming the students and engaging relationally with them, followed by a time of relaxed singing accompanied by guitars and percussion. This 'fellowship time' was a normal part of the school timetable for her Form Class and was followed by a structured English lesson.

The naturalistic in-class observation notes highlighted that the integration of the virtues into the writing activity based around a selection of static images (photos), was challenging for the students and more difficult than the teacher had anticipated. Yet through this difficulty the teacher recognised the need for more explicit planning. Subsequent teaching experiences developed greater confidence in planning for and integrating virtues into her teaching. In an email several weeks later, P4 explained what she had been doing for her CAR and the influence it was having on her professional practice.

> I have tried a few lessons that were solidly integrated within the creative writing unit... I think it taught me that we can more solidly integrate things from the Bible within our teaching in a subtle way by use of examples and stories, especially in English. It seems silly for me not to have done this explicitly before, but this project has helped me to be clearer with my intentions and how to do it. (Personal correspondence, 28th August, 2017)

In the same email she described her next steps which continue the theme of integrating her chosen topic within English writing. Of note is her acknowledgement of the benefits of having *time to think* and the personal and pedagogical effects of this reflective processing.

> We will be moving on to short stories and the use of static images. I will try to help the students find underlying themes of the 'fruit of the Spirit' or lack of. Having the time to think about this has improved my teaching. I feel like it is helping me to have a more biblically based classroom. Even once the project is over, I will continue to find ways to build up my classroom in the ways I have researched and experimented with. (Personal correspondence, 28th August, 2017)

Additional Positive Outcomes from Mentoring of Teacher Participants

Analysis of the data also showed a range of examples where the mentoring received during the release sessions had impacted on the participants' professional thinking and decision-making. P1 noted that one of the teacher-educators had encouraged her to focus on emphasizing the purpose of narrative writing to increase student motivation.

Table 2. Summary of key findings related to the six subsidiary research questions

Research questions	P1	P2	P3	P4
'What personal, professional and contextual factors influence teacher-participants' choice of topic to explore through the collaborative action research processes?'	Senior teacher-leader, awareness that students lacked understanding of assessment criteria and feedback skills in English.	Early career teacher, dissonance over class culture, desire to improve relationships and collaboration.	Experienced teacher-leader, concern for student biblical literacy and inquiry skills.	Experienced teacher-leader, passion for nurturing virtues in student character.
'How do the participant teachers develop, implement and refine their action plans.'	Class discussions, student voice/agency, assessment rubric redeveloped for oral language, practised feedback skills, applied learning to written language unit.	'Strengths' survey, learned about and implemented cooperative groups in Social Science unit, collaborative group practices in written language unit.	Class survey, modelling and applying biblical hermeneutics, student-led collaborative inquiries via applications on digital devices.	Student surveys, trialling activities (songs, posters, story book), integration of virtues within English lessons (static images, short-story writing).
'How might the collaborative action research processes influence teacher-participants' professional practice?'	Improved sense of teacher efficacy, shift from directed teaching to facilitation of student learning, sharing within teaching team.	New pedagogical strategies, improved emotional well-being, collaborative class culture best fit for preferred teaching style.	Strengthened sense of teacher agency, strengthened capacity to facilitate meaningful student-led inquiry via digital applications.	Improved understanding and application of integrating character development into class programme and English written language.
'How might the teacher-participants' action plans impact student engagement and learning?'	Improved student understanding and application of success criteria, skills for self and peer assessment feedback in oral and written language.	Improved peer relationships, collaborative support and quality of learning outcomes within a social science and written language.	Improved student biblical literacy and inquiry skills, motivation to learn through the use of digital devices, enhanced student agency.	Positive teacher student rapport, increased awareness among students of virtues and corresponding behaviour.

Research questions	P1	P2	P3	P4
'What challenges or hindrances did participants experience to enacting their plans?'	Resisting directed teaching and learning how to encourage student voice and self-management.	Overcoming student personality clashes within cooperative groups.	Building own knowledge base and overcoming self-doubt.	Time commitments, complexity of transformational goals.
'What aspects of the half- day fortnightly release sessions were believed to be effective and how might the sessions be strengthened?'	Having quality time away from busyness of school to think and plan. Being able to choose their own topics, Collegial support from fellow-participants and mentors, Critical friends discussion groups In-class naturalistic observations and feedback. Extended cycles of the process to embed the new-learning.			

This was an extension to the original focus on success criteria and feedback. In the following quote, the teacher links purpose to a broader meta-narrative connected to the special character of the school.

> After the discussion with Janette, really exploring purpose and encouraging children to see the purpose in writing a narrative and appreciating that it's a powerful tool they have at their fingertips to bring pleasure to other people… and I think giving them purpose in our unit work, like love your neighbour… to really appreciate it as an individual they've been designed to love others and how important that makes them to their community. So I think focusing on drawing out that deeper level of stuff for them. (Semi-formal interview #2, p. 2)

Another outcome from the CAR project was that the researchers encouraged P3 to develop and present her CAR experiences as a paper at the International Conference for Christian Educators (ICCTE), being hosted by Bethlehem Tertiary Institute the following year (2018). This additional mentoring role of helping the teacher write and submit an abstract for peer review and supporting her during her presentation was reciprocally encouraging to her and the researchers. Furthermore, as a result of the relational connections established via the CAR, the researchers were also able to support P1 in the development, submission and presentation of a paper to the aforementioned conference based on her recently completed Master's thesis.

IMPLICATIONS, LIMITATIONS AND RECOMMENDATIONS

Implications

The first implication from the findings is that Collaborative Action Research has the potential to effectively support professional development and collegial relationships within a school institution. It is not a quick, technicist strategy, and does require provision of time, mentoring personnel, and funding to release teachers. However, principals, teacher-leaders and teachers can be confident that CAR is a robust, transformative, and socio-culturally responsive strategy that can facilitate improved pedagogy and student learning outcomes.

A second implication is the benefits for teacher-educators seeking opportunities to engage in research partnerships with schools. Collaborative Action Research when integrated with a case study method can provide reciprocal benefits to both parties. Not only are teachers mentored through their professional inquiries but authentic opportunities are provided for teacher-educators to gather rich, descriptive, qualitative data. This can lead to opportunities for teacher-educators and their teacher participants to individually or collaboratively disseminate their findings and experiences via educational conferences and publications.

Limitations

The findings of this qualitative case study of a Collaborative Action Research project are highly contextualised and therefore not generalizable to other school contexts. However, readers are invited to reflect on and adapt the processes described to explore and strengthen their own professional practice and institutional cultures. In this way the findings and methodology will have some transferable value to teachers, teacher-leaders and teacher-educators.

Another limitation is what the literature refers to as the Hawthorne effect in which participants may alter their behaviour because they know they are being studied. The data from the focus groups, reflective journaling, interviews and non-participant observations were obtained by the project facilitators. This could have influenced participants to be less likely to report negative effects. McCambridge, Wilton, and Elbourne (2014), conducted a recent critical study of the Hawthorne effect, and showed inconsistent and yet some significant effects can occur. The potential for inauthentic behavioural responses being produced by participants in our Collaborative Action Research project are mitigated by the fact that each teacher had volunteered and that outcomes were not linked to their institutional performance appraisals.

Recommendations

The first recommendation for further research is that a follow-up project be conducted with the original teacher participants to further support their professional growth. This second study could also explore how the outcomes from the first project have continued to influence their teaching and students' learning. The second recommendation is for the CAR strategy combined with the case-study method to be applied to different school contexts and with different sectors of the school system. This would help to strengthen the teacher-educators dispositions, knowledge and skills to more effectively serve teachers and schools through this type of professional development.

A final recommendation arising from this case study is that future CAR projects include a member of the school's leadership team. This was brought to our attention when one of the Associate Principals of the participants' school joined in on several of our fortnightly meetings. Further research could be conducted to explore the advantages and disadvantages of having leaders being active participants in the entire process. This could strengthen relationships between teachers and leaders as they share their vulnerabilities and expertise; inviting one another to contribute to professional solutions.

CONCLUSION

Collaborative Action Research is well supported in educational research literature as an empowering, flexible and robust approach to collegial professional inquiry. With appropriate release time and mentoring, it can be responsive to the situated pedagogical needs that are most relevant to teachers. The collaborative and cyclical nature of this method helps build supportive relationships, and ensures in-depth engagement that can produce positive outcomes for teachers and students. CAR is a non-technicist approach to professional learning that requires vulnerability, perseverance, and willingness to trial innovative ideas.

The success of this case-study was enhanced by well-prepared release sessions which included opportunities for professional reading, collegial critique, and quality planning. Reflective journaling, interviews, focus groups and naturalistic in-class observations ensured accountability and transparency in the process, while also providing rich, triangulated qualitative data for the case study component of the project.

The teacher participants in this case study were able to choose their own topics, which were subsequently negotiated and refined. This freedom to choose supported the teachers' sense of professional judgement, efficacy and motivation. P1 explored success criteria and student assessment feedback. P2 explored co-operative group learning and building a collaborative class culture. P3 explored student-led inquiry via digital device applications. P4 explored virtues and their integration through modelling and the curriculum. These diverse topics and the ways that the teachers worked through them was enriching to everyone in the group. All topics led to practices consistent with effective pedagogy for lifting student achievement. Each participant was motivated to continue their learning. P1 expressed how her experiences are already opening up collegial conversations within her capacity as a team leader. P3 was able to develop her findings into a paper and present it at an international conference. P2 has now commenced her Master of Professional Practice degree.

As teacher-educators it has been a valuable learning opportunity to work alongside four middle school teachers in this project. We are passionate about Collaborative Action Research and hope to build upon what we have learned and continue to provide effective in-service professional development to support teachers and their students.

'Tell me and I forget, teach me and I remember, involve me and I learn.'
Benjamin Franklin

REFERENCES

Bambino, D. (2002). Critical friends. *Educational Leadership 59*(6), 25-27.
Barkhuizen, G. P. (2009). Topics, aims, and constraints in English teacher research: A Chinese case study. *TESOL Quarterly, 43*(1), 113-125.
Borg, S. (2009). English language teachers' conceptions of research. *Applied Linguistics, 30*(3), 358-388.
Brydon-Miller, M., Greenwood, D., & Maguire, P. (Eds.). (2003). Why action research? *Action Research 1*(1), 10-11.
Brydon-Miller, M., & Maguire, P. (2009). Participatory action research: Contributions to the development of practitioner inquiry in education. *Educational Action Research, 17*(1), 79-93. DOI: 10.1080/0965079080 2667469.
Bryman, A. (2004). *Social research methods.* Oxford, England: Oxford University Press.
Carson, T., & Sumara, D. (1997). *Action research as a living practice.* New York, NY: Peter Lang.
Coghlan, D., & Brannick, T. (2014). *Doing action research in your own organisation,* (4th ed.). London, United Kingdom: Sage.
Creswell, J. W. (1998). *Qualitative inquiry and research design: Choosing among five traditions.* Thousand Oaks, CA: Sage.
Creswell, J. W. (2003). *Research design: Qualitative, quantitative and mixed methods approaches* (2nd ed.). London, England: Sage.
Curry, M. (2008). Critical friends groups: The possibilities and limitations embedded in teacher professional communities aimed at instructional

improvement and school reform. *Teachers College Record 110*(4), 733-774.

Denzin, N., & Lincoln, Y. (Eds.). (2003). *The landscape of qualitative research* (2nd ed.). Thousand Oaks, CA: Sage.

Du Four, R. (2004). What is a professional learning community? *Educational Leadership 61*(8), 6-11.

Education Review Office (ERO, 2016a). *School evaluation indicators: Effective practice for improvement and learner success.* Retrieved from http://www.ero.govt.nz/assets/Uploads/ERO-15968-School-Evaluation-Indicators-2016-v10lowres.pdf.

Education Review Office (ERO, 2016b). *Wellbeing for success: A resource for schools.* Retrieved from http://www.ero.govt.nz/assets/Uploads/Wellbeing-resource-WEB.pdf.

Edwards-Groves, C., Grootenboer, P., & Ronnerman, K. (2016). Facilitating a culture of trust in school-based action research: Recognising the role of middle leaders. *Educational Action Research, 24*(3), 369-386. DOI: 10.1080/09650792.2015.1131175.

Eriksson, N., Romar, J., & Dyson, B. (2017). The action research story of a student-teacher: Change is not easy and it takes time, effort and critical reflection. *International Journal of Action Research, 13*(1), 51-74. DOI: 10.3224/ijar.v13i1.05.

Evans, M., Lomax, P., & Morgan, H. (2000). Closing the circle: Action research partnerships towards better learning and teaching in schools. *Cambridge Journal of Education, 30*(3), 405-419. DOI: 10.1080/0305 76 40020004531.

Firkins, A., & Wong C. (2005). From the basement of the ivory tower: English teachers as collaborative researchers. *English Teaching, 4*(2), 62–71.

Fraser, D. (2007). State education, spirituality and culture: Teachers' personal and professional stories of negotiating the nexus. *International Journal of Children's Spirituality, 12*(3), 289-305.

Freire, P. (1998). *Teachers as cultural workers.* Boulder, CO: Westview Press.

Fry, L. (2005). Editorial: Toward a paradigm of spiritual leadership. *The Leadership Quarterly 16*, 619-622.

Gibson, A. (2014a). Exploring spirituality in teaching within a Christian school context through collaborative action research. *ICCTE Journal 9*(1), 1-14.

Gibson, A. (2014b). Principals' and teachers' views of spirituality in principal leadership in three primary schools. *Educational Management Administration & Leadership, 42*(4), 520-535. DOI: 10.1177/1741143213502195.

Gibson, A. (2016). Exploring spirituality in the teacher-leadership role of mentoring through collaborative action research. *TEACH Journal of Christian Education, 10*(1), 33-40.

Goodnough, K. (2011). Examining the long-term impact of collaborative action research on teacher identity and practice: The perceptions of K-12 teachers. *Educational Action Research, 19*(1), 73-86. DOI: 10.1080/09650792.2011.547694.

Gustavsen, B. (2001). Theory and practice: The mediating discourse. In P. Reason & H. Bradbury (Eds.). *Handbook of action research: Participatory inquiry and practice.* London, United Kingdom: Sage Publications.

Hargreaves, A. (2007). Sustainable professional learning communities. In L. Stoll & K. Seashore Louis (Eds.), *Professional learning communities: Divergence, depth and dilemmas.* Berkshire, England: Open University Press.

Houston, N., Ross, H., Robinson, J., & Malcolm, H. (2010). Inside research, inside ourselves: Teacher educators take stock of their research practice. *Educational Action Research 18*(4), 555-569.

Huffman, J., & Jacobson, A. (2003). Perceptions of professional learning communities. *International Journal of Leadership Education 6*(3), 239-250.

Jordon, M. (2015). Extra, extra, read all about it: Teacher scaffolds interactive read-alouds of a dynamic text. *Elementary School Journal, 115*(3), 358-383.

Joubert, L., & Hocking, A. (2015). Academic practitioner partnerships: A model for collaborative practice research in social work. *Australian Social Work 68*(3), 352-363. https://www.tandfonline.com/doi/full/10.1080/0312407X.2015.1045533.

Kapachtsi, V., & Kakana, D. (2012). Initiating collaborative action research after the implementation of school self-evaluation. *International Studies in Educational Administration, 40*(1), 35-45.

Keegan, R. (2016). Action research as an agent for enhancing teaching and learning in physical education: A physical education teacher's perspective. *The Physical Educator, 73,* 255-284.

Kemmis, S., & McTaggart, R. (2005). Participatory action research: Communicative action and the public sphere. In N. K. Denzin, & Y. S. Lincoln, (Eds.), *The Sage Handbook of Qualitative Research* (pp. 559-603). Thousand Oaks, CA: Sage.

Korthagen, F. (2010). Situated learning theory and the pedagogy of teacher education: Towards an integrative view of teacher behaviour and teacher learning. *Teaching and Teacher Education, 26*(1), 98-106. https://www.sciencedirect.com/science/article/pii/S0742051X09001103?via%3Dihub.

Lathouris, D., Piliouas, P., Platkitsi, K., & Stylianou, L. (2015). Collaborative action research in the context of developmental work research. A methodological approach for science teachers' professional development. *World Journal of Education, 5*(6), 74-80.

Lundy, L., McEvoy, L., & Byrne, B. (2011). Working with young children as co-researchers: An approach informed by the United Nations Convention of the Rights of the Child. *Early Education & Development, 22*(5), 714-736. DOI: 10.1080/10409289.2011.596463.

Luttenberg, J., Meijer, P., & Oolbekkink, H. (2017). Understanding the complexity of teacher reflection in action research. *Educational Action Research 25*(1), 88-102.

McCambridge, J., Wilton, J., & Elbourne, D. (2014). Systematic review of the Hawthorne effect: New concepts are needed to study research participant effects. *Journal of Clinical Epidemiology, 67*(3), 267-277. DOI: 10.1016/j.jclinepi.2013.08.015.

McNiff, J. (2010). *Action research for professional development: Concise advice for new action researchers:* Hamilton, New Zealand: Teaching Development Unit, Wāhanga Whakapakari Ako.

Maksimović, J. (2010). Historical development of action research in social sciences. *Philosophy, Sociology, Psychology and History, 9*(1), 119-124.

Meadowcroft, P., & Moxley, R. (2009). Naturalistic observation in the classroom: A radical behavioural view. *Educational Psychology, 15*(1), 23-34. https://www.tandfonline.com/doi/abs/10.1080/00461528009529213.

Mengwasser, E., & Walton, M. (2011). 'Show me what health means to you! Exploring children's perspectives of health. *Pastoral Care in Education, 31*(1), 4-14. DOI: 10.1080/02643944.2012.731424.

Mills, G. (2013). *Action research: A guide for the teacher researcher* (5th ed.). Boston, MA: Pearson.

Ministry of Education. (2007). *The New Zealand curriculum for English-medium teaching and learning in Years 1-13.* Wellington, New Zealand: Learning Media.

Ministry of Education. (2011). *Tataiako: Cultural competencies for teachers of Māori learners.* Wellington, New Zealand: Learning Media.

National School Reform Faculty. (2018). *Your guide to critical friends group (CFG) coaches' training.* Retrieved from https://www.nsrfharmony.org/wp-content/uploads/2018/04/YourGuideToCFGCoachesTraining.pdf.

Nelson, E., & Bishop, P. (2013). Students as action research partners: A New Zealand example. *Middle School Journal, 45*(2), 19-26.

O'Brien, R. (2001). *An overview of the methodological approach of action research.* Retrieved from http://www.web.net/~robrien/papers/arfinal.html.

Pellerin, M. (2011). *University-school collaborative action research as an alternative model for professional development through AISI.* Retrieved from https://www.uleth.ca/sites/default/files/AISI%20V1%201%201%20Fall%202011.pdf .

Piggot-Irvine, E. (2006). Establishing criteria for effective professional development and use in evaluating an action research based programme. *Journal of In-service Education, 32*(4), 477-496.

Ponce, O., & Pagan-Maldonado, N. (2015). Mixed methods research in education: Capturing the complexity of the profession. *International Journal of Educational Excellence 1*(1), 111-135.

Ratts, R., Pate, J., Archibald, J., Andrews, S., Ballard, C., & Lowney, K. (2015). The influence of professional learning communities on student achievement in elementary schools. *Journal of Education and Social Policy, 2*(4), 51-61.

Reason, P., & Bradbury, H. (Eds.). (2001). *Handbook of action research: Participative inquiry and practice.* London, United Kingdom: Sage.

Reichertz, J. (2010). Abduction: The logic of discovery of grounded theory. *Forum: Qualitative Social Research 11*(1), Art. 13. Retrieved from http://nbn-resolving.de/urn:nbn:de:0114-fqs1001135.

Rogoff, B. (2003). *The cultural nature of human development.* New York, NY: Oxford University Press.

Sarantakos, S. (2005). *Social research* (3rd ed.) Melbourne, Australia: Macmillan Education.

Seider, S., & Lemma, P. (2004). Perceived effects of action research on teachers' professional efficacy, inquiry mindsets and the support they received while conducting projects to intervene into student learning. *Educational Action Research 12*(2), 219-238. DOI: 10.1080/09650790 400200246.

Shepherd, N. (2012). Action research as professional development: Educating for performative knowledge and enhancing theological capital. *Journal of Adult Theological Education, 9*(2), 121-138.

Sheridan-Thomas, H. K. (2006). Theme and variations: One middle school's interpretation of mandated action research. *Educational Action Research, 14*(1), 101-118.

Somekh, B., & Zeichner, K. (2009). Action research for educational reform: Remodelling action research theories and practices in local contexts. *Educational Action Research 17*(1), 5-21. DOI: 10.1080/09650790802 667402.

Stingu, M. (2012). Reflexive practice in teacher education: Facts and trends. *Procedia-Social and Behavioural Sciences 33*, 617-621.

Stoll, L., & Seashore Louis, K. (Eds.). (2007). *Professional learning communities: Divergence, depth and dilemmas.* Berkshire, England: Open University Press.

Talbert, J. E. (2010). Professional learning communities at the crossroads: How systems hinder or engender change. In A. Hargreaves, A. Lieberman, M. Fullan, & D. Hopkins, (Eds.), *Second International Handbook of Educational Change* (pp. 555-571), Dordrecht, Netherlands: Springer.

Tripp, D. (2005). *Action research: A methodological introduction.* Retrieved from https://www.researchgate.net/profile/David_Tripp/publications.

Wennergren, A., & Rönnerman, K. (2006). The relation between tools used in action research and the zone of proximal development. *Educational Action Research, 14*(4), 547-568.

Whitehead, J., & McNiff, J. (2006). *Action research: Living theory.* London, United Kingdom: Sage Publications.

Woolner, P., Clark, J., Hall, E., Tiplady, L., Thomas, U., & Wall, K. (2008). Pictures are necessary but not sufficient: Using a range of visual methods to engage users about school design. *Learning Environments Research, 13*(1), 1–22. DOI: 10.1007/s10984-009-9067-6.

Zeichner, K. (2003). Teacher research as professional development for P-12 educators in the USA. *Educational Action Research, 11*(2), 301-326.

Zeni, J. (2009). Ethics and the "personal" in action research. In S. Noffke, & B. Somekh (Eds.), *The Sage handbook of educational action research* (pp. 254–266). London, United Kingdom: Sage.

In: Progress in Education. Volume 55
Editor: Roberta V. Nata
ISBN: 978-1-53614-551-9
© 2019 Nova Science Publishers, Inc.

Chapter 3

BEST PRACTICE IN MATHEMATICS LEARNING: A THEORETICAL-CONCEPTUAL DISCUSSION FOR CONSIDERATION

Bing H. Ngu[1,*], *Huy P. Phan*[1], *Hui-Wen Wang*[2], *Jen-Hwa Shih*[2], *Sheng-Ying Shi*[2] *and Ruey-Yih Lin*[2]
[1]University of New England, Armidale, Australia
[2]Huafan University, New Taipei City, Taiwan

ABSTRACT

The concept of optimal best practice, reflecting the paradigm of positive psychology, gained extensive research interests from scholars in the fields of Psychology and Education. Optimal best practice, from the perspective of academia, is concerned with the maximization of a person's cognitive competence in a specific domain of academic learning. Achieving optimal best practice, in this sense, requires the 'activation and enactment' of the process of optimization. In recent years, with the emergence of the study of positive psychology, educators and researchers have explored and focused on the development of different theoretical and

---
[*] Corresponding Author Email: bngu@une.edu.au.

methodological conceptualizations that could explain a person's experience of optimal best. Our significant theoretical and empirical contributions, which consisted of research development in Australia, Malaysia, and Taiwan, have involved the proposition of the Framework of Achievement Bests.

The Framework of Achievement Bests (Ngu & Phan, 2018), recently introduced, emphasizes a person's optimal best practice in daily settings. Best practice encompasses three major components: acquired knowledge, personal experience, and personal functioning. The coining of this term 'best practice,' in particular, focuses on different levels of best practice that may exist on a continuum, for example: realistic achievement best and optimal achievement best. This book chapter, in line with the scope of progressive education, explores in detail the concept of optimal best practice, situated within the context of secondary school mathematics learning. In particular, reflecting our recent research development, we provide a complex methodological conceptualization for understanding of optimal best practice, which takes into account cognitive load imposition.

Keywords: best practice, optimal cognitive functioning, mathematics learning, optimization, index of optimization, cognitive load imposition

INTRODUCTION: THE IMPORTANCE OF OPTIMAL FUNCTIONING

Optimal functioning is an indicator of personal growth (Phan & Ngu, 2017; Phan & Ngu, In press-2018). "What is the best that I can do for myself" is a reflective question that any person, for that matter, would ask. More importantly, this consideration of exceptional outcome is inspirational, and requires planning, deliberation, and subsequent actions. Optimal functioning is quite prevalent in school, especially in the area of academic well-being. Enriched academic well-being experiences in school settings are synonymous with the notion of optimal cognitive functioning. From the paradigm of positive psychology (M. Seligman, 2011; M. E. Seligman & Csikszentmihalyi, 2000) and situated within the context of academia, it is important for educators to consider different pathways and means that could encourage, facilitate, and foster optimal cognitive functioning. Optimal cognitive functioning in a subject matter, for example, may consist of a student's exceeding performance-based results, or the achievement of mastery competence (Phan et al.,).

One area of our research, which we recently delved into, consists of propositions of different 'methodological conceptualizations' that could address a particular topical theme. This research-based approach is innovative as emphasis is placed on a researcher's synthesis of existing studies, in-depth knowledge, and strongly rationalized postulations. The focus of this discourse is to initiate social dialogues, and to encourage researchers to make theoretical, methodological, and/or empirical contributions to the conceptualized inquiry. A proposition, we contend from our research-based discourse, may be accepted, advanced, and/or revised. Other researchers, for example, may offer their interpretations, viewpoints, and alternatives to a postulation that we propose. Hence, from this personal contention, we argue that our proposed theoretical-conceptual model may have plausible credence, despite its complexity.

THE FRAMEWORK OF BEST PRACTICE: A THEORETICAL OVERVIEW

Successful schooling entails more than just academic achievement. School is central to the facilitation and development of other achievement-related attributes, for example: engagement of mastery and deep learning (Lau, Liem, & Nie, 2008; Slack, Beer, Armitt, & Green, 2003), enjoyment and personal interest for learning (Harackiewicz, Barron, Carter, Letho, & Elliot, 1997; Harackiewicz, Barron, Tauer, Carter, & Elliot, 2000; Harackiewicz, Barron, Tauer, & Elliot, 2002), and experience of positive well-being (Fraillon, 2004; Soutter, 2011). One major attribute that is of value for cultivation is the experience of optimal functioning. Optimal functioning, in this case, is concerned with a person's striving to learn and achieve to the fullest of his/her capability (Phan & Ngu, 2017; Phan, Ngu, & Yeung, 2017). This concept of optimal functioning is positive, in nature, and emphasizes the importance of motivation, enrichment, and self-fulfillment of psychological needs. Basically, optimal functioning is non-deficit and details accomplishment of learning objectives that reflects a person's fullest capacity.

The Framework of best practice, which we introduce and discuss in this chapter, closely relates to the theoretical concept of optimal functioning. 'Best practice,' from our conceptualization, features centrally in human agency by emphasizing on optimal standard of accomplishment. This concept of best practice is not concerned with automated and/or repeated actions, nor is it concerned with transformation of key theoretical concepts into applied practices. In a similar vein, best practice does not necessarily emphasize a person's 'best' or optimal standard of performance, given there are individual variations and people differ. Best practice in academic settings, from our point of view, is concerned with a person's accomplishment of three distinctive areas of personal agency: acquired knowledge, personal experience, and personal functioning. These components may act independently, or they may act in tandem to reflect a person's repertoire of best practice in a subject matter.

Best Practice: Acquired Knowledge

The first component of best practice is that of acquired knowledge. From the perspective of mathematics learning, acquired knowledge reflects two different types, for example: (i) *conceptual knowledge*, which focuses on the abstract principle that underlies a specific mathematics topic, and (ii) *procedural knowledge*, which is knowledge pertaining to application of procedure (i.e., the 'how' to perform a given task) (Rittle-Johnson & Alibali, 1999). Acquired knowledge varies between individuals and differs in terms of understanding complexity, consequently because of the impact of differential instructional designs, life experience, etc. A person's level of best practice in mathematics domain may reflect his/her conceptual knowledge and/or procedural knowledge.

Consider, for example, a Year 9 student, Melissa, who is learning the concept of Algebra with her teacher, Mrs. Cho. Another Year 9 student, Kelvin, is in the other class with Mr. Mueller. The topical theme, at present, is Algebra. The two types of acquired knowledge are as follows:

Conceptual Knowledge

Presented with a linear equation such as, $2x + 5 = 21$, Melisa understands the relational concept of the '=' sign, which indicates a quantitative relation whereby the left side of the equation equals to the right hand side. Moreover, having performed a balance operation (i.e., -5 on both sides) on $2x + 5 = 21$, she can judge that a pair of equations are equivalent with respective to the '=' sign concept (i.e., $2x + 5 = 21$, and $2x + 5 - 5 = 21 - 5$) (Ngu & Phan, 2016a).

Procedural Knowledge

Mr. Mueller has taught his class two different methods of solving linear equations, namely, the 'balance method' and the 'inverse method' (Ngu, Phan, Yeung, & Chung, 2018). Mrs. Cho, in contrast, has only exposed her class to the balance method because she is unaware of the inverse method that is more efficient than the balance method from a cognitive load perspective.

The inverse method and the balance method differs in the critical procedural step in the solution procedure (e.g., -5 on both sides *versus* $+5$ becomes -5). The balance operation requires the interaction of elements on both sides of the equation, whereas the inverse operation requires the interaction of elements on one side of the equation. Thus, the balance method imposes twice as many interactive elements as the inverse method for each operation. Accordingly, the inverse method imposes lower cognitive load than the balance method (Ngu et al., 2018). In sum, the two types of acquired knowledge differ between the two students, consequently because of different external factors (e.g., the role of the teacher). Acquired knowledge in this case depends on appropriate instructional design based on cognitive load theory (Sweller, Ayres, & Kalyuga, 2011).

Best Practice: Personal Experience

The second component of best practice is that of personal experience. Personal experience at school is complex in scope, and covers both classroom and school-based levels of accomplishment of academic and non-academic attributes. Personal experience, in its totality, may indicate the following:

1. *Enriched academic learning experience* in classroom settings that involves the acquisition in terms of not only competence but also mastery of a specific mathematics topic. For example, having been exposed to the inverse method of solving linear equations, students are likely to acquire schema not only for simple one-step linear equations (e.g., $2x = 10$), but also complex one-step linear equations (e.g., $15\%x = 30$). The presence of a percentage, which is a complex element (Ngu & Phan, 2016b) renders the equation, $15\%x = 30$ more complex than $2x = 10$.

2. *Enriched school-based experiences* that are relatively diverse, and involve: (i) students' *emotional functioning* (Ryan & Deci, 2001; Ryff, 1989; M. Seligman, 2011) in terms of their positive (e.g., happiness) and negative (e.g., anxiety) responses, (ii) students' expressed *feelings for schooling* in terms of whether they believe that school, in general, is worthwhile (Opdenakker & Van Damme, 2000; Van Damme, De Fraine, Van Landeghem, Opdenakker, & Onghena, 2002), (iii) students' *perceived view of school* in its entirety, especially in relation to acceptance of diversity, safety, belonging, and appreciation, and (iv) students' proactive *social relationships* with both teachers (Bergeron, Chouinard, & Janosz, 2011; Cornelius-White, 2007; Roorda, Koomen, Spilt, & Oort, 2011) and peers (Lau et al., 2008; A. D. Liem, Lau, & Nie, 2008).

Inclusion of both classroom and school-based level attributes supports a more holistic view of the schooling process. This indication of personal experience, encompassing different academic and non-academic attributes is consistent with previous theorizations that emphasize on the saliency of accomplishment of different classroom (e.g., academic performance in a subject discipline) and school-based (e.g., proactive peer relationship) outcomes. Successful schooling, in this sense, is more global and encompasses a variety of personal experiences that may not necessarily reflect academic achievement.

Personal experience at school, indeed, may serve as an important index of a student's level of best practice. Importantly, of course, indication of personal experience may show achievement and self-fulfillment of both classroom and school-based level attributes. Positive personal experience, for example, may indicate a student's successful best practice because of the following, for example: (i) his/her enjoyment of school, consequently as a result of ample opportunities to partake in extracurricular activities and pastoral care programs, (ii) his/her proactive engagement in social relationships with teachers and peers, and (iii) his/her enrichment of academic learning, such as being exposed to an efficient instructional design that has low cognitive imposition for acquiring conceptual knowledge, and/or procedural knowledge of a mathematics topic. It is possible, of course, that some students may report negative school experiences. Engagement of work-avoidance practices, such as school disengagement (A. D. Liem et al., 2008; Salamonson, Andrew, & Everett, 2009), delinquency, and problem substance use (Henry, 2010; Henry, Knight, & Thornberry, 2012) may indicate negative school experience.

Best Practice: Personal Functioning

The third component of best practice is that of personal functioning. Personal functioning in school settings is relatively complex in terms of scope. This concept of personal functioning, in part, closely aligns to the importance of subjective well-being (Fraillon, 2004; Phan & Ngu, 2015; Ryan & Deci, 2001; Soutter, 2011). One aspect of subjective well-being, in this analysis, entails the striving of optimal functioning in life. Optimal functioning involves self-fulfillment of psychological needs (e.g., autonomy), experience of personal satisfaction, and accomplishment of educational and non-educational outcomes.

Personal functioning in school contexts emphasizes on the saliency of a person's consideration of deliberation, his/her purposive action, and usage of resources that takes into account of efficiency. The notion of 'functioning' itself suggests an individualized state of operation that is dynamic in nature. Personal functioning then, from our point of view, may indicate the following: (i) *engagement of deliberation* (i.e., defined as a person's careful consideration of an act to ensure successful outcome), (ii) *purposive course of action* (i.e., defined as a person's purposive act that takes into account the confinement of resourcefulness), and (iii) *subsequent effective operation* (i.e., defined as a person's consideration and mindfulness to achieve maximization in outputs, taking into account the confinement of resourcefulness) that may result in efficiency. This theorization is similar to that of the concept of *optimization* (Fraillon, 2004; Phan et al., 2018b), which focuses on a person's quest to achieve notional best functioning from actual functioning.

In the context of mathematics learning, personal functioning may yield some interesting results for consideration. Referring back to the previous example of the case of Melissa, it can be inferred that:

Engagement of Deliberation

Melissa deliberates on the question of whether it is worthwhile to spend time and effort to learn another pedagogical method for solving linear equations (i.e., the inverse method) that may facilitate better understanding of Algebra. Her deliberation is supported, in this case, by her focusing on extra research to determine the effectiveness of this pedagogical method.

Engagement of Purposive Action

Recognizing the effectiveness of the inverse method for solving linear equations (e.g., reduces cognitive load imposition: Sweller, 2010; Sweller et al., 2011), Melissa decides to learn this pedagogical method in order to help her understand Algebra better. As part of this learning, Melissa has devised a personal task for completion: to solve linear equations (e.g., $3x - 11 = 28$)

by using both the balance and inverse methods, and to determine which of the two is easier to comprehend.

Effective Operation

Melissa recognizes the effectiveness of the inverse method, and has decided to use this pedagogical method in her learning of linear equations. In particular, to facilitate her learning, Melissa decides to spend sufficient amount of time to acquire conceptual and procedural knowledge of linear equations via the inverse method. For example, regarding the acquisition of conceptual knowledge, Melissa spends adequate time to learn that a pair of equations (i.e., $2x + 5 = 21$, and $2x = 21 - 5$) are equivalent with respective to the '=' sign concept.

THE EFFECTIVENESS OF BEST PRACTICE

The Framework of best practice, which we propose here, signifies a holistic representation of a person's repertoire of knowledge, competence, and experience. Best practice, in this sense, is not indication of a person's 'best,' but rather a combination of three major components of a person's learning: *acquired knowledge, personal experience*, and *personal functioning*. The Framework of best practice, we contend, is meaningful as it reflects the multifaceted nature of educational and/or non-educational success. Its effectiveness in academic settings, however, may entail the following:

1. Recognition of variations (i.e., strengths, weaknesses) in the three components of best practice between individuals. A student, for example, may indicate an exceptional standard of best practice in relation to acquired knowledge only owing to the exposure of appropriate instructional design that incurs low cognitive load imposition. Another student, in contrast, may report on high levels of personal experience and personal functioning, but not acquired knowledge.

2. Best practice, in the context of mathematics learning, progressively develops in terms of complexity as a result of receiving different instructional designs based on cognitive load theory. For example, research has indicated that the inverse method was better than the balance method in assisting students to acquire schema for multi-step equations (e.g., $5x - 3 = 2x + 7$) that involve multiple steps (Ngu et al., 2018).

3. Best practice, in its totality, is contextual and subject to specificity of the situation and/or learning task, at hand. A student, in this case, may indicate an exceptional standard of acquired knowledge for Algebra but not necessarily Calculus. Again, we can attribute such phenomenon to differential instructional practices in the classrooms. Any instruction that disregards the negative impact of cognitive load imposition would hinder learning. At the same time, however, situational circumstance may influence a person's level of best practice. An unfortunate incident at home, for example, is likely to result in indication of a low level of best practice.

In summary, the Framework of best practice is effective for its explanatory account of human behavior. Best practice provides a strong basis for in-depth understanding of quality learning and enriched well-being experiences in school contexts. In a classroom context, best practice may explain deficiencies and offer pathways and means to improve learning and academic performance.

THE FRAMEWORK OF ACHIEVEMENT BESTS

The effectiveness of best practice may be explained from the perspective of achievement bests. The Framework of Achievement Bests, recently introduced by Phan and colleagues (Phan et al., 2018b; Phan, Ngu, & Williams, 2016; Phan et al., 2017), attempts to explain the process of optimization and, more importantly, how a person reaches an optimal level of best practice. Figure 1 shows our adaptation of the original conceptualization of the Framework of Achievement Bests. In this revision of the Framework of Achievement Bests, we emphasize three major theoretical facets: (i) the activation and enactment (AE) of psychological, educational, and psychosocial agencies, (ii) the personal experience of energization, which may then serve to stimulate the buoyancy of intrinsic motivation, effective functioning, personal resolve, mental strength, and effort expenditure, and (iii) the arousal and sustaining of a person's progress from T_1 to T_2. The importance of this revised theoretical model (Phan et al.,), from our perspective, lies in its emphasis on the operational nature of optimal functioning – that is, in terms of theoretical understanding, optimal functioning is defined as the difference between L_1 at T_1 and L_2 at T_2 (i.e., $\Delta_{(L2T2-L1T1)}$).

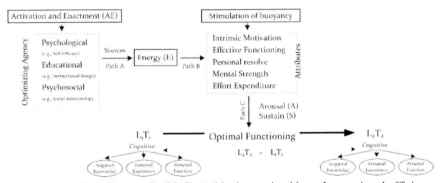

Note: Adapted from Phan et al. (2017). Achieving optimal best: Instructional efficiency and the use of cognitive load theory in mathematical problem solving. *Educational Psychology Review*, 29(4), 667-692. doi: 10.1007/s10648-016-9373-3.

Figure 1. The Framework of Achievement Bests.

An In-Depth Analysis of Optimal Functioning

Fraillon's (2004) seminal review of subjective well-being in school contexts briefly introduced the theoretical concept of optimization, which is defined as the difference between a person's actual best functioning and his/her notional best functioning. A decade later, Phan and colleagues (Phan et al., 2016) expanded on this consideration and proposed two corresponding tenets: realistic achievement best, defined as a person's actual level of functioning at the present time, and optimal achievement best, defined as a person's indication at the present time of the maximization of his/her competence in a subject matter. This theorization, in accord with Fraillon's (2004) original definition, is comparable to that of Vygotsky's (1978) sociocultural theory of cognitive learning pertaining to the zone of proximal development (ZPD). Of interest, however, is the understanding that optimal functioning, in this sense, reflects the maximization of a person's functioning. Other researchers have also proposed similar psychological concepts that emphasize the importance of a person's state of resilience, effort, and proactive accomplishment, for example: personal best goals (G. A. D. Liem, Ginns, Martin, Stone, & Herrett, 2012; Martin, 2011), flourishing (Diener et al., 2009; Diener et al., 2010), thriving (Su, Tay, & Diener, 2014; Wiese, Tay, Su, & Diener, 2018), and personal striving (Phan & Ngu, 2015; Phan et al., 2018a).

We contend that the derivative of the concept of optimal functioning requires the fulfilment of three major criteria: (i) a point of reference, which we coin as L_1, for personal benchmarking and comparison, (ii) the precedence of time difference (i.e., T_1, T_2... T_n), and (iii) the enactment of different facets of human agency in order for a person to progress from T_1 to T_2. Experience of optimal functioning, comparable with a state of flourishing, is depicted as the difference between a person's state of functioning (e.g., cognitive, social, emotional, physical) at T_1 and that at T_2 – that is, the difference between L_1T_1 (i.e., realistic achievement best at T_1) and L_2T_2 (i.e., optimal achievement best at T_2). This difference, denoted as $\Delta_{(L2T2-L1T1)}$, is positive in nature and reflects the importance of personal growth. The Framework of Achievement Bests (Phan et al., 2018b; Phan et al., 2017), in this sense, describes an underlying process known as optimization, which could assist in a person's achievement of optimal functioning. To date, as we have noted, very few theoretical conceptualizations exist to explain how a person reaches a state of optimal best. Drawing from Phan et al.'s (Phan et al., 2017) theoretical proposition and Phan et al.'s (Phan et al., 2018b) recent empirical study, we consider a revised conceptualization of optimization that is more explanatory (Phan et al.,).

What is of considerable interest, from our revision of the Framework of Achievement Bests (Phan & Ngu, 2017; Phan et al., 2017), is the proposition of a theoretical concept that may serve as a central anchor in the achievement of optimal functioning: energy. In this analysis, we postulate that the activation and enactment of psychological (e.g., personal self-efficacy belief: Bandura, 1997), educational (e.g., an appropriate instructional design: Ngu & Phan, 2016a), and psychosocial (e.g., teacher-student relationship: Roorda et al., 2011) agencies in life would create a source of positive 'energy' for action. Positive energy is indicative of operational change, propelling the dynamic functioning of different personal attributes (e.g., intrinsic motivation) that would then arouse and sustain a person's progress. There are three major pathways, as shown in our conceptualization, which depict the totality of optimization – (i) Pathway A: the formation of a source of energy (i.e., AE → E), (ii) Pathway B: the stimulation of buoyancy of intrinsic motivation, effective functioning, personal resolve, mental strength, and effort expenditure (i.e., E → SB), and (iii) Pathway C: the arousal and sustaining of a person's progress across time (i.e., SB → AS).

It is plausible, from our conceptualization, to consider a quantitative methodological development to measure and assess the totality of optimization. We propose an 'optimizing effect', denoted as 'γ', which reflects the combined paths of A, B, and C – that is:

$$\gamma = \text{Path A} + \text{Path B} + \text{Path C} \tag{1}$$

Moreover, our proposition considers another theoretical tenet, which may illustrate the holistic nature of optimization – that is, the Index of Optimization (IO), according to our positioning, equates to the following relationship:

$$IO = \Delta_{(L2T2-L1T1)} \times \gamma \tag{2}$$

where $\Delta_{(L2T2-L1T1)}$ = the difference between realistic achievement best (i.e., L_1) and optimal achievement best (i.e., L_2), and γ (i.e., optimizing effect) = Path A + Path B + Path C (Phan et al., 2018b). The Index of Optimization, in this analysis, may vary in its numerical value (e.g., 0 = a minimal level of optimization, 10 = a high level of optimization), which in turn could highlight the magnitude or strength of the process of optimization. This proposition regarding the 'magnitude of optimization' (e.g., what is the strength of optimization that a teacher would need to ensure that a student is able to achieve an exceptional result in the half-yearly mathematics exam?) is insightful, emphasizing the importance of complexity in a person's state of functioning. For example, a small-to-moderate level of difference between L_1 and L_2 (e.g., where L_2 is not complex and does not differ that much from L_1) would correspondingly suggest a minimal value for the Index of Optimization, whereas a larger level of difference (e.g., where L_2 is complex and differ largely from L_1) would indicate a high value.

The Optimization of Levels of Best Practice

From the preceding sections, we briefly described the theoretical tenets of the process of optimization. Achieving an optimal level of best practice, L_2 at T_2, from a realistic level of best practice, L_1 at T_1, calls for the enactment of optimization. Indeed, from our examination of the literature, very few if any research has yet addressed this topical theme – that is, how does optimization, as a general underlying process, explain the operational nature of $\Delta_{(L2T2-L1T1)}$. In a recent study, using a correlational methodological design, Phan et al., (Phan et al., 2018b) explored the mediating influences of three comparable psychological agencies: effective functioning, personal resolve, and emotional functioning. Structural equation modeling (SEM)(Kline, 2011; Schumacker & Lomax, 2004), in this case, showed that the three mentioned psychological agencies positively mediated the effect of realistic achievement best onto optimal achievement best (e.g., realistic achievement best → effective functioning → optimal achievement best, β = .07, $p < .01$). This evidence, preliminary at this stage of development, is insightful for the purpose of enabling researchers and educators to seek further understanding into the operational nature of optimal functioning.

One notable aspect for consideration in the study of optimal functioning, from our point of view, entails the development of appropriate methodological designs that could effectively measure and assess the process of optimization (Phan et al., 2018b). An in situ experimental intervention, for example, may provide strong grounding into the understanding of clarity of Pathways A, B, and C. In tandem with this emphasis of methodological designs, we also recognize that there is a need to descriptively consider the nature of both realistic and optimal achievement best in the context of academic learning. For example, in relation to mathematics learning, Table 1 describes the two levels of best practice in terms of acquired knowledge, personal experience, and personal functioning.

The present discussion, as shown in Table 1, complements our understanding of the Framework of Achievement Bests by detailing both realistic achievement best and optimal achievement best of the three components of best practice of mathematics learning. In this case, differing from previous conceptualization (Phan et al., 2017), achievement of optimal best may involve: (i) acquired knowledge, which entails both conceptual and procedural knowledge, (ii) personal experience, (ii) personal experience that include both classroom and school-based experiences, and (iii) personal functioning, which entails engagement of deliberation, engagement of purposive action, and effective operation. This indication highlights, specifically, the complexity of achievement of an exceptional level of best practice. In this analysis, the achievement of optimal best does not rest solely with the notion of acquired knowledge; rather, the achievement of optimal best from realistic best indicates that there are individual variations of different components of best practice. For example, within a secondary school context, a student may choose to seek optimal best in personal experience of mathematics, but not for acquired knowledge and/or personal functioning.

Table 1. Realistic and Optimal achievement best

	Realistic achievement best	Optimal achievement best
Acquired knowledge		
1. Declarative	Learning the topical theme of 'linear equations' of Algebra problems. For example, having performed a balance operation, a student can judge that a pair of equations are equivalent with respect to the '=' sign concept: $5x - 1 = 7$ and $5x - 1 + 1 = 7 + 1$ (Balance operation)	Learning the topical theme of 'linear equations' of Algebra problems. For example, having performed a balance operation or an inverse operation, a student can judge that a pair of equations are equivalent with respect to the '=' sign concept: $5x - 1 = 7$ and $5x - 1 + 1 = 7 + 1$ (Balance operation) $5x - 1 = 7$ and $5x = 7 + 1$ (Inverse operation)
2. Procedural	Knowing that there is one procedure (i.e., balance method) for solving linear equations.	Knowing that there are different procedures (i.e., balance method and inverse method) for solving linear equations, and that more effective procedures take into account the negative impact of cognitive load imposition (i.e., inverse method).
Personal experience	Class-based learning experience results in the acquisition of schema for simple one-step equations (e.g., $9x = 36$).	Enriched class-based learning experience results in the acquisition of schema for both simple one-step equations as well as complex one-step equations (e.g., $12\%x = 40$).
	School enjoyment, especially when it comes to learning English and mathematics. Indication of progressive appreciation and enjoyment of other subject disciplines.	School enjoyment and appreciation of different academic disciplines. Indication of keen interest to partake in extracurricular activities and pastoral care programs to boost one's well-being.

	Realistic achievement best	Optimal achievement best
Personal functioning		
1. Engagement of deliberation	Deliberates on choosing an appropriate pedagogical method (e.g., balance method) to successfully solve Algebra problems.	Deliberates on understanding and mastering all the different pedagogical methods available (e.g., balance method and inverse method).
2. Engagement of purposive action	Recognizing the effectiveness of a particular pedagogical method (e.g., substitution method), and choosing to master this method for solving simultaneous linear equations.	Recognizing variations in effectiveness of different pedagogical methods (e.g., substitution method and elimination method). Consider usage of these two pedagogical methods, depending on types of simultaneous linear equation. For example, using the substitution method when one variable is the subject of an equation.
3. Effective operation	Specific in terms of expenditure of resources (e.g., time) to ensure successful completion of tasks.	Consider having a balance in expenditure of resources (e.g., time) and the use of an efficient method to ensure mastery and successful of tasks.

Note: An example of Year 9 mathematics learning.

IMPLICATIONS FOR CONSIDERATION: OPTIMIZING BEST PRACTICE

An important focus to consider is the optimization of best practice. To date, the Framework of Achievement Bests is limited for its restrictive focus on the definition of what constitutes 'best practice,' and hence, its explanatory account of the process of optimization. That is, theorization of achievement bests (Phan et al., 2018b; Phan et al., 2017) at present emphasizes on the importance of acquired knowledge, and very little is known about the achievement of personal experience and personal functioning. We contend that the process of optimization may expand to incorporate the three components of best practice. This inquiry is complex and entails consideration of optimization of the following: (i) conceptual and procedural knowledge (i.e., acquired knowledge), (ii) personal experience, and (iii) engagement of deliberation, engagement of purposive action, and effective operation (i.e., personal functioning). Achieving an exceptional level of best practice may differentiate and involve disparities in terms of successes and failures. Different optimizing agents may influence and optimize different components of best practice, for example:

1. Realistic Best (Conceptual knowledge) → Optimal Best (Conceptual knowledge)
2. Realistic Best (Classroom-based experience) → Optimal Best (Classroom-based experience)
3. Realistic Best (Engagement of deliberation) → Optimal Best (Engagement of deliberation)

The Optimal Outcomes Questionnaire

The Optimal Outcomes Questionnaire (Phan, Ngu, & Williams, 2015) is self-rating (i.e., 1 – 7) and consists of two major subscales: the Realistic Best Subscale and the Optimal Best Subscale. Each subscale has eight items and reflects the nature and characteristics of each achievement best type (Phan et al., 2016). Scores for each subscale range from 8 (i.e., a rating of 1 × 8 items) to 56 (i.e., a rating of 7 × 8 items). Quantitative research studies undertaken by Phan and colleagues, preliminary at this stage, have produced three important lines of evidence: Research pertaining to the Framework of Achievement Bests, at present, indicates three major findings:

1. The factorial structure of the Optimal Outcomes Questionnaire, which shows a two first-order factor model and affirms modest psychometric properties (e.g., $\chi^2/df = 1.98$, CFI = .91, TLI = .90) (Phan et al., 2017) for the subscales.
2. The association between realistic achievement best and optimal achievement best. Phan et al., (Phan et al., 2018b), for example, from structural equation modeling found that realistic achievement best positively predicted optimal achievement best (β = .29, p < .001).
3. The establishment of four distinctive profiles of achievement bests, illustrating corresponding permutations of responses to both the realistic and optimal achievement best subscales (Phan et al., 2018a): (a) high score on Realistic achievement best, high score on Optimal achievement best (i.e., Quadrant 1: coined as the Exceptional profile), (b) high score on Realistic achievement best, low score on Optimal achievement best (i.e., Quadrant 2: coined as the Realistic profile), (c) low score on Realistic achievement best, low score on Optimal achievement best (i.e., Quadrant 3: coined as the Pessimistic profile), and (d) low score on Realistic achievement best, high score on Optimal achievement best (i.e., Quadrant 4: coined as the Unrealistic profile).

The Optimal Outcomes Questionnaire (Phan et al., 2015), from our point of view, is advantageous and may act as a diagnostic tool to seek understanding of students' learning and motivational patterns. In this analysis, Phan et al.'s (Phan et al., 2018a) recent research is insightful for the purpose of providing understanding into an important concept of 'student profiling.' The use of the Optimal Outcomes Questionnaire, according to the authors, is simple and non-intrusive, enabling researchers and educators to gauge into students' perceptions and judgments of their best practice. From an educational point of view, the notion of profiling is beneficial as it could serve as a source of motivation for students to direct their focus of attention to the learning task and/or practical activity. One distinction from this study of profiling is concerned with the encouragement towards and the fostering of the Exceptional profile (i.e., Quadrant 1).

Introducing the Best Practice Questionnaire

Arising from the present discussion is the introduction of the theoretical concept of best practice, which we contend would coincide with the Framework of Achievement Bests (Phan & Ngu, 2017; Phan et al., 2017). This information, from our point of view, is insightful for the purpose of clarity into individual variations between the three components of best practice.

From a quantitative methodological approach, we have developed the Best practice Questionnaire (Phan & Ngu, 2016), which is Likert-scale and consists of three subscales. Table 2 presents sample items of the three subscales. In total, the Best practice Questionnaire has 51 items: (i) 16 items for the Acquired knowledge Subscale (8 items for Conceptual Knowledge, and 8 items for Procedural Knowledge, (ii) 22 items for the Personal experience Subscale (5 items for Academic Learning Experience, and 17 items for School-based Experience), and (iii) 13 items for the Personal functioning Subscale (4 items for Engagement of Deliberation, 4 items for Purposive Course of Action, and 5 items for Effective Operation). Individual scores arising from responses to the different subscales may inform educators and researchers of students' differing levels of best practice (i.e., acquired knowledge, personal experience, and personal functioning). For example, in the context of secondary school mathematics learning, a student may report on exceptional levels for acquired knowledge and personal experience, but not personal functioning. Another student, in contrast, may

Best Practice in Mathematics Learning

indicate an exceptional level for personal experience, but not for acquired knowledge and/or for personal functioning.

An important inquiry that is of value, in this case, relates to the striving of optimal best for the three different components of best practice. This endeavor requires conceptualization, especially given that the Best practice Questionnaire does not contain descriptions of aspired positioning and determination to achieve an exceptional level of best practice. That is, in contrast to the Optimal Outcomes Questionnaire, the Best practice Questionnaire emphasizes the importance of actual functioning, and does not attempt to measure and/or assess the notion of optimal achievement best (e.g., "I can achieve much more in this subject than I have indicated through my work so far"). If this is the case, then how do we determine levels of best practice from responses to the Best practice Questionnaire (i.e., realistic achievement best versus optimal achievement best)? It is plausible to consider a cross-validation approach (Leung & Kember, 2003), which we illustrate in Figure 2. This conceptualization postulates two main associations: (i) the association between realistic achievement best and the three components of best practice, and (ii) the association between optimal achievement best and the three components of best practice.

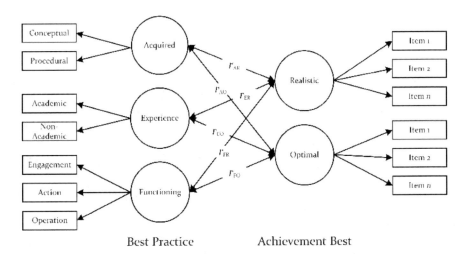

Figure 2. Potential Associations between Best practice and Achievement Best.

Table 2. Realistic and Optimal achievement best

	Component	Sample Items
Acquired Knowledge	*Conceptual Knowledge* (8 items)	I am content with what I know for this topic.
	Procedural Knowledge (8 items)	I know specific procedures that enable me to be successful for this topic.
Personal Experience	*Academic Learning Experience* (5 items)	I appreciate the deep, meaningful learning experience that I have acquired in this subject.
	School-Based Non-Academic Experience (17 items)	I am always happy at school (i.e., *Positive Emotion*, 1 item). I am always uptight when attending school (i.e., *Negative Emotion*, 1 item). I really like attending school (i.e., *Feelings for schooling*, 4 items). I always feel that others are accepting me at school (i.e., *A perceived view of school*, 4 items). I get on with other students at school (i.e., *Relationship with peers*, 4 items). I feel comfortable with my teachers (i.e., *Relationship with teachers*, 3 items).
Personal functioning	*Engagement of Deliberation* (4 items)	I consider carefully a best course of action that would ensure effective learning.
	Purposive Course of Action (4 items)	I purposively use appropriate resources to ensure that I will be successful in my studies.
	Effective Operation (5 items)	I always want to ensure that adequate time is expended to ensure success.

CONCLUSION

This chapter, theoretical and conceptual in nature, continued with an in-depth discussion of the topical theme of optimal functioning. In particular, complementing our other chapter in this book series (Phan et al.,), we introduced an important theoretical concept, coined as the Framework of best practice. The Framework of best practice, in this case, conceptualizes three components of best practice: acquired knowledge, personal experience, and personal functioning. This conceptualization of best practice is poignant for its close alignment with the theory of optimization (Fraillon, 2004; Phan et al., 2017) – that is, optimal best practice may include, in this case, exceptional accomplishment in the fulfilment of acquired knowledge, personal experience, and personal functioning.

The study of optimal functioning in school contexts, often coined as personal best practice (Martin, 2006, 2011), has attracted educational and research interests. One notable inquiry, in this analysis, has consisted of continuing conceptualizations of existing theories into the clarity and understanding of optimal functioning. The Framework of Achievement Bests, introduced in 2016 (Phan et al., 2016), for instance, has led us to undertake a number of empirical research, which has produced some positive yields. For example, from a non-experimental methodological approach, and using the Optimal Outcomes Questionnaire (Phan et al., 2015), we found that students' self-judgments and perceptions of their practice could differentiate into distinct profiles.

Of course, in light of our discussion, we acknowledge that understanding of the theories of optimal functioning is still somewhat limited. One important caveat, which we have mentioned entails the development of appropriate methodological designs that could enable us to effectively measure and assess the process of optimization (Phan et al., 2018b; Phan et al., 2017). Coupled with this is the introduction of the Framework of best practice and its corresponding measure, the Best practice Questionnaire. The Best practice Questionnaire, for example, may provide a diagnostic basis for educators to assess students' reporting of best practice.

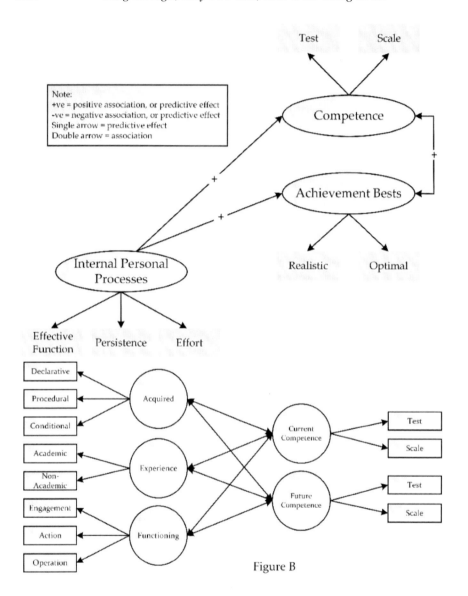

Figure 3. Conceptualization between Best practice and Competence.

One avenue of inquiry for consideration may entail the factorial validation of the Best practice Questionnaire. Cross-cultural validation with different samples, in particular, may affirm the methodological appropriateness and relevance of the questionnaire. At the same time, it is possible to consider the cross-validation of the Optimal Outcomes Questionnaire and the Best practice Questionnaire. Figure 3A, a conceptualization for consideration, shows that the two levels of achievement best may correlate with the construct of cognitive competence, which could include in-class tests and cognitive competence scales (McAuley, Duncan, & Tammen, 1989). A person's current and future cognitive competence scores, measured at T_1 and T_2, may reflect both realistic and optimal achievement bests, respectively. Figure 3B shows, similarly, a conceptualization that may measure and assess both realistic and optimal achievement bests in acquired knowledge, personal experience, and personal functioning. A person's cognitive competence, encompassing both an in-class test and a competence measurement scale (McAuley et al., 1989), on two occasions, may correspond to realistic and optimal levels of best practice.

Finally, best practice is contextual and elicits different patterns in results. In this chapter, we have considered best practice in mathematics learning within the framework of cognitive load theory. It would be of interest for educators to explore best practice for different academic subjects. Becher's (Becher, 1987, 1994) theorization of *intellectual categorization* suggests academic subjects may differentiate into four distinctive categories: 'hard pure theoretical' subjects (e.g., Mathematics), 'soft pure theoretical' subjects (e.g., Ancient History), 'hard applied' subjects (e.g., Home Economics), and 'soft applied' subjects (e.g., ICTs). Intellectual categorization (e.g., hard pure theoretical *versus* hard applied) may give rise to differing patterns in epistemological beliefs, motivation, and approaches to learning (Smith & Miller, 2005). The question then is whether comparative subject matters could elicit different responses for best practice.

REFERENCES

ACU and Erebus International. (2008). *Scoping study into approaches to student wellbeing: Literature review.* Report to the Department of

Education, Employment and Workplace Relations. Sydney, Australia: Australian Catholic University.

Bandura, A. (1986). *Social foundations of thought and action: A social cognitive theory*. Englewood Cliffs, NJ: Prentice-Hall.

Bandura, A. (1997). *Self-efficacy: The exercise of control*. New York: W. H. Freeman & Co.

Becher, T. (1987). The disciplinary shaping of the professions. In B. R. Clarke (Ed.), *The academic profession* (pp. 271 - 303). Berkley, CA: University of California Press.

Becher, T. (1994). The significance of disciplinary differences. *Studies in Higher Education, 19*, 151-161.

Bergeron, J., Chouinard, R., & Janosz, M. (2011). The impact of teacher-student relationships and achievement motivation on students' intentions to dropout according to socio-economic status. *US-China Education Review B 2*, 273-279.

Carver, C. S., & Scheier, M. F. (1999). Optimism. In C. R. Snyder (Ed.), *Coping: The psychology of what works* (pp. 182-204). Oxford, UK: Oxford University Press.

Chen, W. W., & Ho, H. Z. (2012). The relation between perceived parental involvement and academic achievement: the roles of Taiwanese students' academic beliefs and filial piety. *International Journal of Psychology, 47*(4), 315-324. doi: 10.1080/00207594.2011.630004.

Chow, S. S. Y., & Chu, M. H. T. (2007). The impact of filial piety and parental involvement on academic achievement motivation in Chinese secondary school students. *Asian Journal of Counselling*, 14(1 & 2), 91-124.

Cornelius-White, J. (2007). Learner-centered teacher-student relationships are effective: A meta-analysis. *Review of Educational Research, 77*(1), 113-143. doi: 10.3102/003465430298563.

Daulta, M. S. N. (2008). Impact of home environment on the scholastic achievement of children. *Journal of Human Ecology, 23*(1), 75-77.

Diener, E., Wirtz, D., Biswas-Diener, R., Tov, W., Kim-Prieto, C., Choi, D. W., & Oishi, S. (2009). New measures of well-being. In E. Diener (Ed.),

Assessing well-being: The collected works of Ed Diener (pp. 247-266). Netherlands: Springer Science+Business Media B.V.

Diener, E., Wirtz, D., Tov, W., Kim-Prieto, C., Choi, D. W., Oishi, S., & Biswas-Diener, R. (2010). New well-being measures: Short scales to assess flourishing and positive and negative feelings. *Social Indicators Research, 97*(2), 143-156. doi: 10.1007/s11205-009-9493-y.

Fraillon, J. (2004). *Measuring student well-being in the context of Australian schooling:* Discussion Paper (E. Ministerial Council on Education, Training and Youth Affairs Ed.). Carlton South, Victoria: The Australian Council for Research.

Gable, S. L., & Haidt, J. (2005). What (and why) is positive psychology. *Review of General Psychology, 9*(2), 103-110.

Goodenow, C. (1993). The psychological sense of school membership among adolescents: Scale development and educational correlates. *Psychology in the Schools,* 30, 79 - 90.

Harackiewicz, J. M., Barron, K. E., Carter, S. M., Letho, A. T., & Elliot, A. J. (1997). Predictors and consequences of achievement goals in the college classrooms: Maintaining interest and making the grade. *Journal of Personality and Social Psychology, 73*(6), 1284-1295.

Harackiewicz, J. M., Barron, K. E., Tauer, J. M., & Elliot, A. J. (2002). Predicting success in college: A longitudinal study of achievement goals and ability measures as predictors of interest and performance from freshman year through graduation. *Journal of Educational Psychology, 94,* 562-575.

Harackiewicz, J. M., Barron, K. E., Tauer, J. M., Carter, S. M., & Elliot, A. J. (2000). Short-term and long-term consequences of achievement goals: Predicting interest and performance over time. *Journal of Educational Psychology, 92*(2), 316-330.

Hendry, G. D., Phan, H., Lyon, P. M., & Gordon, J. (2002). Student evaluation of expert and non-expert problem-based tutors. *Medical Teacher,* 24(5), 544-549.

Henry, K. L. (2010). Academic achievement and adolescent drug use: An examination of reciprocal effects and correlated growth trajectories. *Journal of School Health, 80*(1), 38 - 43.

Henry, K. L., Knight, K. E., & Thornberry, T. P. (2012). School disengagement as a predictor of dropout, delinquency, and problem substance use during adolescence and early adulthood. *Journal of Youth Adolescence, 41*, 156 - 166.

Hoy, W. K., Tarter, J., & Hoy, A. W. (2006). Academic optimism of schools: A force for student achievement. *American Educational Research Journal,* 43(3), 425 - 446.

Kagitcibasi, C. (1997). Individualism and collectivism. *Handbook of cross-cultural psychology,* 3, 1-49.

Keyes, C., & Haidt, J. (2002). *Flourishing: Positive psychology and the Life Well-Lived:* Washington American Psychological Association.

Kline, R. B. (2011). *Principles and practice of structural equation modeling* (3rd ed.). New York, NY: The Guilford Press.

Lau, S., Liem, A. D., & Nie, Y. (2008). Task- and self-related pathways to deep learning: the mediating role of achievement goals, classroom attentiveness, and group participation. *British Journal of Educational Psychology, 78*(Pt 4), 639-662. doi: 10.1348/000709907X270261.

Lens, W., Lacante, M., Vansteenkiste, M., & Herrera, D. (2005). Study persistence and academic achievement as a function of the type of competing tendencies. *European Journal of Psychology of Education,* 20(3), 275-287.

Lent, R. W., Lopez, F. G., Brown, S. D., & Gore, P. A. (1996). Latent structure of the sources of mathematics self-efficacy. *Journal of Vocational Behavior,* 49(3), 292-308.

Leung, D. Y. P., & Kember, D. (2003). The relationship between approaches to learning and reflection upon practice. *Educational Psychology, 23*(1), 61-71.

Liem, A. D., Lau, S., & Nie, Y. (2008). The role of self-efficacy, task value, and achievement goals in predicting learning strategies, task disengagement, peer relationship, and achievement outcome. *Contemporary Educational Psychology, 33*(4), 486-512. doi: 10.1016/j.cedpsych.2007.08.001.

Liem, G. A. D., Ginns, P., Martin, A. J., Stone, B., & Herrett, M. (2012). Personal best goals and academic and social functioning: A longitudinal perspective. *Learning and Instruction, 22*(3), 222-230. doi: 10.1016/j.learninstruc.2011.11.003.

Ma, X. (2003). Sense of belonging to school: Can schools make a difference? *Journal of Educational Research,* 96(6), 1 - 9.

MacCallum, R. C., & Austin, J. T. (2000). Applications of structural equation modeling in psychological research. *Annual Review of Psychology,* 51(201 - 226).

Markus, H. R., & Kitayama, S. (1991). Culture and the self: Implications for cognition, emotion, and motivation. *Psychological Review,* 98(2), 224-253.

Martin, A. J. (2006). Personal bests (PBs): A proposed multidimensional model and empirical analysis. *British Journal of Educational Psychology,* 76(4), 803-825.

Martin, A. J. (2011). Personal best (PB) approaches to academic development: Implications for motivation and assessment. *Educational Practice and Theory, 33*(1), 93-99.

McAuley, E., Duncan, T. E., & Tammen, V. V. (1989). Psychometric properties of the Intrinsic Motivation Inventory in a competitive sport setting: A confirmatory factor analysis. *Research Quarterly for Exercise and Sport, 60,* 40-58.

Muthén, L. K., & Muthén, B. O. (1998 - 2012). *Mplus User's Guide* (7th ed.). Los Angeles, CA: Muthén & Muthén.

Ngu, B. H., & Phan, H. P. (2016a). Comparing balance and inverse methods on learning conceptual and procedural knowledge in equation solving: A Cognitive load perspective. *Pedagogies: An International Journal, 11*(1), 63-83.

Ngu, B. H., & Phan, H. P. (2016b). Unpacking the complexity of linear equations from a cognitive load theory perspective. *Educational Psychology Review, 28,* 95-118.

Ngu, B. H., & Phan, H. P. (2018). Achievement Bests framework, cognitive load theory, and equation solving. In O. B. Cavero (Ed.), *New pedagogical challenges in the 21st Century* (pp. 287-306). Rijeka, Croatia: InTech Open Science| Open Minds.

Ngu, B. H., Phan, H. P., Yeung, A. S., & Chung, S. F. (2018). Managing element interactivity in equation solving. *Educational Psychology Review, 30*(1), 255-272. doi: 10.1007/s10648-016-9397-8.

Opdenakker, M. C., & Van Damme, J. (2000). Effects of schools, teaching staff and classes on achievement and well-being in secondary education: Similarities and differences between school outcomes. *School effectiveness and school improvement, 11*(2), 165 - 196.

Phan, H. P. (2016). Longitudinal examination of personal well-being: Validating newly developed concepts. In E. Ortega (Ed.), *Academic achievement: Student attitudes, social influences and gender differences* (pp. 113-130). New York, NY: Nova Publisher.

Phan, H. P., & Ngu, B. H. (2014). *The Academic Well-being Experience Questionnaire* (AWEQ). UNE. Armidale, NSW.

Phan, H. P., & Ngu, B. H. (2015). Validating personal well-being experiences: A quantitative approach. *Education,* 136(1), 34-52.

Phan, H. P., & Ngu, B. H. (2016). Optimal outcomes: A focus on theoretical tenets for consideration. In J. Porter (Ed.), *Deep learning: Fundamentals, methods and applications* (pp. 33-60). New York, NY: Nova Publishing.

Phan, H. P., & Ngu, B. H. (2017). Positive psychology: The use of the Framework of Achievement Bests to facilitate personal flourishing. In A. A. V. Boas (Ed.), *Well-being and Quality of Life* (pp. 19-33). Rijeka, Croatia: Intech: Open Science|Open Minds.

Phan, H. P., & Ngu, B. H. (In press-2018). Expanding on the theoretical concept of 'Optimization' for effective learning: Establishing empirical evidence from an Eastern sociocultural context. In A. D. Liem & T. S. Hong (Eds.), *Student motivation, engagement, and growth: Asian insights*. Singapore: Routledge.

Phan, H. P., & Ngu, N. H. (2016). *The Best practice Questionnaire*. The University of New England. Armidale, NSW.

Phan, H. P., Ngu, B. H., & Alrashidi, O. (2016). Roles of student well-being: A study using structural equation modeling. *Psychological Reports,* 119(1), 77-105. doi: 10.1177/0033294116656819.

Phan, H. P., Ngu, B. H., & Williams, A. (2015). *The Optimal Outcomes Questionnaire*. Education. UNE. Armidale, Australia.

Phan, H. P., Ngu, B. H., & Williams, A. (2016). Introducing the concept of Optimal Best: Theoretical and methodological contributions. *Education, 136*(3), 312-322.

Phan, H. P., Ngu, B. H., & Yeung, A. S. (2017). Achieving optimal best: Instructional efficiency and the use of cognitive load theory in mathematical problem solving. *Educational Psychology Review, 29*(4), 667-692. doi: 10.1007/s10648-016-9373-3.

Phan, H. P., Ngu, B. H., Wang, H. W., Shih, J. H., Shi, S. Y., & Lin, R. Y. (2018a). Introducing the theoretical concept of 'profiling': A cross-cultural perspective. In *Exploring learning experiences from around the world*. New York, NY: Nova Science.

Phan, H. P., Ngu, B. H., Wang, H. W., Shih, J. H., Shi, S. Y., & Lin, R. Y. (2018b). Understanding levels of best practice: An empirical development. *PLOS One, 13*(6), e0198888. https://doi.org/10.1371/journal.pone.0198888.

Rand, K. L. (2009). Hope and optimism: Latent structures and influences on grade expectancy and academic performance. *Journal of Personality, 77*(1), 231 - 260.

Rittle-Johnson, B., & Alibali, M. W. (1999). Conceptual and procedural knowledge of mathematics: Does one lead to the other? *Journal of Educational Psychology, 91*(1), 175-189. http://dx.doi.org/10.1037/0022-0663.91.1.175.

Rogoff, B., Turkanis, C. G., & Bartlett, L. (2001). *Learning together: Children and adults in a school community*. New York, NY: Oxford.

Rogosa, D. (1979). Causal models in longitudinal research: Rationale, formulation, and interpretation. In J. R. Nesselroade & P. B. Balles (Eds.), *Longitudinal research in the study of behaviour and development* (pp. 263-302). New York: Academic Press.

Roorda, D. L., Koomen, H. M. Y., Spilt, J. L., & Oort, F. J. (2011). The influence of affective teacher-student relationships on students' school engagement and achievement: A meta-analytic approach. *Review of*

Educational Research, 81(4), 493-529. doi: 10.3102/0034654311421793.

Ryan, R. M., & Deci, E. L. (2001). On happiness and human potentials: A review of research on hedonic and eudemonic well-being. *Annual Review of Psychology, 52*, 141-166.

Ryff, C. D. (1989). Happiness is everything, or is it? Explorations on the meaning of psychological well-being. *Journal of Personality and Social Psychology, 57*(6), 1069 - 1081.

Salamonson, Y., Andrew, S., & Everett, B. (2009). Academic engagement and disengagement as predictors of performance in pathophysiology among nursing students. *Contemporary Nurse, 32*(1 - 2), 123 - 132.

Schumacker, R. E., & Lomax, R. G. (2004). *A beginner's guide to structural equation modeling* (2nd ed.). Mahwah, NJ: Lawrence Erlbaum Associates, Inc.

Seligman, M. (2010). *Flourish: Positive psychology and positive interventions.* Paper presented at the The Tanner Lectures on Human Values, The University of Michigan.

Seligman, M. (2011). *Flourish: A visionary new understanding of happiness and well-being.* New York: Simon & Schuster.

Seligman, M. (2011a). *Flourish.* North Sydney, NSW: Random House Australia.

Seligman, M., & Csíkszentmihályi, M. (2000). Positive psychology. *American Psychologist, 55*, 5-14.

Sheldon, K. M., & King, I. (2001). Why positive psychology is necessary. *American Psychologist, 56*, 216-217.

Slack, F., Beer, M., Armitt, G., & Green, S. (2003). Assessment and learning outcomes: The evaluation of deep learning in an online course. *Journal of Information Technology Education, 2*, 305-317.

Smith, S. N., & Miller, R. J. (2005). Learning approaches: Examination type, discipline of study, and gender. *Educational Psychology, 25*(1), 43-53. doi: 10.1080/0144341042000294886.

Snyder, C. R. (2002). Hope theory: Rainbows in the mind. *Psychological Inquiry, 13*, 249-275.

Snyder, C. R. (2004). Hope and depression: A light in the darkness. *Journal of Social and Clinical Psychology*, 23, 347-351.

Snyder, C. R., Harris, C., Anderson, J. R., Hollerman, S. A., Irving, L. M., Sigmon, S. T., Sandra, T., Yoshinobu, L., Gibb, J., Langelle, C., & Harney, P. (1991). The will and the ways: Development and validation of an individual-differences measure of hope. *Journal of Personality and Social Psychology*, 60, 570-585.

Soutter, A. K. (2011). What can we learn about wellbeing in school? *Journal of Student Wellbeing*, 5(1), 1 - 21.

Su, R., Tay, L., & Diener, E. (2014). The development and validation of the Comprehensive Inventory of Thriving (CIT) and the Brief Inventory of Thriving (BIT). *Applied Psychology: Health and Well Being*, 6(3), 251-279. doi: 10.1111/aphw.12027.

Sweller, J. (2010). Element interactivity and intrinsic, extraneous, and germane cognitive load. *Educational Psychology Review*, 22(2), 123-138. doi: 10.1007/s10648-010-9128-5.

Sweller, J., Ayres, P., & Kalyuga, S. (2011). *Cognitive load theory*. New York: Springer.

Triandis, H. C., Bontempo, R., Villareal, M. J., Asai, M., & Lucca, N. (1988). Individualism and collectivism: Cross-cultural perspectives on self-ingroup relationships. *Journal of Personality and Social Psychology*, 54(2), 323.

Van Damme, J., De Fraine, B., Van Landeghem, G., Opdenakker, M. C., & Onghena, P. (2002). A new study on educational effectiveness in secondary schools in Flanders: An introduction. *School Effectiveness and School Improvement*, 13(4), 383 - 397.

Vanthournout, G., Gijbels, D., Coertjens, L., Donche, V., & Van Petegem, P. (2012). Students' persistence and academic success in a first-year professional bachelor program: The influence of students' learning strategies and academic motivation. *Education Research International*, 2012, 10 pages.

Von Glaserfeld, E. (1997). Amplification of a constructivist perspective. Issues in Education: *Contributions from Educational Psychology*, 3, 213-210.

Wiese, C. W., Tay, L., Su, R., & Diener, E. (2018). Measuring thriving across nations: Examining the measurement equivalence of the Comprehensive Inventory of Thriving (CIT) and the Brief Inventory of Thriving (BIT). *Applied Psychology: Health and Well Being, 10*(1), 127-148. doi: 10.1111/aphw.12119.

Yao, X. (2000). *An introduction to Confucianism.* Cambridge, UK: Cambridge University Press.

In: Progress in Education. Volume 55 ISBN: 978-1-53614-551-9
Editor: Roberta V. Nata © 2019 Nova Science Publishers, Inc.

Chapter 4

VIRTUAL EDUCATIONAL GUIDANCE TOOLS FOR PREVENTING UNIVERSITY DROP-OUT

Ana B. Bernardo[*], Antonio Cervero, Constanza López, María Esteban and Ellián Tuero
Department of Psychology, University of Oviedo, Spain

ABSTRACT

Educational guidance is a counselling process that addresses students' personal and academic development, although traditionally it has mainly focused on students' academic and vocational decisions. Despite education legislation attempting to ensure the effectiveness of this service, there are many difficulties when it comes to practice, from a lack of teacher training, to a lack of material resources and economic support. However, new computer and web-based tools and programs present an opportunity to increase the motivation of students and improve educational guidance services. We describe an on-line guidance project for secondary school students, the results of which seem promising for improving the quality of guidance and the students' decision-making processes about their academic futures, something which may in turn influence a reduction in drop-out rates, especially from university courses.

---

[*] Corresponding Author Email: bernardoana@uniovi.es.

Keywords: virtual education, drop-out, educational tools, permanence

1. INTRODUCTION

Educational guidance is a complex process that has been conceptualized in various ways and has had various objectives over time. Nowadays it addresses various aspects of a student from an integrated, holistic perspective. It can be defined as a process of personal, social, academic and vocational counselling that facilitates the subject's decision-making, anticipating the difficulties they may encounter, and improving their integration or development in education or work (Molina 2004).

Educational guidance can be delivered though specific programs which touch upon the various aspects they aim to address. We find programs focusing on personal development or students' social integration, programs aimed at facilitating students' teaching-learning processes, programs of family guidance (including so-called parent schools, which have become relatively well-known), guidance programs for university degrees (also known as professional or careers guidance), and diversity programs (Henao, Ramírez and Ramírez 2006). All of these programs fall within a framework of an overall strategy which aims for the student to adapt well to their social environment.

Education legislation in Spain has developed in step with the concept of educational guidance. Law 14/1970, 4th August, on Education and Financing for Educational Reform (LGE), was based on the Education White Book, and defined guidance from a fundamentally professional and academic perspective, stating that educational and professional guidance must be a service that continued throughout the education system, allowing students to make responsible decisions based on their abilities, aptitudes and vocations. The law indicated that students had the right to educational and professional guidance throughout their school lives that would address learning problems, and facilitate the choice of further study and work, especially in the final stages of the various educational cycles.

Organic Law 1/1990, 3rd October, General Plan of the Education System (LOGSE), included educational guidance in its preamble, and expressly cited it as a quality criterion for schools, making it clear that it was part of teaching, and identifying it as a student right and a principle of the education system, although limiting it specifically to educational psychology and careers guidance fields.

Organic Law 2/2006, 3rd May, on Education (LOE), together with the amendments made to it by Organic Law 8/2013, 9th December, for Improvement to Education Quality (LOMCE), maintained educational and vocational guidance as one of the basic principles of the education system, and considered it to be one of the system's aims. This legislation also stated that teachers were responsible for guidance, both in their specific tutoring functions and, in an integrated manner, in the curriculum content along with giving responsibility to guidance departments. It also maintained that educational guidance was a student right, but defined it as part of an integrated education process, specifying its four areas of intervention (dealing with diversity, academic and vocational guidance, psychosocial development, and intervention in a socio-community context).

Despite these legal directives and despite the growing importance of educational guidance as a basic process in overall student development, schools still face many difficulties when it comes to application. The Organization for Economic Co-operation and Development and the Spanish Ministry of Education, Culture and Sport (OCDE and MECD 2004) identified some of those difficulties. They include its short-term nature, the fact that it is focused on the world of work and the academic arena, the cost of implementation together with the problem of funding, and above all the training deficit in teachers who are charged with managing it, and the lack of material and technological resources. These factors, together with difficulties in conceptualizing educational guidance, seem to apply in other places, as various studies in different countries have shown (Fung 2017; González 2008). These problems have a pernicious effect on the application of educational guidance, something which is reflected in studies into student perception. Students often see it as useless or ineffective (when it exists at all), both in secondary school (Bernardo et al. 2017) and at university (González-Ramírez, Contreras-Rosado and Reyes 2015).

This is where we might appreciate the potential of technological resources in alleviating some of these limitations in planning and delivery of educational guidance. The educational potential of ITC has been demonstrated in numerous studies and in various aspects of the teaching-learning process (Schneckenberg, Ehlers and Adelsberger 2011). Including ITC with didactic objectives increases student interest and motivation, and improves achievement (Del Moral, Villalustre and Neira 2014; García-Valcárcel and Tejedor 2017). It facilitates collaboration and cooperative learning while developing transversal skills in using technology (García-Valcárcel, Basilotta and López 2014). It provides better access to up-to-date information, in terms of both amount and quality (Marín, Reche and Maldonado 2013). It provides tools which are necessary for better educational inclusion (Rodríguez and Arroyo 2014), and it has great potential to make communication between all those involved in the teaching-learning process easier (Marqués 2013), although some studies demonstrate that this potential is being under-utilized (Álvarez, Cervero and Urbano 2016).

Educational guidance, as an educational service, is not outside the scope of this consideration and various attempts have been made to make the most of the potential of ITC in improving quality. However, before looking at those, which we will examine in part 3, we will first look at what academic and vocational options the system offers students who have finished secondary education.

2. AFTER SECONDARY EDUCATION, WHAT?

Students normally finish obligatory secondary education (ESO) after four years, when they are 16 years old (if they advance at the usual rate). They can then follow one of three academic-vocational paths. Before examining those in detail, we must note three situations where these usual paths may not apply.

First, if a student wants to change their academic path or do courses from a path they had not previously chosen. There are various procedures and entrance tests for this, some of which are aimed at people who had previously dropped out and which have a minimum age requirement.

Second, if a student wants to change to a course which has its own particular structure and organization, such as foreign languages, courses in art, or sports studies. We do not deal with these courses here in order to simplify the analysis and because they are much less common.

The third situation is if a student wants to take a year off to gain life experience and a clearer idea of their future. While a gap year like this is a common practice in other European and American countries, it is almost unheard of in countries like Spain (Barbero 2018).

Once students successfully complete their secondary education, they can choose from three main paths to continue their academic life, which are described in the LOE and LOMCE legislation: the academic path, which means two more years of non-obligatory secondary education (called "bachillerato"), which in turn provides access to higher education; the technical education path, which facilitates access to vocational training; and the path directly to employment, which includes specific training both for active workers and the unemployed in search of work.

The aim of the bachillerato is to give the students training, knowledge and skills which help them to take part in society, to begin their working life with some security, and to allow them to enter higher education. It lasts two years in which the student may select one of three branches; arts, humanities and social sciences, or sciences. Students receive the qualification bachillerato once they pass all of their subjects and a final examination.

Once students have the bachillerato, they can enroll in university courses by following the procedures laid down by each university, all of which must follow the basic government regulations in Royal Decree 412/2014, 6th June, which establishes the basic requirements for admission procedures for university degree courses.

These courses are governed in turn by Royal Decree 1393/2007, 29th October, which establishes the organization of university teaching, and regulates its structure in three cycles: **bachelor's degrees, master's degrees** and doctorates, within the framework of Organic Law 6/2001, 21st December, on Universities (LOU) and its subsequent amendments.

Bachelor's degrees are intended to give the student general training in their discipline allowing them to undertake professional work. They generally comprise 240 ECTS credits which are spread over four years (60 credits per year), although there are exceptions such as degrees in medicine which last six years. ECTS means European Credit Transfer System, a framework that standardizes university credits for European higher education systems, understanding that each credit entails 10 hours of classes and 15 hours of autonomous learning activities for the students.

Master's degrees are intended to give the student advanced, specialized or multidisciplinary training aimed at academic, professional or research specialization. They normally comprise between 60 and 120 ECTS credits.

Doctoral degrees are intended to give the student advanced training in research techniques. They vary in how they are organized and finish when the student completes a period of organized training and research making up the doctoral program.

Vocational training includes a mix of educational programs to form students in a variety of skilled professions and to help them find work. In this case it is important to differentiate between the education system's vocational training, which is regulated by the LOE, and professional training to foster employment, which is marked by the design of activities within a workplace framework.

Vocational training system is made up of basic, intermediate and advanced vocational training, which is usually organized into modules of varying length. Students can enroll in basic vocational training having finished the first cycle of secondary education as long as they meet certain requirements. In order to enroll in intermediate courses, students would have to have graduated secondary education, or the equivalent, have an advanced academic qualification, or pass an entrance test once they are 17 years old. For advanced vocational training, the requirements are the bachillerato qualification or equivalent, an advanced academic qualification, or passing an entrance test that students must be 19 or over to take.

The third option is for students to directly enter the labour market. The most common choices are to actively search for work or to study for the competitive exams to be able to work in the public sector (these exams are called "oposiciones" in Spain). Entering the labour market does not mean the end of training options, or the need for training, as this is where professional training to foster employment takes place.

This training is governed by Law 30/2015, 9th September, the objective of which is to regulate the planning, execution and evaluation of activities in the system of professional training to foster employment, which is done within the European Union framework of regulation of training and qualification.

This system (or subsystem if we look at it from the point of view of vocational training as a whole) is intended to foster training in businesses, active workers and unemployed workers that responds to their needs, organized as both training provision and on-demand training. It is governed by Royal Decree 395/2007, 23rd March, which regulates the subsystem of professional training to foster employment. The training provision aims to offer both active and unemployed workers training which meets the need of the labour market, with the worker requesting training from an already existing public provision. On-demand training responds to the specific training needs in business and their workers. It is part of a company's training activities, although financially supported by the state through individual training permits, and is planned and managed by the business where the worker works.

3. TRADITIONAL GUIDANCE OR ONLINE GUIDANCE

With all the options students have to choose from once they finish their secondary education it is no wonder that educational guidance counsellors spend a significant amount of their time giving information about the academic-vocational paths that the student might take. Nevertheless, this does not mean that they can ignore their other obligations, nor can they reduce offering information to a mere rote process. Instead they must engage deeply in the process and with the decisions the students are faced with, always focusing on the students' own interests and individual characteristics.

Technological tools are of special interest here, particularly what is called online guidance, which includes those programs that autonomously provide students with academic-vocational guidance (Noaman and Ahmed 2015). Various researchers have looked at the use of online tools to facilitate student decision-making about future academic-vocational options due because of the positive effect of offering online platforms in friendly low-stress environments that the students can access from any internet connected device. Some students feel satisfied just with online support, saying that it is a complement to face to face counseling (Kalamkarian and Karp 2017).

The inclination towards one method or the other depends on cultural context. For example, secondary schools in the USA have an academic counseling team available to their students from the moment they begin secondary education until graduation, or even beyond. The main objective is to work on students' weak points and reinforce their strengths by the counsellors working closely with the students and their families, paying special attention to the first year, in which they produce timelines based on an individual analysis of each student, looking at their learning styles, coping strategies, and organizational skills (Workman 2015). Other countries use different resources; for example, Mindler, in India, is one of the main vocational counseling platforms which provides an objective, impartial review for someone looking for vocational counseling. U-explore, the main company in the UK in this area, offers various services to both high schools and universities, employing various methods from traditional face-to-face guidance, through to comprehensive software which lets users explore degree options and qualifications and access resources and modules to successfully face the world of work. They also offer Pathways Tracker, which allows the school, college or university to record student interactions and generate reports, and allows teachers to target programs to ensure success in the students' chosen direction.

The majority of educational guidance resources which use ITC in their implementation (see Table 1) have three related sections: a first section which gives students information about possible academic-vocational paths they can take at the end of the various educational levels; a second, more practical section which includes various tools and applications to help the student make decisions; and a third section, which varies from one resource to another, which provides the student with materials and activities to develop educational, learning and self-regulation strategies.

The guidance process does not end with secondary education but continues throughout vocational training and university. The most common format for universities in Europe is welcome days or orientation days provide students with an introduction to the program they have chosen. This might occasionally include immersion courses where new students are given guidelines and tips. In addition, many universities have their own guidance services and tutoring or mentoring programs.

In American universities the most common format is to give new students access to various orientation platforms with their student ID. These orientation platforms combine a guide with information that helps students in their transition to online learning and allows them access to information they need to succeed in their courses. The California-based company Comevo produces software designed to make maximum use of technology which is useful for both teachers and students at universities all over North America (see Table 2). Software like Comevo's Launch offers teaching staff intuitive configuration that lets them easily create, edit and manage the content they want, and gives the students unlimited access to comprehensive, easy-to-use, online orientation. This system operates a cloud-based service model where Comevo stores, maintains and backs up the content from each institution. This has two big advantages: it reduces the time demands on teaching staff responsible for student orientation, and it eliminates the need for resources such as on-campus servers, and the associated costs.

It is important to highlight the particular significance online tools have taken on over the last decade, as they have been shown to be beneficial in various parts of the student learning process: self-regulation, metacognition, learning strategies, time management, effort regulation and critical thinking.

Table 1. Guidance resources using ITC (compiled by the authors)

Resource	Description
Itinerarios educativos Pasas (ItePasas) https://bit.ly/2KY5n3e	An academic-vocational guidance tool focused on taking decisions regarding the vocational path for secondary students and students in vocational training. It provides information about professional sectors and training pathways and includes a self-evaluation test about the vocational options that best fit the students' profile.
MyWayPass http://bit.ly/2gYhQAo	A tool developed within a "gamification" framework, the student is faced with a kind of video game where they go on a journey into space, visiting planets where they can find resources which encourage self-knowledge and information about the various academic and vocational pathways.
Uddannelseszoom https://goo.gl/2fcw3t	A guidance tool which guides the students in the search for relevant information about curricula, rates of unemployment, wages, and retirement. It also gives information about the educational and social environment based on evaluations from past and current students doing those courses.
Programa INESEM ORIENTA https://bit.ly/2NMaNfr	A 90-minute program which aims to guide the student and help them to choose the most appropriate training according to their preferences and expectations. It starts from optimizing the curriculum and focuses on giving the student the strategies they will need to determine their own academic-vocational interests and to successfully pass the various tests needed to find a job.
Was-studiere-ich.de https://goo.gl/tcfiWC	A guidance tool which includes a 15-minute test. It is aimed at students who still do not have a clear idea of what they want to study in the future, and gives information based on the student's interests, likes, and abilities.
Proyecto GR (Gran recorrido) https://bit.ly/2xqR4hg	A project aimed at students over 16 years of age regardless of qualifications, focusing on helping them make decisions in the vocational path. The objective is to increase student self-awareness and it includes various tools and questionnaires to help students think about themselves so that they end up having a better idea of what courses or jobs they might find most satisfying.
Proyecto Orión http://bit.ly/2fW710A	A project designed by the University of Comillas in Madrid, consisting of ten 50-minute teaching units focusing on taking vocational decisions and which provides support materials.
Studifinder https://goo.gl/GYEDow	A tool offering support to students all over Germany, via a detailed search of courses depending on their interests, abilities, and work habits, which aims to help students choose courses which fulfill their expectations.

Table 2. Orientation resources using Comevo's Launch software (compiled by the authors)

Resource	Description
University of Maine at Augusta (ONSO) https://goo.gl/qvM1KG	A tool which gives the student information about the institution they are going to be part of and its benefits. It has nine required sections and two additional optional modules which include photos, videos and activities.
Ohio University (eCampus) https://goo.gl/tbuUJR	A program for new undergraduates offering key information about the university, how to access online tools, advice, policies, enrollment information etc., and noting those aspects that raise questions. After each section there is an evaluation and a final test in which the student must score 70%. Once this final test is passed, the responsible guidance counsellor contacts the student to resolve any outstanding issues. The program usually takes about an hour to complete.
Long Beach City College https://goo.gl/i6A59B	This university college offers an online orientation designed to familiarize the student with various elements: general campus and safety/security information, the programs on offer, support services, financial help, the academic calendar, counseling services, policies etc. It is split into nine sections and once the student successfully completes at least 80% they can do the final test.
Santa Barbara City College https://goo.gl/pdioze	This institution offers online orientation designed to give the student the information they need in order to attend, and to make the adaptation process as easy as possible. There are 11 sections which detail key elements the student must be aware of: one example is the Gateway Program in which tutors, who work with instructors, provide students with help both in and out of the classroom in their first years at university. It also includes the Schall Career Center which helps students choose courses, write resumes and look for jobs.
Oregon State University Orientation (eCampus) https://goo.gl/ed1ZSH	This orientation program is divided into six sections in which the students are given information about the university through interactive video-tutorials covering important procedures, written instructions, documents they must print, and optional materials of interest. It takes about an hour and a half to complete.

Nevertheless, in the course of their academic training students have to acquire a set of skills which allow them to choose their training path realistically, examine their self-awareness of their capabilities, understand their motivations and examine the educational options open to them and their path into the world of work (Broadbent and Poon 2015), which can only be done by involving the student in the decision-making process and cultivating their critical thinking (McGill 2016).

4. THE IMPORTANCE OF PSYCHO-EDUCATIONAL GUIDANCE IN PREVENTING UNIVERSITY DROP OUT

Guidance should be part of a school's planning and delivered through two routes. One, as we saw earlier, through the work of teaching staff assigned to be form tutors (or home room teachers), giving educational, academic and vocational guidance to the students. The other path is through secondary schools' guidance departments, made up of teachers but having at least one education or psychology professional. The functions of these departments include organizing and managing educational and vocation guidance, educational psychology, and the tutorial scheme of work (Royal Decree 83/1996, 26th January, approving the Organic Regulations on Secondary Schools).

The most common decision students make when they finish secondary education in Spain is to go to university. Almost half of Spanish secondary school students (47%) opt for undergraduate courses, which is slightly lower than the Organization for Economic Co-operation and Development –from now on OCDE- average of 54% of young adults starting undergraduate or equivalent courses (Hernández and Pérez 2017). Just over a third (34%) of Spanish students enroll in vocational training, which is much lower than the average in the European Union, which is 48% (Eurostat 2016).

Students as a whole seem to have a certain amount of inertia which makes them more likely to follow the traditional secondary school-university path, and which leads them to undervalue vocational training (Del Cerro and Ramón 2017), possibly due to historical prejudice. If we add in poorly chosen university courses, in which educational guidance plays an important role, the result is a high university drop-out rate. In OCDE countries the average drop-out rate is about 30%, although it varies, with countries such as Japan, Denmark and Australia around 20% and countries such as the USA and Sweden, around 50% (OCDE 2013).

Many studies have shown the influence of educational guidance on student decision-making processes which can lead to dropping out. Tuero, Cervero, Esteban and Bernardo (2018) found that educational guidance played an important role as one of the variables influencing drop out, and Bernardo, Esteban and Cerezo (2014) showed its influence on the various choices facing university students of remaining, dropping out or changing courses.

Bearing all of this in mind, we have designed the E-Orientation project, a resource which makes the most of ITC potential, and aims to give teachers a tool that includes various functions to allow delivery of quality educational guidance.

5. E-ORIENTATION: DESIGNING MY OWN LIFE PROJECT

5.1. Presenting the Virtual Psycho-Educational Guidance Classroom

The E-Orientation project is configured as a MOOC (massive open online course) supported by a teacher by means of a blended-learning methodology (b-learning) during tutoring hours at high school. It consists of one session every second week (five in total) where classmates can interact as a group while accessing content and doing the activities systematically about one of its modules.

In order to promote accessibility, the Moodle platform students are also provided with an individual account (see Figure 1), which gives them access from any internet-connected device and allows them to complete optional complementary activities during their spare-time.

Figure 1. Access to the virtual classroom.

The first session, called "Landing in reality," is an introduction (see Figure 2) to familiarize students with the program and its objectives, learn to use the virtual classroom and to complete a pre-test questionnaire. This questionnaire includes questions about the students' characteristics, and their understanding and use of self-regulation strategies. The same questionnaire is used at the end of the project (post-test) to allow us to evaluate its effectiveness and fitness for purpose.

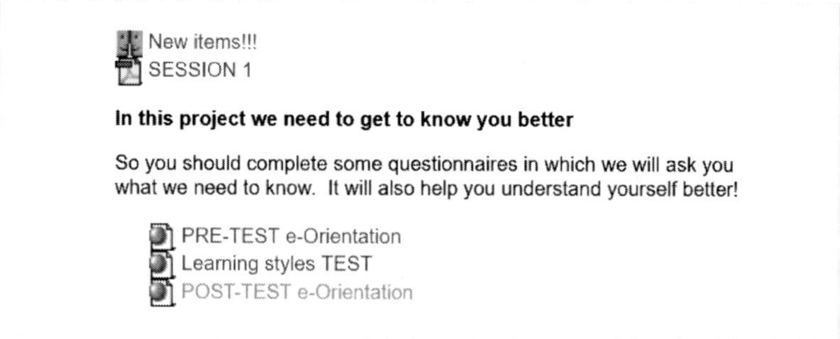

Figure 2. First session, pre-test.

Session two is called "Living in the 21st century" (see Figure 3) and aims to make students think about their environment, explaining economic and socio-political aspects of the knowledge-based society and highlighting the commitments and responsibilities that being part of that society involves. Before accessing the content, students complete a test to help identify their dominant learning styles (active, pragmatic, reflexive or theoretical) in order to later select the most appropriate activities in each lesson.

```
SESSION 2. Module topic 1: Living in the 21st century

In this session, and in the module content, you will learn more about the global village you live in

Session content
We will give you some information to think about. Whenever you feel that you need to, or whenever you like, you can come back to this session and look at it again. You can also search for similar topics and create your own
block of content!
    INTRODUCTORY VIDEO: Surviving in the 21st Century!

Fundamental Activities (to do in class)
We will do these activities during the class session with the teacher present. They are essential to put what you see into practice. Try to do the activities to the best of your abilities, because the more effort you put in here,
the better your results will be.
    ACTIVE STYLE: Activity 'Discovering Transgenics'
    PRAGMATIC STYLE: Activity 'Diagnosing my neighbourhood and/or school'
    REFLEXIVE STYLE: Activity 'Observing the school'
    THEORETICAL STYLE: Activity 'Really understanding Coca-Cola'

Complementary Activities (to do wherever you like)

Here are some more activities about the topics covered in this session. You can do these activities whenever you wish, in your free time, when you have nothing to do etc. Remember, these activities are just as important as
the others, but you decide when to do them.
    ACTIVE STYLE: Activity 'Expressing myself'
    ACTIVE STYLE: Activity 'Investigating Crowdfunding'
    PRAGMATIC STYLE: Activity 'The potential of social networks'
    PRAGMATIC STYLE: Activity 'Sustainable cities or viable cities '
    REFLEXIVE STYLE: Activity 'Increasing my knowledge'
    REFLEXIVE STYLE: Activity 'About the downturn'
    THEORETICAL STYLE: Activity 'Deep research'
    THEORETICAL STYLE: Activity 'Supersize me'

UPLOADING COMPLEMENTARY ACTIVITIES
You can upload the extra activities you might have done here (they might be in your preferred learning style or any of the other learning styles if you wish to see what you think about those)
    Send activities

Self-regulation report for session 2
    Report
```

Figure 3. Second session, module topic 1: "Living in the 21st century."

Then students complete a micro-lesson which includes a video of the session content and gives them access to the platform to complete the activities. One of those is obligatory during the session with the teacher present, and is recommended to be in the student's preferred learning style, although they can choose an alternative, or do it later online any time as many times as they wish in whatever learning style they select. To end the session, the students complete a worksheet which evaluates the self-regulation strategies used while learning within each unit of contents, the knowledge gained and they satisfaction with the module they have just completed.

SESSION 2. Module topic 1: Living in the 21st century

In this session, and in the module content, you will learn more about the global village you live in

Session content

We will give you some information to think about. Whenever you feel that you need to, or whenever you like, you can come back to this session and look at it again. You can also search for similar topics and create your own block of content

- INTRODUCTORY VIDEO: Surviving in the 21st Century!

Fundamental Activities (to do in class)

We will do these activities during the class session with the teacher present. They are essential to put what you see into practice. Try to do the activities to the best of your abilities, because the more effort you put in here, the better your results will be.

- ACTIVE STYLE: Activity "Discovering Transgenics"
- PRAGMATIC STYLE: Activity "Diagnosing my neighbourhood and/or school"
- REFLEXIVE STYLE: Activity "Observing the school"
- THEORETICAL STYLE: Activity "Really understanding Coca-Cola"

Complementary Activities (to do wherever you like)

Here are some more activities about the topics covered in this session. You can do these activities whenever you wish, in your free time, when you have nothing to do etc. Remember, these activities are just as important as the others, but you decide when to do them.

- ACTIVE STYLE: Activity "Expressing myself"
- ACTIVE STYLE: Activity "Investigating Crowdfunding"
- PRAGMATIC STYLE: Activity "The potential of social networks"
- PRAGMATIC STYLE: Activity "Sustainable cities or viable cities "
- REFLEXIVE STYLE: Activity "Increasing my knowledge"
- REFLEXIVE STYLE: Activity "About the downturn"
- THEORETICAL STYLE: Activity "Deep research"
- THEORETICAL STYLE: Activity "Supersize me"

UPLOADING COMPLEMENTARY ACTIVITIES

You can upload the extra activities you might have done here (they might be in your preferred learning style or any of the other learning styles if you wish to see what you think about those)

- Send activities

Self-regulation report for session 2

- Report

Figure 4. Third session, module topic 2: "Taking decisions and designing my own work/life project."

The third session, entitled "Taking decisions and designing my own work/life project" (see Figure 4), gives information on what steps students need to follow to make decisions optimally. It focuses on practical strategies to achieve this.

The fourth session, called "And after obligatory secondary education, what?" (See Figure 5), gives information about the different academic or vocational paths that students can follow after finishing obligatory secondary education. It details the academic requirements, means of access, structures and organization of the different options.

As the images show, the three central sessions with the three module topics have the same structure. They all start with an explanation of the topics, which is given in text or audio-visually according to the student's choice. Following that they offer basic and optional activities grouped by each student's learning style. Finally, the students complete a worksheet about learning self-regulation.

Figure 5. Fourth session, module topic 3: "And after obligatory secondary education, now what?"

Figure 6. Fifth session, post-test.

The project finishes with the fifth session (see Figure 6) in which the students summarize the skills they have gained during the program, this is done as a group brainstorming activity about the usefulness of the program and individual reflections about it. The post-test completes the project, in which the student evaluates the program and can comment on its usefulness.

5.2. Participants

The results of our study into the implementation of the E-Orientation project are from two different samples. One sample was made up of Spanish students from four of the five bachillerato options in a public high school in Gijón and from the three options in a concertado high school in Oviedo (the three types of high schools in Spain are public, or state funded, independent concertados high schools which receive some public funds but operate with relative autonomy, and private schools which receive no public money). The students followed the program within the framework of their schools' own educational guidance counselling processes. The groups were selected according to the availability of staff on the research team who carried out the project, as well as the availability of material and human resources in the selected high schools.

This sample comprised 120 students (see Figure 7), 40.8% were from the concertado high school in Oviedo and 59.2% from the high school in

Gijón. All of the students were in their first year of the bachillerato. There were slightly fewer girls (45.8%) than boys (54.2%), almost all were between 15 and 17 years old, with the exception of 2.5% who were 18. There was a relatively even split between the branch of bachillerato being taken, with 43.3% doing humanities and social sciences, and 56.7% doing the science branch.

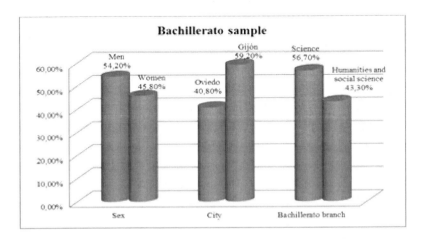

Figure 7. Bachillerato sample.

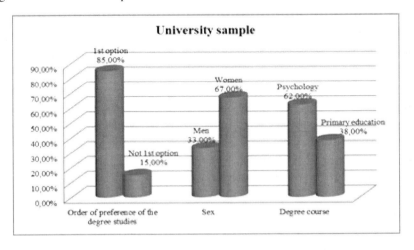

Figure 8. University sample.

We also demonstrated the program to sample of university students in the educational psychology field and asked them if, after having seen the program, they would evaluate retrospectively whether it would have been useful had they completed that program at secondary school. This sample consisted of 127 undergraduate students of psychology and primary education with the following characteristics (see Figure 8).

5.3. Instrument

As previously indicated, the students completed a pre-test questionnaire in the first face-to-face class which collected information about the students' initial situations, their perceptions about their academic-vocational futures and their learning self-regulation processes. In the final session the students completed the post-test questionnaire, which was the same as the pre-test, allowing us to examine the effectiveness of the project.

The questionnaire was designed ad hoc and was made up of 29 items in three blocks with different response types so that multiple-choice questions were mixed in with open questions and questions with 5-point Likert-type scale responses.

The first block had eleven items focused on sociodemographic and personal information such as: sex, age, residence, high school, type of bachillerato, parents' professions, etc.

The second block had seven items and evaluated strategies for self-regulation and learning including variables such as: time spent on homework, study sessions planning, main tasks while studying, monitoring processes, obtained marks, etc.

The third block, with ten items, focused on the guidance received to date and the students' views on the future, on collecting information about the professional sector or field the student was interested in, and on checking the students' understanding of the various academic paths they had looked at.

5.4. Procedure

The face-to-face sessions were done during school hours, during student tutoring time. They were carried out every two weeks alternating between a face-to-face session, run by one of the research team, and an hour of reflection about the previous week's session, run by the school's guidance counsellor. The students were able to access the virtual class from any internet-connected device to do the program's complementary optional activities.

The online format of the pre-test questionnaire and the post-test questionnaire were part of the tools available in the virtual classroom included as a link to the Google Forms platform for the students to complete. This let us save the responses as .xls or .csv files to then export for statistical analysis.

5.5. Results

The first aspect we examined was the students' views about academic-vocational guidance they received during secondary school, focusing on the time just before starting university. We found statistically significant differences between the students at high school and the university students (χ^2 = 17.078; p ≤ .001). A surprisingly high proportion of students, especially those at university, said that they had not received any kind of guidance. Around half of the students in each group said that they had been given guidance, but that they had not found it particularly useful (see Figure 9).

Given these results, the need for guidance programs to make the most of the motivational capability of technological resources is obvious. This can be seen in the results of the satisfaction survey from the high school students which are given in Table 3 separated by bachillerato branch (sciences, or humanities and social sciences), although the differences between the two branches are not significant. The organization into three blocks was the

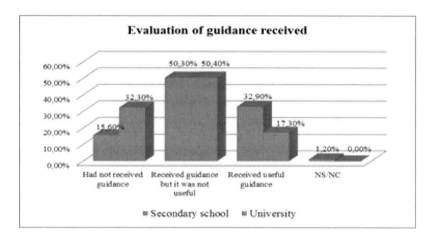

Figure 9. Evaluation of orientation given to high school and university students.

highest scoring variable, with other aspects scoring between 3 and 5 such as; usefulness in improving self-awareness, availability of information, and improved decision-making capability (see Table 3).

The university students studying psychology tended to evaluate the e-orientation tool more highly than the students studying primary education, although the difference between the scores was only significant for the final item, showing that the psychology students demonstrated more interest in the material and felt it would have been useful in their previous phase of education (see Table 4).

CONCLUSION

We have seen how the need to improve the quality of educational guidance processes affects various countries and the problems that can affect both individuals, who find their academic progress or entry into employment more difficult, and society, wasting already scarce resources on a service that fails to reach its potential. This waste of resources is both direct (investment in improving the service which appears to have had little effect)

Table 3. Difference in mean evaluation scores for the tool from students studying sciences and students studying humanities and social sciences (Student-t test for independent samples - SPSS.24)

	Sciences		Humanities & Social Sciences		DMSc-HSS	$t_{(120)}$	p	d
	M	SD	M	SD				
Organizing the content into blocks and topics makes it easier to understand.	3.78	.878	3.63	8.17	.15	.922	.358	...
The tools for self-awareness have helped me to identify my aptitudes and interests, strengths and weaknesses.	3.18	1.078	3.40	.995	-.22	-1.183	.239	...
The information given by e-orientation and the activities made it easier for me to make decisions about my future study and work.	2.94	1.020	3.10	.955	-.16	-.847	.398	...
I believe that after completing the e-orientation project I am in a better position to make decisions.	3.01	1.000	3.06	.978	-.05	-.236	.814	...

Note. M = mean; S.D. = standard deviation; DMSc-HSS = difference in means; d = Cohen's d (effect size).

and indirect cost (losses owing to poor guidance leading to students dropping out).

In this chapter we have focused on one of the objectives of educational guidance, that of academic-vocational guidance, with the inclusive perspective of counselling for academic-vocational decisions within an framework of the student's own personal development and adaptation.

Table 4. Difference in mean evaluation scores for the tool from psychology students and students studying primary education (Student-t test for independent samples - SPSS.24)

	Psychology		Primary education		$DM_{Psych-PEd}$	$t_{(125)}$	p	d
	M	SD	M	SD				
The e-orientation methodology (learning through self-regulation and content selection according to learning strategy) seems to be useful.	4.08	.86	3.88	.76	.20	1.33	.185	...
I like the design of the modules (self-regulation, micro-lessons, activities according to learning style).	4.05	.77	3.88	.70	.176	1.29	.199	...
The topics (living in the 21st century, taking decisions, and options on finishing secondary education) are useful and contribute to better student decision-making.	4.14	.83	4.17	.75	-.027	-.19	.852	...
I think that e-orientation helps users better understand themselves and improve their capabilities, encouraging better academic-vocational decision-making.	4.10	.82	3.81	.89	.29	1.87	.064	...
I would have liked to use this program in the guidance classes in my school.	4.32	.89	3.65	1.06	.671	3.84	.000	.71

Note. M = mean; S.D. = standard deviation; DMPsych-PEd = difference in means; d = Cohen's d (effect size).

In order to achieve that, neither the student nor the guidance process can be considered in isolation as mechanical processes that operate outside the students' cultural context. It is essential to give students references with which they can understand their environment, and make the most of all that it offers to make the process easier.

Information and communication technologies are developing at a staggering pace and are becoming more and more firmly fixed in the educational arena. They represent an opportunity to improve guidance processes, not only because of their motivational nature, but because they can easy communication with teachers and other students, and provide ubiquitous access to information both in terms of quantity and quality.

We performed a brief analysis of some international projects which attempt to include technological tools in guidance processes, and presented our own project, E-Orientation, which is part of those.

The results from this lead us to conclude that these resources are welcomed by students and improve the effectiveness of educational guidance. They seem to indicate a promising new path in which guidance services may at last play the important role they should in the overall education process and, in short, the student's life plan.

REFERENCES

Álvarez, Lucía, Antonio Cervero, and Antonio Urbano. (2016). "Análisis del uso de herramientas digitales en los campus virtuales para la comunicación y evaluación del alumnado universitario [Analysis of the use digital tools in the virtual campus for communication and evaluation of University students]." In *Investigación en el ámbito escolar: un acercamiento multidimensional a las variables psicológicas y educativas*, coordinated by José Jesús Gázquez et al., 163–168. Almería: ASUNIVEP. [*Research in the school environment: a multidimensional approach to psychological and educational variables*]

Barbero, María. (2016.) *Por qué realizar un año sabático en el extranjero? UNIR da las claves de esta experiencia educativa* [*Why do a gap year abroad? Join gives the keys of this educational experience]*. Accessed July 20, 2018. https://bit.ly/2up22zX.

Bernardo, Ana, Antonio Cervero, María Esteban, Ellián Tuero, Paula Solano, and Joana Casanova. (2017). "Proyecto E-Orientación, una necesidad desde el campo de la orientación educative [Project E-Orientation, a necessity from the field of educational guidance]." *Revista d´Innovació Docent Universitària*, 9:81–95. Accessed June 14, 2018. doi: 10.1344/RIDU2017.9.7. [*Magazine of University Teaching Innovation*]

Bernardo, Ana, María Esteban, and Rebeca Cerezo. (2014). "La importancia de empezar con buen pie: Influencia de la etapa previa al ingreso y primer curso en la universidad en el abandono de titulación [The importance of good start: Influence of the stage prior to entry and first course University in the drop out titulation]." In *Cuarta Conferencia Latinoamericana sobre el Abandono en la Educación Superior* (IV CLABES). Colombia: Medellín. [*Fourth Latin American Conference on Abandonment in Higher Education*]

Broadbent, Jaclyn, and Walter Poon. (2015). "Self-regulated learning strategies & academic achievement in online higher education learning environments: A systematic review." *The Internet and Higher Education* 27:1–13. Accessed June 14, 2018. doi: 10.1016/j.iheduc.20 15.04.007.

Del Cerro, Franciso, and Franciso Javier Ramón. (2017). "Compromiso y empleabilidad de los recién titulados de formación profesional. Conclusiones para un rediseño de la modalidad formativa [Engagement and employability of the student newly titled of vocational training. Conclusions for a redesign of the training modality]." *Revista de Educación a Distancia* 54:1–15. Accessed July 19, 2018. http://dx.doi.org/10.6018/red/54/12. [*Distance Education Magazine*]

Del Moral, María Esther, Lourdes Villalustre, and María del Rosario Neira. (2014). "Variables asociadas a la cultura innovadora con TIC en escuelas rurales [Variables linked to the innovative culture with ICT in rural schools]". *Revista de Currículum y Formación del Profesorado* 18:9–25. [*Curriculum magazine and faculty formation*]

Eurostat (2016). *Almost half of upper secondary pupils in the EU enrolled in vocational education.* Luxemburgo: Eurostat Publishing.

Fung, Mario. (2017). "Las funciones que desempeñan el personal de Orientación y sus implicaciones jurídicas en la prestación de los servicios educativos [The role of counselors and its legal impact on Educational Services]." *Revista Gestión de la Educación* 7 (1): 37-72. Accessed July 20, 2018. doi: 10.15517/rge.v7i1.27570. [*Education Management Journal*]

García-Valcárcel, Ana, and Franciso Javier Tejedor. (2017). "Percepción de los estudiantes sobre el valor de las TIC en sus estrategias de aprendizaje y su relación con el rendimiento [Student perception of the value of ict's in their learning strategies and their relation to performance]." *Educación XX1* 20:137–159. doi: 10.5944/educXX1.13447.

García-Valcárcel, Ana, Verónica Basilotta, and Camino López. (2014). "Las TIC en el aprendizaje colaborativo en el aula de Primaria y Secundaria [ICT in Collaborative learning in the classrooms of Primary and Secondary Education]." *Revista Científica Iberoamericana de Comunicación y Educación -Comunicar-* 21:65–74. doi: 10.3916/C42-2014-06. [*Iberoamerican Scientific Journal of Communication and Education –Communicate*]

González, Julio R. (2008). "La orientación profesional en América Latina: Fortalezas, debilidades, amenazas y oportunidades [Vocational guidancd in Latin America: Strenghs, weaknesses, threats and opportunities]." *Revista Mexicana de Orientación Educativa* 5: 44–49. [*Mexican Magazine of Educational Guidance*]

González-Ramírez, Teresa, José Antonio Contreras-Rosado, and Salvador Reyes. 2015. "Utilización y valoración de los servicios de orientación desde la perspectiva de los universitarios [Utilization and evaluation of guidance services from the perspective of college students]." *Paper presented at the XVII International Congress of Educational Research.* Cádiz.

Henao, Gloria Cecilia, Luz Ángela Ramírez, and Carlota Ramírez. (2006). "Qué es la intervención psicopedagógica: Definición, principios y componentes [What is the psycho-pedagogical intervention? Definition, principles and components]." *Agora USB* 6: 215–226.

Hernández, Juan, and José Antonio Pérez. (2017). *La Universidad Española en Cifras 2015/2016* [*The Spanish University in figures 2015/2016*]. Madrid: CRUE.

Kalamkarian, Hoori S., and Melinda Mechur Karp. (2017). *Student attitudes toward technology-mediated advising systems.* Accessed July 1, 2018. https://goo.gl/aum1jw.

Law 30/2015, 9th September, which regulates the system of vocational training for employment in the workplace. *Officer Newsletter of the State*, number 217, on September 10, 2015.

Law 14/1970, 4th August, on Education and Financing for Educational Reform. *Officer Newsletter of the State*, number 187, on August 6, 1970.

Marín, Verónica, Eloísa Reche, and Guadalupe A. Maldonado. (2013). "Ventajas e inconvenientes de la formación online [Advantages and disadvantages of online training]." *Revista Digital de Investigación en Docencia Universitaria* 1: 33–43. doi: 10.19083/ridu.7.185. [*Digital Journal of Research in University Teaching*]

Marqués, Pere Ramón. (2013). "Impacto de las Tic en la educación: Funciones y limitaciones [Impact of ICT in education: Functions and limitations]." *Revista de Investigación 3 Ciencias* 2:1–15. [*Research Journal 3 Sciences*]

McGill, Craig M. (2016). "Cultivating Ways of Thinking: The Developmental Teaching Perspective in Academic Advising." *New Horizons in Adult Education and Human Resource Development* 28:50–54. doi: 10.1002/nha3.20131.

Molina, Denyz Luz. (2004). "Concepto de orientación educativa: Diversidad y aproximación [Concept of educational guidance: diversity and approach]." *Revista Iberoamericana de Educación* 35:1–22. [*Iberoamerican Journal of Education*]

Noaman, Amin Y., and Fekry Fouad Ahmed. (2015). "A new framework for e academic advising." *Procedia Computer Science* 65:358–367. doi: 10.1016/j.procs.2015.09.097.

OCDE and MECD. (2004). *Orientación profesional y políticas públicas. Cómo acortar distancias* [*Career guidance and public policy. How to shorten distances*]. París: OCDE Publishing.

OCDE. (2013). *Education at a Glance 2013. OCDE indicators*. Paris: OCDE Publishing.

Organic Law 1/1990, 3rd October, General Plan of the Education System. *Officer Newsletter of the State*, number 238, on October 4, 1990.

Organic Law 2/2006, 3rd May, on Education. *Officer Newsletter of the State*, number 106, on May 4, 2006.

Organic Law 6/2001, 21st December, on Universities. *Officer Newsletter of the State*, number 307, on December 24, 2001.

Organic Law 8/2013, 9th December, for Improvement to Education Quality. *Officer Newsletter of the State*, number 295, on December 10, 2013.

Royal Decree 1393/2007, 29th October, which establishes the organization of university teaching. *Officer Newsletter of the State*, number 260, on October 30, 2007.

Royal Decree 395/2007, 23rd March, which regulates the subsystem of professional training to foster employment. *Officer Newsletter of the State*, number 87, on April 11, 2007.

Royal Decree 412/2014, 6th June, which establishes the basic requirements for admission procedures for university degree courses. *Officer Newsletter of the State*, number 138, on Jun 7, 2014.

Royal Decree 83/1996, 26th January, approving the Organic Regulations on Secondary Schools. *Officer Newsletter of the State*, number 45, on January 26, 1996.

Rodríguez, Marisol, and María José Arroyo. (2014). "Las TIC al servicio de la inclusión educativa [ICT in the service of inclusive education]." *Digital Education Review* 25: 108–126.

Schneckenberg, Dirk, Ulf Ehlers, and Heimo Adelsberger (2011). "Web 2.0 and competence-oriented design of learning-Potentials and implications for higher education." *British Journal of Educational Technology* 42:747–762. doi: 10.1111/j.1467-8535.2010.01092.x.

Tuero, Ellián, Antonio Cervero, María Esteban, and Ana Bernardo. (2018). "Por qué abandonan los alumnos universitarios? Variables de influencia en el planteamiento y consolidación del abandon [Why do university students drop out? Influencing variables regarding the approach and consolidation of drop out]." *Educación XX1* 21: 131–154. doi: 10.5944/educxx1.20066.

Workman, Jamie L. (2015). "Exploratory students' experiences with first-year academic advising." *The Journal of the National Academic Advising Association* 35:5–12. doi: 10.12930/NACADA-14-005.

In: Progress in Education. Volume 55 ISBN: 978-1-53614-551-9
Editor: Roberta V. Nata © 2019 Nova Science Publishers, Inc.

Chapter 5

INFLUENCES OF CULTURAL CAPITAL ON JUNIOR SECONDARY SCHOOL STUDENTS' MUSICAL PREFERENCES IN HONG KONG, CHINA

Siu-Hang Kong[*], *PhD*
Department of Music,
Hong Kong Baptist University, Hong Kong, China

ABSTRACT

The relationship between individuals' possession of cultural capital and their musical preferences has been extensively examined in Western society; however, little attention has been given to it in contemporary Chinese contexts. Based on Bourdieu's (1973, 1986) concept of cultural capital, this study focuses on junior secondary school students' (Grades Seven to Nine) preferred musical listening styles, and their perception of how their parents' and their own cultural capital have shaped their musical preferences in contemporary Hong Kong society. Two research questions are addressed: (1) How does parental cultural capital influence students'

---

[*] Corresponding Author Email: erickonghkbu@gmail.com.

cultural capital? (2) To what extent does students' cultural capital shape their musical preferences in contemporary Hong Kong society? A survey questionnaire was distributed to nine Hong Kong secondary schools in the summer of 2015, followed by an interview survey conducted in the spring of 2016. Based on a synthesis of the 1,614 completed questionnaires and 28 in-depth individual interviews, the quantitative and qualitative findings provide nuanced insights into students' perceptions of their musical preferences, and how one's cultural capital shapes one's musical preferences, in a Hong Kong context. This study finds that the students' music listening not only served as an aesthetic and leisure activity, but also as a means of inculcating cultural capital—proficiency of English—that is legitimate in Hong Kong and deemed an influential factor in school performance. The study also shows that through technological advancements, more specifically a readily-available platform for accessing comprehensive musical resource databases, a new factor has emerged that weakens the relationship between familial social status and students' musical preferences and leads to more autonomous music listening behaviour. In addition, students' musical cultural capital, which is transformed from their parents' cultural capital, may directly and explicitly inform their musical listening behaviour. Further supplementing and revisiting Bourdieu's cultural capital by considering technological invention and conceptualising cultural capital in Hong Kong society, this study offers a new insight on how cultural capital influences one's musical preferences and contributes to students' academic success in contemporary Chinese societies. Given the extensive penetration of technology in all sectors, the study also offers recommendations on how music educators could assist students' music listening by using technological devices to develop their music learning in a more enriched and complete manner.

Keywords: musical preferences, cultural capital, junior secondary school students, Hong Kong

INTRODUCTION

Bourdieu's theory of cultural capital (1973) has been influential for more than four decades, and does much to explain the impact of the possession of cultural capital on musical preferences and the art of living in the dominant class. Cultural capital is defined as the legitimised cultural knowledge needed to understand and decode the dominant culture in society and secure further advantages from academic success (Bourdieu, 1973).

Cultural capital can be expressed in many forms—reflecting the internalisation of behaviour, disposition, cultural knowledge, and habitus attained in prolonged socialisation or through investment in education. The possession of cultural capital is exclusive to middle-class individuals and enables one to decode high-brow culture in society; hence, possession of cultural capital is often regarded as a social marker indicating one's place in the social hierarcy (Bourdieu, 1986). Furthermore, intergenerational transmission of cultural capital from parents to their children occurs in unconscious ways and without deliberate inculcation (Bourdieu, 1973, 1986); the transmission of cultural capital through socialisation ensures the reproduction of one's social status in one's offspring.

Possession of cultural capital informs one's musical preferences (Bourdieu, 1989). The relationship between cultural capital and musical preferences has been extensively studied in sociological research (for example, see DiMaggio & Useem, 1978; Holt, 1998; Peterson & Kern, 1996; Van Eijck, 2001). One's possession of cultural capital influences one's disposition towards appreciation of the arts, and one's social status can be reflected in one's cultural participation. Drawing on the concept of cultural capital (1973), Bourdieu advanced his theory of homology (1989), which holds that early socialisation helps individuals internalise the class-specific dispositions and tastes that are homologous with and correspond to their social status. Therefore, the lifestyles of the members of a class fraction are similar. According to Bourdieu's homology, individuals from a high social class possess exclusive cultural knowledge and cultural capital that is necessary for the appreciation and understanding of high-brow culture; hence, individuals from upper social strata and who are better educated understand and prefer to consume high-brow culture (e.g., opera, classical music, visiting art galleries), while individuals from lower social strata, having less cultural capital, are more likely to appreciate mass and popular culture. Distinctive, class-specific musical preferences are regarded as a form of cultural participation indicative of a social status that excludes those of lower socioeconomic status (Bourdieu, 1989).

Cultural capital not only reflects social position, but also actively reproduces educational and social inequality. Bourdieu (1973) proposed that class inequality in academic attainment was legitimated by the education system and facilitated by cultural capital. Schools welcome students possessing cultural capital, which is closely related to their social and family background, and which is a factor contributing to their success and failure in the school system (Bourdieu, 1973). Individuals enter schools possessing different endowments of cultural capital. Students from higher-class families endowed with more cultural capital more readily understand the dominant culture, further facilitating their development of cultural competence, which is rewarded by the school. Individuals' initial differences in cultural capital perpetuate existing social inequalities, and are eventually converted into educational credentials, reproducing the individuals into their parents' social class positions (Aschaffenburg & Maas, 1997). Therefore, higher-class individuals are privileged in the education system, and enhance their chances to obtain education credentials that help to legitimate social inequalities. Parents' social class are thus reproduced and reflected in their children. However, Vryonides (2007) argued that participation in cultural activities does not bestow direct educational advantages on students, but serves as symbol for cultural distinction (Bourdieu, 1984), which induces students' intellectual development indirectly.

While Bourdieu's theory has been extensively examined by and influential in sociological and educational studies for decades, its generalisability and transposability to locations other than France, and to periods beyond the 1960s and 1970s, is questionable (van Rees, Vermunt, & Verboord, 1999). The conceptualisation and measurement of cultural capital varies largely between locations and periods of time. In addition, the mechanisms by which social and economic factors reflect cultural consumption and preferences remain unknown (van Rees et al., 1999), and social factors other than cultural capital may also significantly impact individual's cultural consumption. Furthermore, Bourdieu's contention that one's cultural consumption may contribute to "self-realisation" is implausible (Chan & Goldthorpe, 2007; van Rees et al., 1999), as modern society is sufficiently economically advanced that one's lifestyle is less grounded in social stratification, and the choice of lifestyle is shifting from class-specific habitus to freedom (Chan & Goldthorpe, 2007; van Rees et al., 1999).

Bourdieu's theory of cultural capital was founded when digital technology was not yet widely used, and thus does not account for the influence of the Internet on cultural participation and music listening. Music is now more accessible in people's daily lives than ever before, due to the advancement and prevalence of technology. People therefore have many more opportunities for, and more convenient to access music listening and integrating music into their daily lives (Heye & Lamont, 2010). Technological advances have led to an explosion of diverse music listening platforms that have radically changed the ways in which people participate in music activities (Krause & North, 2016), particularly exemplified in the significance of mass media (Rösing, 1984). Music is nowadays largely heard in technologically communicated and digital forms, and the prevalence of mobile devices has changed how music is consumed (Heye & Lamont, 2010). Music listening is no longer restricted to live performances, physical recordings, or radio broadcasts, but is now also available through such new and diverse digital media such as smart phones, laptop or desktop computer, and tablets, all of which can readily access millions of musical works from virtually all genres. Given the proliferation of smartphones, students can also perceive the popularity of songs through social media and music listening apps—such as Facebook, WeChat Moments, and Spotify—rather than seeking or relying on the opinions of peers and parents (Fung, 2014). Parental influence on students' musical preference has thus become less influential. Digital technology affords one the autonomy to enjoy more individualistic musical listening preferences that are less grounded in one's social status.

Bourdieu's theory of cultural capital provides a theoretical framework for examining social status and its relationship to musical preferences, both in France and in English-language societies. However, language familiarity, a factor neglected in Bourdieu's study, also influences one's musical preferences. Lyrics and music are two elements inextricably linked in a song and convey messages to a music listener in different and multiple aspects. Abril and Flowers (2007) maintained that a song can transmit two levels of information—formalistic and referential. At the formalistic level, a song's musical sound can transmit inherent information about its musical elements (e.g., melody, rhythm, style); at the referential level, a song's lyrics convey concrete messages and extramusical meanings to the listener. Therefore, one's familiarity with the language of the lyrics determines one's affective response to the song. Fung (1994) found college students' preferences for world music were positively associated with their familiarity with and study of foreign languages. In Abril's (2005) study, a significant association was found between familiarity with a language and a song's language; in the study, language barriers negatively influenced participants' affective response to and judgement of foreign-language musical works. Subsequent research has also found that song enjoyment was dependent on the lyrics being written in a familiar language; the listener's connectedness to and identification with the song's underlying culture; and the musical styles to which the listener is exposed in his or her home environment (Abril & Flowers, 2007; Brittin, 2014).

AN OVERVIEW OF CONTEMPORARY HONG KONG SOCIETY

Hong Kong (officially the Hong Kong Special Administrative Region of the People's Republic of China (PRC)) has an area of 1,106 square kilometres and a population (in 2017) of over 7.4 million, making it the fourth most densely populated territory in the world (Census and Statistics Department, 2018b). Chinese and English are both official languages of Hong Kong, with Cantonese being the mother tongue of 89% of its population. Although most residents are Chinese, the English language occupies a dominant position in Hong Kong (Carmichael, 2009), and is widely used in the government, legal, professional, and business sectors. Public- and government-aided secondary schools in Hong Kong are categorised into bands, based on students' public examination results; most English-medium schools are in better bands and enroll mainly high-achieving students, while most Chinese-medium schools are in the lower bands, with intakes of low-achieving students (see Tsang, 2008). English-medium schools are often regarded as better at preparing students for entrance into universities in Hong Kong, in which most lectures are conducted in English. Therefore, competition among primary school students to enter English-medium secondary schools is keen, enabling schools to have their pick of Hong Kong's best students, which has led to the schools' being associated with sense of elitism (Tsang, 2008).

Its historical, economic, and political background makes Hong Kong distinctive from other regions of China. Hong Kong was colonised by Britain after the First Opium War (1839-42), which sheds light on its renowned blending of Eastern and Western cultures. On 1st July 1997, sovereignty over Hong Kong was transferred from the United Kingdom to the PRC, and Hong Kong became a special administrative region, governed under the "one country, two systems" policy. Hong Kong thus maintains a high degree of autonomy and a different political and economic system from other regions of China. Based on the Financial Development Index and per capita income, Hong Kong has the potential to become one of the most competitive cities in the world (International Institute for Management Development, 2016; Nelid, 2016).

Purpose of Study

The relationship between cultural capital and musical preference has been extensively studied in Western society; however, little attention has been given to the role of social influences in forming students' musical preferences in the Chinese context. Rapid social changes have challenged the applicability of Bourdieu's concept of cultural capital, which was proposed four decades ago, in contemporary social contexts. With reference to Hong Kong, China, this study focuses on how cultural capital shapes junior secondary school students' (Grades Seven to Nine) preferred music styles of listening in contemporary Hong Kong society, and asks:

1) How does parental cultural capital influence students' cultural capital?
2) To what extent does students' cultural capital shape their musical preferences in contemporary Hong Kong society?

METHOD

In early summer, 2015, a questionnaire was used to collect quantitative data from students attending Grades Seven to Nine in eight secondary schools in different districts of Hong Kong. In each school, teachers selected two to three sample classrooms from each grade; all students in the target classrooms were then invited to complete the questionnaire in class, as instructed by their teachers; 32-40 students in each class participated in the questionnaire survey. The survey questionnaire aimed at gathering data in four major areas: (1) students' general information (demographics and instrumental learning background); (2) parental educational attainment; (3) students' musical preferences; and, (4) students' language proficiency. Students' responses were captured for quantitative data analysis using closed-ended and multiple-choice questions, as well as four-point (0 = never to 3 = always) and five-point (1 = strongly disagree to 5 = strongly agree) Likert scales.

To explore and provide an in-depth understanding of students' perceptions of their musical preferences, students who had completed the questionnaires were invited to participate in interview surveys. In a recruitment process administrated by the school teachers, 28 students were recruited for interviews, 15 of whom were instrumental learners. The qualitative survey consisted of semi-structured, in-depth individual interviews, conducted in Cantonese in Hong Kong. Clarification and dimensional follow-up questions were introduced when further probing was needed. Interview data were transcribed verbatim, followed by open coding. The interview data were coded analytically and, as concepts emerged from the data, were divided into categories, based on their properties and dimensions.

FINDINGS

A total of 1,614 questionnaires were collected from nine Hong Kong secondary schools; four schools in the New Territories, four in Kowloon, and one on Hong Kong Island. Seven of the nine schools sampled were co-educational, one was a boys' school, and one was a girls' school. Demographic information for the student respondents is presented in Table 1.

Table 1. Demographic information of the student respondents

Demographic information		No. of respondents (%)
Grade of study		
	7	569 (37.24%)
	8	367 (25.98%)
	9	555 (36.32%)
Gender		
	M	764 (49.01%)
	F	790 (50.67%)

Parental Educational Attainment and Instrumental Learning Background

This study measured parents' educational attainment level and instrumental learning background as proxy for cultural capital. Table 2 captures respondents' parents' educational attainment level (i.e., Primary education or below, Secondary education, or Tertiary or Postgraduate education) and instrumental learning background (i.e., with or without previous instrumental learning).

Table 2. Parental educational attainment and instrumental learning background

Parents' education attainment	No. of respondents (%)
Father's education attainment	
Primary Education or below	124 (11.2%)
Secondary Education	642 (57.8%)
Tertiary Education or above	344 (31.0%)
Total	1110
Mother's educational attainment	
Primary Education or below	134 (11.8%)
Secondary Education	715 (62.8%)
Tertiary Education or above	289 (25.4%)
Total	1138
Father's instrumental learning background	
No instrumental learning	1301 (89.2%)
Had instrumental learning	157 (10.8%)
Total	1458
Mother's instrumental learning background	
No instrumental learning	1317 (90.5%)
Had instrumental learning	139 (9.5%)
Total	1456

Medium of Students' Music Listening

Students were asked to use four-point rating scales (from 0 = never to 3 = always) to indicate the frequency with which they used three different media for music listening (Table 3): (i) theatre or concert hall; (ii) CD or DVD; and, (iii) Internet (YouTube etc.), mobile phone, radio, television etc. Based on the mean scores, Internet, mobile phone, radio or television were the most popular platforms for students' music listening (mean = 2.70).

Table 3. Medium of students' music listening

	Mean* (SD)
Theatre	.81 (0.77)
CD	1.26 (1.02)
Internet or mobile phone	2.70 (0.70)

*from 0 = never to 3 = always.

Students' Musical Preferences and Their Language Proficiency

The relationship between the frequency of students' listening to the 13 musical styles and their perceived proficiency in five languages (i.e., Mandarin, Cantonese, English, Korean, and Japanese) was examined using Pearson's bivariate correlation analysis. Table 4 shows students' perceived proficiency in Korean and Japanese was strongly and positively correlated with their listening to popular songs from Korea ($r = .513, p < .01$) and Japan ($r = .455, p < .01$), respectively. In addition, students' perceived proficiency in Mandarin and English was positively correlated to the frequency with which they listened to popular songs from mainland China ($r = .346, p < .01$) and English-language popular songs ($r = .192, p < .01$), respectively.

Table 4. Correlation between students' perceived language proficiencies and the frequency of their listening to 13 musical styles

Frequency of listening	Perceived Proficiency				
	Mandarin	Cantonese	English	Korean	Japan
Pop from mainland China	.346**	-.096**	-.079**	.113**	.002
Pop from Taiwan	.174**	.082**	-.044	.146**	.045
Pop from Korea	.144**	.037	.059*	.513**	.023
Pop from Japan	.024	-.007	-.047	-.006	.455**
Pop from Hong Kong	-.020	.135**	.077**	.027	.034
English Pop	.092**	.032	.192**	.114**	.020
Jazz Music	.156**	-.051*	.125**	.106**	.101**
Music from Broadway Musical	.079**	.028	.149**	.167**	.073**
Other pop	.143**	-.017	.130**	.227**	.090**
Classical Music	.123**	.019	.172**	.078**	.097**
Chinese Folk Songs	.160**	-.091**	.034	.091**	.083**
Chinese Instrumental Music	.133**	-.052*	.047	.085**	.079**
Chinese Opera	.107**	-.071**	.011	.098**	.086**

**. Correlation is significant at the 0.01 level (2-tailed).
*. Correlation is significant at the 0.05 level (2-tailed).

In the interview survey, 19 student respondents considered song lyrics a determining factor in their musical preferences, particularly if they found the meaning of the lyrics was connected to them: "The lyrics have a story, and I will see whether the story is connected to me." Students favoured songs written in a language with which they were familiar; as one student said, "because I am a Mandarin speaker, I like pop music in Mandarin more, [as I can] understand the lyrics." Also, being able to understand the lyrics of a song allowed students to interpret those lyrics and affected their emotions; as one student said, "I like old English songs. I can understand the lyrics. It is sweet."

However, unfamiliarity with the language in which lyrics are written may be an obstacle to understanding them; thus, students less often listened to songs with lyrics written in an unfamiliar language; as one student said, "I would like English songs more if I could understand the lyrics." Although an unfamiliar language may be an obstacle to understanding song lyrics for some respondents, some students stated they might learn a new language through music listening. Five respondents reported they had learnt English by listening to English songs, with one stating:

> I like Western pop songs. The songs always talk about parties, the musical pulse is fast and breezier. I don't understand the words, but I would check up the translation... I often listen to English songs to learn English. It really helps.

Parental Educational Attainment and Students' Language Proficiency

The relationship between overall parental education attainment and students' perceived proficiency in five languages was examined using Pearson's bivariate correlation analysis. The results (see Table 5) show that students' perceived proficiency in English was strongly and positively correlated to their parents' education level ($r = .350, p < .01$).

Table 5. Correlation between overall parents' education and students' language proficiency

Language	Overall parental education
Mandarin	.062*
Cantonese	-.062*
English	.350**
Korean	.010
Japan	-.009

**. Correlation is significant at the 0.01 level (2-tailed).
*. Correlation is significant at the 0.05 level (2-tailed).

Parents' Cultural Capital and Students' Enrolment in Instrumental Learning

As shown in the cross-tabulation (Table 6), students' instrumental class enrolment rate raised as their parents' level of cultural capital increased.

Table 6. Cross-tabulation showing parents' cultural capital and students' instrumental learning

Parental cultural capital	No. of respondents	
	Students who were not learning instruments	Students who were learning instruments
Father's educational attainment		
Primary education or below	80	41
Secondary education	362	268
Tertiary education and postgraduate	152	178
Mother's educational attainment		
Primary education or below	86	45
Secondary education	406	295
Tertiary education and postgraduate	119	160
Father's instrumental learning background		
No previous instrumental training	771	512
Had instrumental training	59	95
Mother's instrumental learning background		
No previous instrumental training	776	525
Had instrumental training	43	91

Chi-square test results demonstrated significant association between students' enrolment in instrumental classes and their: (i) father's educational attainment ($X^2 = 18.23(2), p = .000$); (ii) mother's educational attainment ($X^2 = 25.60 (2), p = .000$); (iii) fathers' instrumental learning background ($X^2 = 26.74 (1), p = .000$); and, (iv) mother's instrumental learning background ($X^2 = 37.66 (1), p = .000$). In addition, multiple linear regression analysis comparing parental education attainment and parental musical background indicated parental instrumental learning background was a stronger predictor of students' instrumental class enrolment rate ($F(2,1164) = 34.03, \beta = .189, p<.01$).

Influences of Students' Instrumental Learning on Their Music Listening

In the interview survey, students were asked their perceptions on how instrumental learning influenced their music listening. Nineteen respondents who were learning instruments all agreed that their instrumental learning had different impacts on and benefits for their music listening. All agreed they would search for the songs they were learning in their instrumental class on the Internet, and seven students stated they were better able to analyse the musical elements in their favourite music after learning instruments.

"Learning guitar would help me to know more about intonation and arrangement."

"I now listen to classical music more often and observe how others play. Moreover, I watch performances by other people on YouTube. I pay attention to the rhythm and dynamics."

"Usually there are guitars in pop songs. I pay attention to how the performers play and how they strike the strings."

DISCUSSION

Based on a synthesis of the quantitative and quality findings, this study provides insight into students' perceptions of their musical preferences and how their cultural capital shapes their music preferences, in the Hong Kong context. The study shows that students' music listening did not only serve as an aesthetic and leisure activity, but also as a learning activity for inculcating a form of cultural capital—i.e., their level of proficiency of English—that is highly valued in Hong Kong. Technology provides a readily-available platform for accessing huge musical resources, but is a newly-emerged factor that weakens the association between familial social status and students' musical preferences and leads to more autonomous musical preferences. The following section discusses two research questions: (1) How does parental cultural capital influence students' cultural capital? (2) To what extent does students' cultural capital shape their musical preferences in contemporary Hong Kong society?

First, this study had proven a positive relationship between parents' and students' cultural capital. Consistent with Bourdieu's (1973) model of intergenerational transmission of cultural capital, a Chi-square test in this study showed a positive relationship between parental cultural capital and students' enrolment in instrumental class (see Table 6). Furthermore, multiple linear regression revealed that students whose parents had higher levels of cultural capital—particularly an instrumental background—were more likely to learn musical instruments. This is also in keeping with Lareau's (2011) concept of concert cultivation, which holds that parents with higher social status more actively organise activities for their children, and more actively enhance their children's cultivation of cultural capital. Parents' cultural capital may inform their social status and possession of economic capital. Parents with higher economic capital may find it more possible to afford to organise cultural activities for their children, which requires substantial and continuous financial resources. Consistent with the findings in this study, well-educated and musically-trained parents may cultivate children's musical talents by enrolling students into private instrumental classes. Based on Bourdieu's concept of cultural capital (1986), the author argues that parental cultural capital can be transformed into parental support (e.g., physical and financial support) for enrolling students into instrumental classes outsides home, which can then further students' musical development—a type of cultural capital.

In addition, the quantitative data of this study show a positive relationship between parental education level and students' English language proficiency, one which may, in turn, influence students' musical preference indirectly. Pearson's bivariate correlation showed a positive relationship between parental education attainment and students' English proficiency ($r = .350$, $p < .01$). English, as the city's second main language, plays an important role in Hong Kong's Chinese society and has a correspondingly high status therein (Guo, 2017), as evidenced by its being a major curriculum subject and a medium of instruction in schools (Adamson, 2004; Hu & McKay, 2012). Also, mastering English is an important asset for entering good schools and attaining a good job. Thus, Hong Kong students generally strive to acquire a higher standard of English, and English is deemed dominant and conceptualised as cultural capital.

Second, this study provides insights on how parental and student cultural capital shape students' musical preferences. Participants' proficiency in the language used in the music, a factor neglected in Bourdieu's study, significantly influenced their musical preferences in this study. Student respondents showed a higher frequency of listening to songs written in languages with which they were familiar (see Table 4). As language barriers may impede students' affective responses to foreign-language songs (also see Abril, 2005), understanding a song's lyrics was paramount to determining students' musical preferences. This suggests language familiarity is a major factor in determining students' musical preferences (for example, see Abril, 2005; Brittin, 2014; Fung, 1994).

Furthermore, students' proficiency in English, which was greatly influenced by their parents' education level, was also found to be closely related with students' preferences for English-language songs. Bourdieu (1989) argued one's possession of musical knowledge determined one's musical preferences and contended there was an association between one's knowledge of and disposition towards a particular aspect of culture. However, different from Bourdieu's argument, this study found English proficiency—a non-musical and class-related form of cultural knowledge—directly impacted Hong Kong students' musical preferences. Listening to English-language songs often served the educational purpose of teaching students English in Hong Kong (for example, see Cheung, 2001; Cockrill & Lui, 2013; de Kloet, 2010). According to the qualitative data, students perceived that their English proficiency could be enhanced by listening to English popular songs. Owing to the legitimate position of the English language in Hong Kong, most parents believed that being proficient in English gives students a brighter future and better job opportunities (Cheung, 2001). In addition, parents with more cultural capital may more willing to support their children's English learning by encouraging their listening to English-language popular songs, deeming it a tool for acquiring a cultural capital advantage that would enable them to excel in schools, and hence reproduce their parents' social status. This study supports that students whose parents had higher educational attainment showed greater English language proficiency and a greater preference for English-language songs, and reveals the interplay between English learning and musical preferences for English-language popular music. To supplement Bourdieu's theory of cultural capital (1989), I propose that English language proficiency, as a class-related form of cultural capital, enhances students' musical preferences for English-language popular music in contemporary Hong Kong, a non-English-speaking society.

This study finds that parental cultural capital and support enhanced students' instrumental learning; in turn, the musical knowledge gained through instrumental learning influenced students' music listening. Instrumental learners in this study showed an analytical approach to appreciating music. Some instrumental learners articulated that they would focus on orchestration, and listen to and learn from the performance techniques shown by performers in the video or music. Possession of musical knowledge may enable students to focus on musical elements and influence how they decode music, which may influence how they perceive the music and how it benefits their instrumental learning. Students' instrumental playing could enhance their music listening, as instrumental learners may have higher levels of musical ability and musical knowledge (Elliott & Silverman, 2015), and may appreciate music more analytically (Leder, Belke, Oeberst, & Augustin, 2004; Rössel, 2011). Such a music listening strategy may also benefit their instrumental learning. Moreover, their instrumental learning may also influence the musical styles to which students listen. Instrumental learners in this study tended to search for songs they were learning in their instrumental classes; this may broaden their musical listening styles and expose them to more varieties of music.

The study shows the influence of cultural capital on students' musical preference; on the other hand, technological advancement has radically changed people's music-consuming behaviour, which may have, in turn, reduced the ability of Bourdieu's theory of cultural capital to explain individuals' musical preferences, in current contexts. The high penetration of the Internet—a readily-accessible platform with huge musical resources—in our daily lives may also contribute to the decline in concert attendance. In this study, Internet, radio, television, and smartphone apps were found to be students' most popular platforms for music listening (mean = 2.70; from 0 = never to 3 = always), while attendance at theatres for music listening (mean = 0.81; from 0 = never to 3 = always) was the least popular (See Table 3). In the past, the theatre was the sole venue for consuming highbrow music, such as opera and classical music, meaning appreciation thereof required purchasing tickets for physical attendance at specific sites and times; this may have excluded individuals from less-wealthy families. Due to today's advanced technology, countless sites on the Internet provide online music stores and song downloads, both paid and free-of-charge, and smartphones allow people to listen to music anywhere and at any time. Highbrow music can now be readily accessed wherever Internet access is available and appreciating it is no longer an exclusively middle-class prerogative. Previously unreachable audiences are now exposed to previously unexplored music, particularly classical music, which had usually been offered in theatres only (Crawford, Gosling, Bagnall, & Light, 2014). Online music streaming is now the most prevailing medium for music consumption, and has had far-reaching effects on people's listening behaviour (Heye & Lamont, 2010; Krause & North, 2016). By the end of 2016, 112 million users had subscribed to and paid for music streaming services globally, and music streaming is now the main source of revenue for digital music businesses (IFPI, 2017). Music streaming apps have changed musical consumption patterns radically, by offering audiences access to a huge catalogue of songs for a low monthly subscription fee, or even for free. Moreover, music listening on the Internet may provide an alternative for parents who are too busy to accompany their children to concert theatres (Kong, 2016, 2017a, 2017b). According to the Census and Statistics Department, in 2016, more than half of Hong Kong employees worked from 40 to 49 hours (median = 44 hours) per week, while about 3.8 million employees worked more than 60 hours a week (Census and Statistics Department, 2018a). Parents' long working hours have contributed to their lack of time to accompany their children to and participate in music activities outside of the home (Law & Ho, 2009). The Internet and smartphones may be an alternative to theatre attendance, allowing people to listen to music without leaving their homes, outside of set concert hours. I propose the individualistic and autonomous music listening behaviour attributed to today's new music technology challenges Bourdieu's argument that musical preferences are homologous to one's social status.

CONCLUSION

This study finds that a students' cultural capital (i.e., instrumental learning), transformed from a parents' cultural capital, may directly and explicitly inform their musical listening behaviour. In addition, the students' music listening not only serves as a leisure activity, but also as a means of learning English, which is deemed legitimate in Hong Kong and is seen as a cultural capital that helps students excel in schools. In addition, the study also shows that the Internet, as a readily-available platform for accessing comprehensive musical resource databases, is a new emerging factor that weakens the relationship between familial social status and students' musical preferences, leading to more autonomous music listening behaviours. Supplementing Bourdieu's cultural capital through the consideration of technological invention and a conceptualisation of cultural capital in Hong Kong society, this study offers new insights into how cultural capital influences one's musical preferences and contributes to students' academic success in contemporary Chinese societies. Given the extensive penetration of technology in all sectors, this study also suggests music educators could assist students' music listening by using technological devices to develop their music learning in a more enriched and complete manner.

REFERENCES

Abril, C. R. (2005). Multicultural dimensions and their effect on children's responses to Pop songs performed in various languages. *Bulletin of the Council for Research in Music Education, 165*, 37–51.

Abril, C. R., & Flowers, P. J. (2007). Attention, preference, and identity in music listening by middle school students of different linguistic backgrounds. *Journal of Research in Music Education, 55*(3), 204–219.

Adamson, B. (2004). China's English. In *China's English: A History of English in Chinese Education* (pp. 195–210). Hong Kong: Hong Kong University Press.

Aschaffenburg, K., & Maas, I. (1997). Cultural and educational careers: The dynamics of social reproduction. *American Sociological Review, 62*(4), 573.

Bourdieu, P. (1973). Culture reproduction and social reproduction. In B. S. Association & R. K. Brown (Eds.), *Knowledge, education, and cultural change: papers in the sociology of education* (Vol. 2, pp. 71–112). London: Harper & Row Publishers Barnes & Noble Import Division.

Bourdieu, P. (1986). The forms of capital. In J. G. Richardson (Ed.), *Handbook of theory and research for the sociology of education* (pp. 241–258). New York: Greenwood Press.

Bourdieu, P. (1989). *Distinction: A social critique of the judgement of taste.* London: Routledge.

Brittin, R. V. (2014). Young listeners' music style preferences: patterns related to cultural identification and language use. *Journal of Research in Music Education, 61*(4), 415–430.

Carmichael, S. (2009). *Language rights in education: A study of Hong Kong's linguistic minorities.* Retrieved from https://www.law.hku. hk/ccpl/pub/Documents/Occasional_Paper_19.pdf .

Census and Statistics Department. (2018a). *2017 Report on annual earnings and hours survey.* Hong Kong. Retrieved from https://www.statis tics.gov.hk/pub/B10500142017AN17B0100.pdf .

Census and Statistics Department. (2018b, August 17). *Population.* Retrieved August 18, 2018, from https://www.censtatd.gov.hk/hkstat/ sub/so20.jsp .

Chan, T. W., & Goldthorpe, J. H. (2007). Social stratification and cultural consumption: The visual arts in England. *Poetics, 35*(2–3), 168–190.

Cheung, C. K. (2001). The use of popular culture as a stimulus to motivate secondary students' Englsih learning in Hong Kong. *ELT Journal, 55*(1), 55–61.

Cockrill, A., & Lui, Y. (2013). Western popular music consumption by highly involved Chinese music fans. *Journal of Retailing and Consumer Services, 20,* 263–271.

Crawford, G., Gosling, V., Bagnall, G., & Light, B. (2014). Is there an app for that? A case study of the potentials and limitations of the participatory turn and networked publics for classical music audience engagement. *Information, Communication & Society, 17*(9), 1072–1085.

de Kloet, J. R. (2010). *China with a cut: Globalization, urban youth and popular music.* Amsterdam: Amsterdam University Press.

DiMaggio, P., & Useem, M. (1978). Social class and arts consumption: The origins and consequences of class differences in exposure to the arts in America. *Theory and Society, 5*(2), 141–161.

Elliott, D. J., & Silverman, M. (2015). *Music matters: A new philosophy of music education.* New York; Oxford: Oxford University Press.

Fung, A. Y. H. (2014). The iTunization of pop: Mobile music and youth social networks. *Perfect Beat, 15*(1), 23–43.

Fung, C. V. (1994). Undergraduate nonmusic majors' world music preference and multicultural attitudes. *Journal of Research in Music Education, 42,* 45–57.

Guo, K. (2017, June 2). Middle class hierarchy report sparks online debate. *China Daily*. China.

Heye, A., & Lamont, A. (2010). Mobile listening situations in everyday life: The use of MP3 players while travelling. *Musicae Scientiae, 14*(1), 95–120.

Holt, D. B. (1998). Does cultural capital structure American consumption? *Journal of Consumer Research, 25*(1), 1–25.

Hu, G., & McKay, S. L. (2012). English language education in East Asia: Some recent developments. *Journal of Multilingual and Multicultural Development, 33*(4), 345–362.

IFPI. (2017). *Global music report 2017*. Retrieved from http://www.ifpi.org/downloads/GMR2017.pdf.

International Institute for Management Development. (2016). *The IMD World Competitiveness Scoreboard*. Retrieved March 12, 2017, from http://www.imd.org/uupload/imd.website/wcc/scoreboard.pdf.

Kong, S. H. (2016). A study of parental support for junior secondary school students' musical activities in Hong Kong. *Journal of Youth Studies, 19*(1), 119–133.

Kong, S. H. (2017a). Influence of parental cultural capital and support for students' participation in music activities: A study of junior secondary school students in Hong Kong. *Music Communication, 1*, 63–71.

Kong, S. H. (2017b). Parental cultural capital and parental support for students' participation in music listening and instrumental learning: A study of junior secondary school students in Beijing, China. In *Progress in Education: Volume 42* (pp. 169–192). New York: Nova Science Publishers, Inc.

Krause, A. E., & North, A. C. (2016). Music listening in everyday life: Devices, selection methods, and digital technology. *Psychology of Music, 44*(1), 129–147.

Lareau, A. (2011). *Unequal childhoods: Class, race, and family life*. Berkeley: University of California Press.

Law, W. W., & Ho, W. C. (2009). Parental involvement in and support for musical participation: A study of young Hong Kong students. *Journal of Youth Studies, 12*(1), 150–171.

Leder, H., Belke, B., Oeberst, A., & Augustin, D. (2004). A model of aesthetic appreciation and aesthetic judgments. *British Journal of Psychology, 95*(4), 489–508.

Nelid, B. (2016). *Irresistible cities: World's 25 top tourism destinations*. Retrieved February 14, 2017, from http://edition.cnn.com/2016/01/28/travel/most-visited-cities-euromonitor-2016 .

Peterson, R. A., & Kern, R. M. (1996). Changing highbrow taste: From snob to omnivore. *American Sociological Review, 61*(5), 900–907.

Rösing, H. (1984). Listening behaviour and musical preference in the age of "transmitted music." *Popular Music, 4*, 119–149.

Rössel, J. (2011). Cultural capital and the variety of modes of cultural consumption in the opera audience. *Sociological Quarterly, 52*(1), 83–103.

Tsang, W. (2008). *Evaluation study on the implementation of the medium of instruction guidance for secondary schools*. Retrieved September 6, 2017, from http://www.fed.cuhk.edu.hk/~hkier/content/document/publications/newsletter/newsletter24.pdf .

Van Eijck, K. (2001). Social differentiation in musical taste patterns. *Social Forces, 79*(3), 1163–1185.

van Rees, K., Vermunt, J., & Verboord, M. (1999). Cultural classification under discussion- Latent class analysis of highbrow and lowbrow reading. *Poetics, 26*(5–6), 349–365.

Vryonides, M. (2007). Social and cultural capital in educational research: Issues of operationalisation and measurement. *British Educational Research Journal, 33*(6), 867–885.

In: Progress in Education. Volume 55
Editor: Roberta V. Nata

ISBN: 978-1-53614-551-9
© 2019 Nova Science Publishers, Inc.

Chapter 6

DIGITALLY ENHANCED SPACES: A NEW INNOVATION?

Damian Maher
STEM Education Futures Research Centre,
University of Technology Sydney, Australia

ABSTRACT

Many contemporary classrooms are now being designed to be flexible and open. Such designs reflect designs that were trialed in classrooms during the mid-1960s to the late seventies when the open plan classroom became popular. Many of these spaces reverted back to closed traditional classrooms with the experiment failing. Starting in the early 2000s such open plan flexible learning spaces again came into vogue. This time around technology played a big part in the use of such spaces. The underlying pedagogical approaches to teaching and learning have also developed from a teacher-centred to a more student-centred approach. This chapter explores the initial open plan movement in the sixties and seventies and then investigates some of the changes that now shape the practices within contemporary learning spaces.

INTRODUCTION

It is widely recognised that the material landscape of education (school architecture, classroom furniture, spatial organisation, and learning tools) influences the teaching and learning process (Tondeur, Herman, De Buck & Triquet, 2017). Buildings are loaded with messages regarding how one should talk, behave, interact, and so on (Gislason, 2007; Peponis & Wineman, 2002).

Buildings communicate ideas, form perceptions and guide actions, as might a teacher. Given this strong influence the school environment has gained the label of 'third teacher' (Strong-Wilson & Ellis, 2007). The design of learning spaces is thus important as it impacts on teaching and learning.

Environmental scientists have published studies showing a close correlation between human productivity and space design (Nair, 2011). This research clearly demonstrates that students and teachers do better when they have variety, flexibility, and comfort in their environment—the very qualities that many traditional classrooms lack (Nair, 2011).

The traditional idea of the learning space is shifting away from the familiar classroom arrangement and towards activity-based learning spaces where students can actively participate in, and take charge of, their learning (Lundström, Savolainen, & Kostiainen, 2016).

The design of these learning spaces has gone through cycles. One such cycle is the flexible open-plan design. During the mid-1960s through to the late 1970s many classrooms went from being an enclosed room for one class to become open spaces, which allowed for a number of classes and their teachers to work in different ways within that space. Around the late 1970s many of these spaces were closed for a number of different reasons and converted back to the one-class one-room model. Again, in early 2000s there was resurgence in the open learning space design. Many schools and universities across a number of countries are now embracing this concept again.

The focus of this chapter is to chart the early open space design classroom in the 1960s examining reasons why this design lost favour and then focus on what has changed in the design of the new open learning spaces. One of the key changes that support a modern open plan design argued in this chapter is the introduction of technology- in particular networked computers and mobile devices. In looking at the modern spaces the role that technology can play in supporting these open spaces is examined and how they support contemporary ways of learning and teaching. In the final section of the chapter, the pedagogical aspects that support teaching and learning in the contemporary learning spaces are explored. Literature relating to primary, secondary and tertiary education is drawn upon to support concepts examined in this chapter.

INFLUENCES ON CLASSROOM DESIGN IN THE LATE 20TH CENTURY

Many classrooms prior to the sixties (and some today) were designed on the factory model of learning to equip young people with the skills needed for the industrial revolution. The design of classrooms based on this model reflected a traditional paradigm of learning where tables were in rows and where the teacher was positioned at the front, facing a substantial number of students where knowledge was transmitted in a top-down fashion (Beichner 2014). In this kind of setting, the teacher is the focal point, which conveys an implicit message of power, with the teacher having the entitlement to speak, with the students listening in a passive, non-participatory manner (Van Note Chism 2006).

Starting in the mid-sixties to late seventies, the design of the classroom began changing across many countries. This change originated in the UK after world II. This change was brought about by the Butler Act of 1944 which set out free compulsory secondary education (Wright, 2018). Given the shortage of materials and the need to build classrooms to accommodate the secondary students there was a need to be creative in classroom design to use minimal amounts of materials.

The first school designated open plan was built in 1959 in the rural Oxford shire village of Finmere in the UK (Ministry of Education, 1961).

Brogden, (1983) suggested it was the rural setting that also contributed to the design where classes (given the small population size to draw upon) were often multi-age and did not move beyond the two-roomed model.

The open plan design spread to the United States, Australia and other developed countries and was known as the open plan movement. In the United States the movement was adopted in part by America's concern over falling educational standards at a time when competition with Soviet Union was high and the Cold War was raging. In the fifties, critics began blaming the U.S. public system for falling educational standards and the failure to beat the Soviets to the launch of a space craft (Phillips, 2014). It was thought the open plan movement would remedy academic problems in schools. Postwar elementary schools built in the United States thus reflected both ongoing educational debates and the unique circumstances of the postwar era (Ogata, 2008).

The movement also brought changes to teaching practices. "The best of the open classrooms had planned settings where children came in contact with things, books, and one another at 'interest centers' and learned at their own pace with the help of the teacher" (Cuban, 2004). All of this was done in newly designed learning spaces.

The experiment of the late 20th century in relation to open learning spaces failed. One reason is that: "Teachers found the open space distracting, as did children, especially those with learning disabilities or attention deficit and hyperactivity disorder" (Trejos, 2001). Another factor was that there was a perception that academic standards were slipping and this was a result of the learning that was occurring in the open classroom (Cuban, 2004). Another suggestion for the failure is that while the spaces changed the practices of some teachers did not (Upholt, 2017). Given that there was limited training for teachers as to how to use these open spaces it is not surprising that the pedagogical approaches did not always take advantage of the spaces.

Education is often blamed for society's woes in general. The open plan design was in part seen as a quick fix to society's problems. As stated in a newspaper report in 1973: "Since it looks and sounds easy, school boards anxious to be "with it" and to seem responsive to local critics have pressured administrators into imposing the open classroom, without giving it time to grow roots. Poorly implemented, some open schools have resulted in undisciplined bedlam" (Hechinger, 1973, p. 60).

As a result of the challenges with the open plan design many of the schools that had been designed as open learning spaces began to build walls to replicate the traditional one teacher per class model. There was move also a move back towards teaching the basics.

THE RESURRECTION OF THE OPEN PLAN CLASSROOM- 21ST CENTURY LEARNING

In the early 2000s the move once again began back towards the open plan design. Significant public investment has been made in schools in many countries since the turn of the century to support open plan classrooms (Mulcahy, Cleveland & Aberton, 2015). The move has now been formalised at a national level in many countries with the construction of built environments that respond to student needs through the creation of new learning spaces including England, Australia, Portugal, Finland and the Netherlands amongst others (Loughlin 2013). Attention is being given to the idea that arrangements of space critically influence patterns of learning and teaching in education (Li et al. 2005). As Newton and Gan (2012) describe:

> During the past decade innovative school design has focused on student centred learning within rich digital learning environments. Many schools are shifting from the 'cells and bells' environment of classroom teaching into larger, more fluid spaces with a range of furniture settings.

Lippman (2010) suggests that learning environments should be designed as integrated systems that afford individual, one-to-one, small group, and large group activity settings. In addition, he suggests that students are more likely to construct knowledge for themselves and share their understandings with others when provided with an environment that allows for a flow of activity.

However, it should be noted that on contrast to this move towards open spaces and student-centred learning, there has also been a move towards high stakes outcomes-based testing in a number of countries which limits the educationally possibilities of these spaces. Such testing is seen in Australia by way of National Assessment Program - Literacy and Numeracy (NAPLAN) test which was introduced in 2008. "Currently, every year all Students in Years 3, 5, 7 and 9 are assessed on the same days using national tests in Reading, Writing, Language Conventions (Spelling, Grammar and Punctuation) and Numeracy" (Klenowski & Wyatt-Smith, 2012, p. 1). Without a move away from such high stakes testing it may mean that the current open plan classrooms are again disbanded and a move towards closed classrooms takes place. Time will tell in regards to this.

One of the ways that learning spaces can be conceptualised has been set out by David Thornburg (2013). He uses four metaphors to describe how contemporary classrooms can be used which are Campfires, Watering Holes, Caves and Life. In relation to the construct of Campfires, this is a place where stories are told and where the expert imparts knowledge. The traditional classroom can be considered in this way where the teacher directs learning, but it can also include stories of students and guests to the classroom.

The second metaphor that Thornburg draws on is the Watering Hole which represents a social space for learning. This is where students learn with their peers and importantly, where they are both learner and teacher at the same time. This includes both the teacher and the students. An important aspect here is that teachers need to model the process of learning to students. In the age of the internet teachers cannot be the traditional holders of knowledge that they once were and so this aspect of learning for them is important.

The third metaphor is that of the Cave where a space for reflective learning is provided. Often in schools, the library has been the place where students can undertake reflective learning. This space is of more importance than ever where the introduction of the internet has meant there are large volumes of information available and often students skim the surface of such knowledge. What is also needed is a space where they can engage in deep learning in a reflective way which the Cave can provided.

The final metaphor used by Thornburg is Life. Using this metaphor, the importance of real-world learning is of significance where learning is about just-in-time rather than just-in case. This conceptualisation of learning is what often underpins project-based learning for example.

Learning is enhanced, deepened and made more relevant when the spaces described above are connected in meaningful ways to provide opportunities for:

- active and interactive participation
- collaborative project work
- information retrieval and sharing
- discussion and presentation
- production of new knowledge
- teacher and student-led activities
- connection with experts
- local and global networks' (Ministerial Council on Education, Employment, Training and Youth Affairs, 2008, p. 5).

As can be seen, contemporary learning spaces need to provide for a variety of learning experiences far greater than a traditional classroom affords. Not only do these the spaces need to support such learning, they need to be connected to each other in ways that support learning.

In understanding the design of learning spaces, the age of students is important. Barrett, Davies, Zhang and Barrett (2017) investigated flexibility (which is a measure of how well designed the classroom space is for the particular age of the pupils) of learning spaces in the UK, which involved 3776 students from years 1 to 6. They found that for younger pupils, complex room shapes enabled the differentiation into different learning zones and creation of intimate spaces. For older pupils, they found that larger and squarer rooms enabled flexible working for either group work or whole class learning. What is important, as highlighted by Higgins, Hall, Wall, Woolner and McCaughey (2005) is that the most successful design elements in classrooms are likely to have elements of flexibility that can adapt to new curriculum demands and new challenges.

Technology Supported Learning

One of the major changes that has occurred in the relation to contemporary learning spaces is the technology that now supports such spaces and the link such technology provides beyond the learning spaces. The types of technologies available in and out of classrooms have ballooned and include: desktops, mobile devices, augmented and virtual realities, robotics, interactive surfaces, maker spaces, gaming and gamification, etc.

The advent of such technologies has brought about the advent of the digitally connected learning space. The technology that now supports contemporary spaces includes features such as connected devices, which provide connectivity for students and teachers to the wider world through the use of video conferencing and other similar communicative technologies.

One of the significant inventions that has impacted on how these open modern learning spaces can be used is the mobile device which can include laptops, tablets, iPods and smartphones. It was only in 2010 that the iPad was first introduced into schools and from that point Wi-Fi was installed in schools to support the mobile connected ways of learning that can occur in open-learning spaces. Building of the Wi-Fi network took some time (and is still on-going in many schools). It has only thus been very recent then, that the opportunities to work with mobile connected devices in schools have been possible.

It is important that technology supports learning as young people are digitally connected and learn through these technologies in ways that previous generations have not and this is changing learning both in and outside of the classroom. "Forcing them to put their personal technology away during class contradicts the way they live their lives and gives students one more reason to expect that what they learn in school will have little relationship to reality" (Beichner, 2014, p. 9). One important point to note that there are instances where other learning experiences are important (such as physical education, discussion or drama for example) and so mobile devices should be put away.

"Technology has also brought unique capabilities to learning. Whether by stimulating more interaction through the use of personal response systems or by videoconferencing with international experts, IT has altered learning spaces" (Oblinger, 2006, p. 1.2). Because of the use of technology, the modern learning spaces are blended learning spaces bringing together both the physical and the virtual learning spaces.

In conceptualising a blended learning space there are different ways this can be considered. One scenario is where students have opportunities to work together face-to-face in the classroom while interacting online with content and other people outside of the classroom. With the second scenario, the technology is used outside of the classroom (at home for example) to connect students to each other and their teachers. In this second scenario, the technology is being used to extend the boundaries of the classroom through both time and space.

In consideration of the physical and virtual spaces, as noted by Ellis and Goodyear (2016), the links between the physical and the virtual become less clear and more permeable. "This permits and promotes redistributions of study activity in space and time, with many students demanding greater flexibility in order to fit study around other aspects of their lives…" (p. 150).

Work has been carried out at the university level to investigate the effects of blended learning. It has been found that the different environments (F2F and online) can support different types of learning. In a study conducted by González-Gómez, Jeong, Rodríguez and Cañada-Cañada (2016), it was found that students were better equipped for solving general science problems during F2F classroom and laboratory activities when online video lessons and instructions outlining the theoretical and practical aspects of laboratory work can be watched at any point in time prior to or after in-class sessions. How these two mediums work together is less well known.

In understanding the nature of a blended learning environment and classroom learning, the construct of orchestration can support such understanding. The definition of orchestration in a Technology Enhanced Learning (TEL) environment as defined by Prieto, Sharma and Dillenbourg (2015) is one ... "of managing multiple activities at different social levels using multiple technological tools, often in formal education" (p. 269).

Prieto, Holenko Dlab, Gutiérrez, Abdulwahed and Balid (2011) have developed a model of orchestration in regards to TEL spaces, which includes eight aspects as set out in the table below:

Table 1. Orchestration aspects

Orchestration aspect	Description
Design	This aspect is related to the planning of the learning activities and the tools used to enact them. It includes the conceptualization of learning designs, but also their implementation (setting up of the situation in the technological environment)
Management	This aspect deals with the regulation of the learning activities, and involves issues related to the management of the class, time, tools, artifacts and groups
Adaptation	This aspect is related to the capability of changing the design to both the local context of the classroom and the emergent events during the enactment of the learning activities
Awareness	This aspect deals with being aware of what happens in a learning situation
Roles of the teacher and other actors	This aspect refers to the role that the different actors (teachers and students) take in the orchestration
Pragmatism	This aspect deals with making TEL research results available to average (as opposed to TEL-expert) teachers, fitting with the constraints of the authentic settings of their everyday teaching practice
Alignment	This aspect is related to the coordination of the elements to be orchestrated (learning activities at various social levels, spaces, tools and scaffoldings used) in order to attain the learning goals
Theories	This aspect has to do with the theories and models used to orchestrate learning

This model can support architects and teachers to understand how contemporary spaces can be designed to support teaching and learning where digital technologies are part of the process.

THE USE OF SPACE–THE PEDAGOGICAL PERSPECTIVE

A more nuanced focus on the theoretical aspects of learning has developed in tandem with the development of the digitally supported contemporary learning spaces. The pedagogical change in some parts of the world has moved from teacher-led instruction to constructivist approaches to learning (Jonassen & Land 2012; Prain et al. 2013).

In these newly designed spaces the focus of learning is more around a student-centred approach (Newton & Gan, 2012) moving away from a teacher-centred focus. The students work in collaborative groups as do the teachers. The students can work in learning centres for different subjects and teachers move amongst the groups. The teacher became a facilitator of learning rather than a provider of direct instruction. As noted earlier, there are also opportunities for students to work individually.

The teaching philosophy behind a student-centred approach to leaning is based on a social constructivist idea on learning underpinned by the theories of John Dewey, Piaget and Vygotsky. Social constructivism is premised on the idea that interactions between the learner and situations or environments lead to individuals constructing their own knowledge (Vygotsky, 1978).

Another important aspect of social constructivism is that the learner is actively involved in the construction of knowledge, as opposed to being a passive recipient (Jaworski, 1996).

Ziegenfuss (2010) argues that teachers now "must develop authentic activities that connect learning to what students do or will be doing outside of the classroom" (p. 86). A focus is moving away from students having content knowledge specific to a particular subject to one where young people are capable of adaption, critique and creativity (Wright, 2018). This supports the concept of lifelong learning where it is important to support young people *how* to learn rather than *what* to learn.

The role of teachers is thus evolving to support more student-centric approaches to learning to better prepare learners for the future workforce and new approaches where classroom design is supporting this shift (Freeman, Becker, & Cummins, 2017). A project undertaken by Churchie

Grammar school (in East Brisbane, Australia) which was funded by the Australian Research Council, found that after moving into a new precinct there was an increased level of classroom activities that employed a more active and responsive pedagogical orientation (interactive instruction, providing feedback, class discussion and questioning) (Churchie, n.d.). This has the effect of supporting a more dynamic learning experience.

In a modern classroom students have access to many of the materials they need via computers or other networked devices such as tablets or mobile phones and spend more time working independently. The teacher spends less time providing direct instruction but instead can work more in an advisory role.

The design of the classroom reflects the informal group-based independent nature of learning that is being carried out in them. In this learning environment students are being encouraged to develop self-regulation skills which Sharples et al. (2016) argue is a necessary skill for young people to develop if they are to become successful lifelong learners. It is important that the types of skills needed for both teachers and students is identified and that the opportunity to learn such skills are provided.

Whilst the contemporary spaces afford many opportunities for learning, they do also have limitations. One such issue is noise. As noted by Kariippanon, Cliff, Lancaster, Okely and Parrish (2017): "Flexible learning spaces often have the capacity to hold more students than a traditional classroom, can be more open plan, and do not have walls or dividers to provide isolated spaces" (p. 10). Ways that spaces are being designed to reduce this is in the use of pods or dedicated withdrawal rooms that form part of the integrated learning space. Given that this one of the major concerns of design of learning spaces in the sixties and seventies it remains to be seen how this aspect plays out in the new learning spaces.

Another challenge associated with the use of digital technologies is access. Most young people have access to smart phones. In the United States for example, this is reported to be 95% (Anderson & Jiang, 2018), which is similar to many other developed countries. Whilst phones are useful their size means a number of educational activities such as working on documents cannot be carried out on them easily. Whilst some schools may provide access in schools to such networked devices such as tablets or laptops not all students have access to devices in their homes. This means teachers need to be aware of student circumstances and plan pedagogical activities accordingly.

A further challenge to digitally connected learning spaces is the attitude of teachers and authorities regarding the use of mobile devices in classrooms. There are a number of countries and authorities who view the use mobile devices, and in particular smart phones, as a negative influence on learning. At the time of writing this chapter France had just passed a law banning mobile devices for students up to the age of 15 years of age which includes smart phones, tablets and smart watches (ABC News, 2018).

In New South Wales, Australia a review was underway by the Education Department where there was a suggestion by others of the possibility of also banning mobile phones (Lu, 2018). Many schools already ban phones in Australia and other countries beyond France. St Paul's Catholic College in New South Wales is one example (SBS, 2018). A move to ban mobile devices does not support the types of learning experiences young people have outside of school and does not support a flexible connected mobile way of learning associated with new learning spaces.

CONCLUSION

As has been highlighted in this chapter, there has been a resurgence of the open plan classroom. In this new reiteration, the push for such design has not been prompted by aspects relating to limitations of resources or aspects of national progress as it was in the late sixties to the late seventies, but a renewed focus of pedagogical possibilities which incorporate the use of digital technologies.

The types of technologies that can be employed to support teaching and learning has dramatically increased providing opportunities for students to access experts and peers from around the globe. The boundary that divides inside and outside the classroom has dissolved with the assistance of internet-based applications. Due to these changes the way that students work in the classroom has diversified and contemporary spaces have been built to reflect such diversity.

The traditional classroom where all teachers face the front and lecture has been replaced with flexible arrangements that allow students to work in different ways at the same time. Ways they might work include individual work, group work and whole class work.

The pedagogical principles underpinning teaching and learning in schools have changed from being teacher-centred to student-centred. Students now have more responsibility for their learning and can make choices how they work within the open learning spaces. This has changed the way teachers work with students where they act in a more facilitative role but also use direct instruction where appropriate.

Whilst there have been many changes there are aspects that impact on the effectiveness of these new spaces as outlined in the chapter which include aspects of noise, legislation that requires very traditional teacher-centred types of learning (e.g., high stakes testing), and limitations on the use of technology in schools. It remains to be seen then, if the new open learning spaces will work and thus stand the test of time this time around.

REFERENCES

ABC News. (2018). *France passes new law banning smartphones, tablets and smartwatches in Schools*. Retrieved from http://www.abc.net.au/news/2018-08-01/france-bans-smartphones-and-tablets-in- classrooms/10060590 .

Anderson, M. & Jiang, J. (2018). *Teens, Social Media & Technology 2018*, Pew Research Center report. Retrieved from http://www.pewinternet.org/2018/05/31/teens-social-media-technology-2018/.

Barrett, P., Davies, F., Zhang, Y. & Barrett, L. (2017). The holistic impact of classroom spaces on learning in specific subjects. *Environment and behavior*, *49*(4), 425-451.

Beichner, (2014). History and evolution of active learning spaces. *New Directions for Teaching and Learning*, *137*, 9–16.

Brogden, M. (1983). Open plan primary schools: Rhetoric and reality. *School Organisation*, *3*(1), 27-41.

Churchie (n.d.). *Innovative learning environments and teacher change project*. Retrieved from https://www.churchie.com.au/academic/new-generation-learning-spaces/australian-research-council-project.

Cuban, L. (2004). The open classroom. *Education Next*, *4*(2). Retrieved from https://educationnext.org/theopenclassroom/.

Dillenbourg, P. (2013). Design for classroom orchestration. *Computers & Education*, *69*, 485-492.

Ellis, R. A. & Goodyear, P. (2016). Models of learning space: integrating research on space, place and learning in higher education. *Review of Education*, *4*(2), 149-191.

Freeman, A., Becker, S. A. & Cummins, M. (2017). *NMC/CoSN horizon report: 2017 K-12*. The New Media Consortium.

Gislason, N. (2007). Placing education: The school as architectural space. *Philosophical Inquiry in Education*, *16*(3), 5-14.

González-Gómez, D., Jeong, J. S., Rodríguez, D. A. & Cañada-Cañada, F. (2016). Performance and perception in the flipped learning model: An initial approach to evaluate the effectiveness of a new teaching methodology in a general science classroom. *Journal of Science and Education Technology*, *25*(3), 450-459.

Hechinger, F. (1973). 'Open classroom' found to be no instant cure all. *The New York Times*. Retrieved from https://www.nytimes.com/1973/01/08/archives/-open-classroom-found-to-be-no-instant-cureall-disaffection-appears.html .

Higgins, S., Hall, E., Wall, K., Woolner, P. & McCaughey, C. (2005). *The impact of school environments: A literature review*. London, England: Design Council.

Jaworski, B. (1996). *Investigating mathematics teaching: A constructivist enquiry*. London-Washignton DC: The Falmer Press.

Jonassen, D. & Land, S. (2012). *Theoretical foundations of learning environments* (2nd ed.). Abingdon: Routledge.

Kariippanon, K. E., Cliff, D. P., Lancaster, S. L., Okely, A. D. & Parrish, A. M. (2017). Perceived interplay between flexible learning spaces and teaching, learning and student wellbeing. *Learning Environments Research*, 1-20.

Klenowski, V. & Wyatt-Smith, C. (2012). The impact of high stakes testing: The Australian story. *Assessment in education: Principles, policy & practice*, *19*(1), 65-79.

Li, P., Locke, J., Nair, P. & Bunting, A. (2005). Creating 21st century learning environments. PEB Exchange, Programme on Educational Building, 2005/10. Retrieved from https://ideas.repec.org/p/oec/eduaaa/2005-10-en.html.

Lippman, P. C. (2010). *Evidence-based design of elementary and secondary schools*. Hoboken, N.J.: John Wiley & Sons.

Loughlin, J. (2013). How photography as field notes helps in understanding the building the education revolution. *The Australian Educational Researcher*, *40*(5), 535–548

Lu, A. (2018). *Smartphone ban in NSW schools an option, as Government launches study into phone use*. Retrieved from http://www.abc.net.au/news/2018-06-21/ban-on-smartphones-in-nsw-schools-on-the-cards/9893186 .

Lundström, A., Savolainen, J. & Kostiainen, E. (2016). Case study: developing campus spaces through co-creation. *Architectural Engineering and Design Management*, *12*(6), pp. 409-426.

Ministerial Council on Education, Employment, Training and Youth Affairs (Mceetya) (Australia). (2008).*Learning spaces framework: Learning in an online world*. Ministerial Council on Education.

Ministry of Education. (1961). *Building Bulletin 3*, Village Schools London, HMSO.

Mulcahy, D., Cleveland, B. & Aberton, H. (2015). Learning spaces and pedagogic change: envisioned, enacted and experienced. *Pedagogy, Culture & Society*, *23*(4), 575-595.

Nair, P. (2011). The classroom is obsolete: It's time for something new. *Education Week*. Retrieved from https://www.edweek.org/ew/articles/2011/07/29/37nair.h30.html?print=1 .

Newton, C. & Gan, L. (2012). Revolution or missed opportunity. *Architecture Australia*, *101* (1), 74–78.

Oblinger, D. (Ed.). (2006). *Learning spaces*. Washington, DC: Educause. Retrieved from https://www.educause.edu/ir/library/pdf/PUB7102a.pdf

Ogata, A. F. (2008). Building for learning in postwar American elementary schools. *Journal of the Society of Architectural Historians, 67*(4), 562-591.

Peponis, J. & Wineman, J. (2002). Spatial structure of environment and behavior. In R. B. Bechtel & A. Churchman (Eds.), *Handbook of environmental psychology*, (pp. 271-291). New York: John Wiley & Sons, Inc.

Phillips, D. C. (Ed.). (2014). *Encyclopedia of educational theory and philosophy*. Sage Publications.

Prain, V., Cox, P., Deed, C., Dorman, J., Edwards, D., Farrelly, C., et al. (2013). Personalised learning: Lessons to be learnt. *British Educational Research Journal, 39*, 654–676.

Prieto, L. P., Holenko Dlab, M., Gutiérrez, I., Abdulwahed, M. & Balid, W. (2011). Orchestrating technology enhanced learning: a literature review and a conceptual framework. *International Journal of Technology Enhanced Learning, 3*(6), 583-598.

Prieto, L. P., Sharma, K. & Dillenbourg, P. (2015). Studying teacher orchestration load in technology-enhanced classrooms. In *Design for teaching and learning in a networked world*, (pp. 268-281). Springer, Cham.

SBS. (2018). *Review of smartphone use in NSW schools*. Retrieved from https://www.sbs.com.au/news/review-of-smartphone-use-in-nsw-schools.

Strong-Wilson, T. & Ellis, J. (2007). Children and place: Reggio Emilia's environment as third teacher. *Theory into Practice, 46*, 40-47.

Sharples, M., de Roock, R., Ferguson, R., Gaved, M., Herodotou, C., Koh, E. & Wong, L. H. (2016). *Innovating pedagogy: Open university innovation report, 5*. Milton Keynes: The Open University.

Tondeur, J., Herman, F., De Buck, M. & Triquet, K. (2017). Classroom biographies: Teaching and learning in evolving material landscapes (c. 1960-2015). *European Journal of Education, 52*(3), 280-294.

Trejos, N. (2001). 70s open classrooms fail test of time. *Washington Post*. Retrieved from https://www.washingtonpost.com/archive/local/2001/05/13/70s-open-classrooms-fail-test-of-time/_6385962e-f844-4d5b-9217-d680d451c85d/?noredirect=on&utm_term=.65c293db1627.

Upholt, B. (2017). Back to the future with a new kind of open classroom school. *One Day Magazine*. Retrieved from https://www.teachforamerica.org/one-day-magazine/back-future-new-kind-open-classroom-school.

Van Note Chism, N. (2006). Challenging traditional assumptions and rethinking learning spaces. In D Oblinger (Ed.), *Learning Spaces*. Washington, DC: Educause.

Vygotsky, L. (1978). *Mind and society*. Cambridge, MA: Harvard University Press.

Wright, N. (2018). *Becoming an Innovative Learning Environment. The making of a New Zealand secondary school*. Singapore; Springer.

Ziegenfuss, R. M. (2010). *Education in the 21st century: Toward an expanded epistemic frame of leadership*. Unpublished doctoral thesis, University of Pennsylvania (Order No. 3410471). Available from Education Database. (499974761).

In: Progress in Education. Volume 55 ISBN: 978-1-53614-551-9
Editor: Roberta V. Nata © 2019 Nova Science Publishers, Inc.

Chapter 7

ELEMENT INTERACTIVITY AS A CONSTRUCT FOR THE ANALYSIS OF SCIENCE PROBLEM-SOLVING PROCESSES

Munirah Shaik Kadir[1,*], *Alexander Seeshing Yeung*[1] *and Anne Forbes*[2]

[1]Australian Catholic University, Sydney, Australia
[2]Macquarie University, Sydney, Australia

ABSTRACT

Element interactivity is a construct used by cognitive load theory researchers to explain the complexity in learning tasks. Despite advances in cognitive load research, element interactivity in science problem solving has not been vastly studied. In this book chapter, we illustrate how element interactivity gives rise to different types of cognitive load (intrinsic, extraneous, and germane) when middle school students solve a complex science problem. Analyzing learning tasks in terms of element interactivity assesses their suitability for targeted students, thus lowering the chances of cognitive overload, and therefore facilitating the cognitive processes for effective learning.

---

[*] Corresponding Author Email: Munirah.Kadir@acu.edu.au.

INTRODUCTION

The purpose of this chapter is to revisit the conceptualization of cognitive load theory (CLT; Sweller, 1988; Sweller, Ayres, & Kalyuga, 2011) by examining the cognitive processes involved during science problem solving, with a focus on element interactivity, or the degree to which learning comprises elements that cannot be learned in isolation. Despite accumulated knowledge about cognitive load and how it may affect learning, there is limited research on the links between element interactivity, cognitive load, and students' problem solving in science.

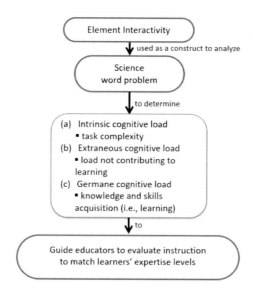

Figure 1. Overview of chapter.

To address these gaps in the literature, we used element interactivity as a construct to determine how the interaction of elements in a science word problem may incur various types of cognitive load. Our illustration of the analysis could guide educators to design learning tasks and instruction that match students' existing knowledge levels (i.e., expertise) in the domain, to optimize learning. We will illustrate element interactivity by examining how solving a science problem on 'speed' imposes three types of cognitive load on the students, which can then be used to modify and optimize the

Element Interactivity in Problem-Solving 187

suitability of learning tasks. The analysis of a science word problem will determine (a) the complexity of the science problem (intrinsic cognitive load), (b) cognitive load that does not contribute to learning (extraneous cognitive load), and (c) cognitive load that contributes to knowledge and skills acquisition (germane cognitive load). Figure 1 presents the overview of this chapter.

COGNITIVE PROCESSES INVOLVED IN SCIENCE PROBLEM SOLVING

Understanding human cognitive processes is important for us to make sense of students' learning capabilities and limitations. Figure 2 illustrates a model of the human cognitive processes when students are involved in learning tasks such as science problem solving. The model is based on the components of the human working memory (WM) advanced by Baddeley and Hitch (2000), which was illustrated by Chinnappan and Chandler (2010) and modified by Kadir, Ngu, & Yeung (2015).

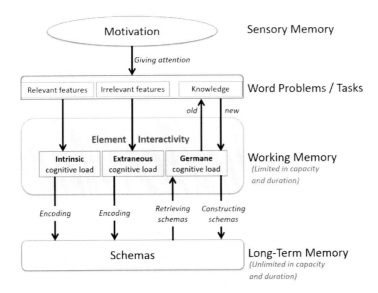

Figure 2. Model of human cognitive processes related to element interactivity during learning.

Sensory Memory

The sensory memory of the brain (top of the model in Figure 2) receives incoming signals and information when students are given a cognitive task. When students are sufficiently motivated to give the cognitive task enough attention, the input from the sensory memory is passed on and processed in the WM of the brain system (Baddeley, 1986). That is, active processing begins when the learner is motivated or has the intention of attempting the cognitive task.

Working Memory

Working memory (WM) is defined by Baddeley (1986) as "the temporary storage of information that is being processed in any range of cognitive tasks" (p. 43). It is a cognitive structure where current and active mental processing takes place but can only manage to process a few elements of information at any time because it has a limited capacity (Miller, 1956) and duration (Peterson & Peterson, 1959). If WM limitations are exceeded, learning and understanding is compromised. On the contrary, if the processing of the elements is within the capabilities of WM, the information will be successfully processed, and learning will occur. Whenever students are involved in any form of mental activity, their WM experiences cognitive load (middle of the model in Figure 2).

The three types of cognitive load identified by cognitive load theory (CLT) are: intrinsic, extraneous, and germane (Paas, Renkl, & Sweller, 2003). Interacting elements in the learning material impose intrinsic cognitive load (Ayres, 2013). Sub-optimal instruction results in inefficient problem-solving methods, which imposes extraneous cognitive load on WM (Sweller et al., 2011). The processing, encoding, and organization of new science knowledge into schemas to be retained in long-term memory (LTM) for future use (Figure 2), is called germane cognitive load. Learners require enough WM resources to be available for the cycle of constructing, retrieving, and automating schemas (germane cognitive load in Figure 2) for successful learning and this should be the primary aim of effective instruction. The involvement of the three types of cognitive load in terms of element interactivity will be described later.

Long-Term Memory

When information is successfully processed through WM, schemas are constructed and transferred to LTM and stored there (bottom of the model in Figure 2). In contrast to WM, LTM has unlimited capacity (Landauer, 1986) as there are no known limits to its immeasurably large storage space (Newell & Simon, 1972). Hence, it can store an infinite amount of information that has been processed by WM (i.e., schemas).

Schemas

Schemas are "general knowledge structures that encapsulate numerous elements of information into a single element" (Carlson, Chandler, & Sweller, 2003, p. 629). Successful learning results in the construction of schemas, which are hierarchically organized and stored in LTM (Kalyuga, Ayres, Chandler, & Sweller, 2003) for easy retrieval (Valcke, 2002). Whenever the need arises, these schemas are retrieved from LTM, interact with new elements in WM, and then higher-level schemas are generated (Newell & Simon, 1972), and stored in LTM. These new schemas are especially useful for problem solving as they help the learner to classify a variety of problem states and to select the most suitable solution for a specific problem (Chi, Glaser, & Rees, 1982). Schemas reduce element interactivity and WM load during problem solving because multiple and interacting elements in a schema can be treated as a single element (Sweller et al., 2011).

Schema Automation

Learning new concepts or solving new science problems requires controlled and conscious effort, which imposes a heavy burden on WM

(Carlson et al., 2003). However, with extensive practice over time, cognitive processing becomes automated, resulting in schema automation (Ericsson, 2005). Schema automation is critical for problem solving transfer (Sweller et al., 2011), where learners apply learned knowledge to new situations and contexts. Automated schemas enable information to be processed with less effort through the limited WM (Carlson et al., 2003). This facilitates the construction of new schemas of higher complexity, which increases learners' expertise in the domain (Ericsson, 2006).

ANALYSIS OF A SCIENCE PROBLEM IN TERMS OF ELEMENT INTERACTIVITY

Element interactivity can be measured by estimating the number of interacting elements that need to be simultaneously processed before the learning task can be successfully understood or completed (Sweller & Chandler, 1994). This measurement has been used by several researchers in various learning areas (e.g., Carlson et al., 2003; Leahy, Hanham, & Sweller, 2015; Tindall-Ford, Chandler, & Sweller, 1997). To assess element interactivity, relevant assumptions about the learners are required, since a single element for an expert who has existing domain-specific schemas may equate to many elements for a novice (Sweller et al., 2011).

In the element interactivity analysis that follows, assumptions about learners include: (a) a good understanding of the language used in the problem so as to understand the problem statement (i.e., the general message of the word problem was considered as one element); (b) relevant knowledge of the concept of speed; (c) basic mathematical skills expected of lower secondary students (i.e., an operation such as multiplication, addition, or division was considered as one element); and (d) necessary skills to interpret a table of values (i.e., table interpretation was considered as one element) to solve the problem. While element interactivity in intrinsic cognitive load is frequently assessed, it is not usually done for extraneous and germane cognitive load. To illustrate the element interactivity in all three forms of cognitive load, we analyzed the science word problem on 'speed' (Figure 3) within each type of load. The word problem was retrieved from Kadir, Foong, Wong, & Kuppan (2011). The following section first defines and then analyzes each type of cognitive load (i.e., intrinsic, extraneous, and germane) in terms of element interactivity in the word problem.

Intrinsic Cognitive Load

According to Sweller (2010), "the level of intrinsic cognitive load for a particular task and knowledge level is assumed to be determined by the level of element interactivity" (p. 124).

In order to solve the word problem on speed, students needed to understand its objective by reading the words and studying the numbers and units (i.e., magnitudes) in the problem statement. An additional element was that students needed to attend to the data table containing multiple values of time and average speed. Intrinsic cognitive load constitutes the element interactivity involved with simultaneously understanding the words and magnitudes in the problem statement as well as the interpretation of the table of values. Since magnitudes for the total distance and total time were not directly provided in the problem, students needed to deal with four main sub-goals of the problem in order to calculate average speed by: (1) calculating the distance travelled during each of the three time intervals by manipulating the average speed formula; (2) adding individual distances to get the total distance travelled; (3) deriving the time from the time intervals (e.g., 12 pm to 2 pm means a time interval of 2 hours); and (4) summing the times to get the total time travelled for the journey. Novices would be expected to experience a high level of element interactivity in the problem to solve these sub-goals resulting in a high intrinsic cognitive load. They would perceive this problem as complex because of the high number of interacting elements that need to be processed concurrently in their limited WM space.

The table below shows the average speed of a car at different timing, from the [3] time the car left its start point (12pm) to the time it reached its destination (6 pm).

Based on the information in the table, **calculate the average speed** of the car for the entire journey (Leave your answer in km/h).

Time Interval	12 pm to 2 pm	2 pm to 3 pm	3 pm to 6 pm
Average speed	75 km/h	0 km/h	70 km/h

a

To effectively solve this problem, students need to apply this formula: Average speed = total distance travelled by car / total time taken			
However, students are required to manipulate the formula using the concept of algebra to find the distance, which is not given in the problem:			
distance = average speed X time			
Method 1 using the step by step method		Method 2 using the combined method	
Step 1 line 1 line 2	Distance travelled from 12pm-2pm = 75 km/h X 2 h = 150 km	Step 1 line 1 line 2 line 3 line 4	Average speed = total distance travelled by car / total time = [(75X2) + (0X1) + (70X3)]/ 2+1+3 = (150 km + 0 km + 210 km) / 6 h = 360 km / 6 h = 60 km/h
Step 2 line 1 line 2	Distance travelled from 2pm-3pm = 0 km/h X 1 h = 0 km		
Step 3 line 1 line 2	Distance travelled from 3pm-6pm = 70 km/h X 3 h = 210 km		
Step 4 line 1 line 2	Total distance travelled by car = 150 km + 0 km + 210 km = 360 km		
Step 5 line 1 line 2	Total time taken by car = 2 h + 1 h + 3 h = 6 h		
Step 6 line 1 line 2	Average speed = total distance travelled by car / total time = 360 km / 6 h = 60 km/h		

b

Note. (a) Problem statement. (b) Methods to solve the science problem on speed.

Figure 3. Science problem on speed.

Extraneous Cognitive Load

The presentation style of instructional materials influences extraneous cognitive load (Leahy et al., 2015). Since extraneous cognitive load does not contribute to learning (Sweller, 2010), it should be minimised. Reducing extraneous cognitive load frees up WM resources to manage the complexity of the learning material and may contribute to learning. Element interactivity is not commonly used to explain extraneous cognitive load (Beckmann, 2010). While Sweller (2010) proposed that element interactivity should be a major source of extraneous cognitive load as well as intrinsic cognitive load, it was not until recently that researchers have started to explore how extraneous cognitive load can be attributed to element interactivity (e.g., Kadir et al., 2015).

Students who experience sub-optimal instruction tend to engage in cognitive activities that do not enhance schema acquisition, which impose unwanted extraneous cognitive load (Sweller et al., 2011). An example of such an activity is the 'backward-working phase' (Larkin, McDermott, Simon, & Simon, 1980) or the 'means-ends analysis' (Newell & Simon, 1972), where problem solvers simultaneously consider: (a) the current problem state, (b) goal state, (c) differences between the current problem state and the goal state, (d) problem solving operators that are able to reduce the differences between the two states, and (e) sub-goals that have been established (Sweller, 1988). The simultaneous processing of elements (a) to (e) results in element interactivity that imposes extraneous cognitive load.

Problem solving experts work through solutions with procedural moves that are mostly automated, and through retrieval of relevant problem-type schemas that exist in their LTM (Reed, 1993), which are then integrated with the information in the problem to arrive at a solution (Van Lehn, 1989). Expert problem solvers draw "on the extensive experience stored in their long-term memory and then quickly select and apply the best procedures for solving problems" (Kirschner, Sweller, & Clark, 2006, p. 76), reducing the element interactivity that constitutes extraneous cognitive load.

Instructional designs may introduce extraneous cognitive load in specific ways (Sweller et al., 2011). Figure 3b illustrates two methods, Method 1 and Method 2, of teaching students to solve the word problem. Method 1 comprises six operational lines while Method 2 combines the six operational lines into a one-step solution. Every operational line in the solution for Method 1 has low element interactivity because each involves two elements undergoing just one operation (e.g., multiplication, addition, or division) between them. Thus, each operational line, when considered in isolation, constitutes a low cognitive load. Method 1 is suitable for teaching novices to solve the problem since each operational line clearly shows the knowledge being applied and the procedures that follow. The low element interactivity helps students to manage their thought processes more effectively without overloading their WM.

By way of contrast, Method 2 comprises one step with high element interactivity, involving nine values undergoing three different operations (i.e., multiplication, addition, and division) simultaneously, requiring much WM resources. For example, to complete the single step in Method 2, students have to simultaneously:

1) apply the formula to calculate average speed = total distance / total time taken,
2) substitute the respective quantities for each variable (i.e., total distance and total time),
3) calculate the quantities of total distance and total time taken from the table of values because they are not directly provided, which requires an algebraic manipulation of the formula of average speed (i.e., average speed = total distance / total time), making total distance the subject (i.e., total distance = average speed X total time),
4) calculate the time travelled in hours from each of the three time intervals given in the table of values by multiplying the average speed in that time frame by the time in hours to determine the total distance covered within that time interval,
5) repeat this step for the other two time frames and sum all three to determine the total distance travelled, and
6) divide the answer by the total time taken for the journey.

The concurrent processing of the above mathematical procedures, along with the interpretation of the table of values and application of conceptual knowledge, involves a high level of element interactivity and therefore, a high cognitive load.

While Method 2 technically has a higher element interactivity compared to Method 1, the solution involves fewer operational lines, and is the preferred option of experts (Star & Newton, 2009). Experts would recall most of the required procedural and conceptual knowledge as automated schemas (Kirschner et al., 2006), so the reduction in the number of operational lines is actually a reflection of less element interactivity. Requiring experts to use many operational lines introduces extraneous cognitive load.

For the benefit of novices who are learning to solve such complex problems for the first time, teachers should firstly introduce Method 1 during instruction. This is because novices lack or have unstable links to existing schemas (Ericsson, 2006) and would not be able to handle much element interactivity. After sufficient problem-solving practice, students would gain more knowledge and develop more stable links to schemas. Teachers may then progress to intermediate stages of problem solving. Intermediate stages to bridge the element interactivity gap between Method 1 and Method 2 could include strategies that comprise fewer steps by combining certain mathematical procedures that are more easily managed.

Germane Cognitive Load

Germane cognitive load occurs when the learner devotes WM resources to deal with the intrinsic cognitive load of the learning material, contributing directly to the learner's development of cognitive structures such as schema development and automation that increase performance (Sweller et al., 2011). Sweller (2010) and Beckmann (2010) suggest that germane cognitive load should be seen as a result of element interactivity and associated cognitive behaviors that contribute to learning. Kadir et al. (2015) elaborated that germane cognitive load is imposed on WM when existing relevant schemas are retrieved from LTM to interact with the new information in WM (derived from the learning task) to form new higher-level schemas (representing the newly-formed knowledge) which are again stored in LTM. This process, when repeated, will develop learners' expertise in the domain.

As illustrated in Figure 3b, the process of solving the speed problem involves four interacting elements: (1) the concept of average speed = total distance/total time, (2) total distance and total time for each of the three time intervals: 12pm-2pm, 2pm-3pm, and 3pm-6pm requires interpretation of a table of values, (3) matching of variable and value in a formula (i.e., symbolic representation of relations), and (4) mathematical procedures involving interacting values. After instruction, students should have been exposed to all four elements: (1), (2), (3,) and (4). The retrieval of (1) as a schema from LTM (which is probably not stable at the initial stages of new learning), to interact with (2), (3), and (4) constitutes germane cognitive load because the practice consolidates and automates the mental process (see Figure 2). Students who have had practice in solving similar problems would know how to interpret the table of values to make sense of it, apply the average speed formula, and process the multiple interacting elements in the problem to derive the correct solution (i.e., apply scientific concept, recall related formula, and use mathematical skills to solve the problem), as illustrated in Figure 3b Method 2. Ideally, these processes would be recalled as automated schemas from LTM to interact with the new elements in the problem to facilitate the problem-solving process, imposing germane cognitive load. Novice or intermediate level students who may not have these schemas in their LTM would experience extraneous cognitive load on their WM while executing these processes, thus reducing available WM to actually solve the essence of the problem.

The speed problem has been designed to differentiate between students who understand the concept of average speed and those who do not. Before beginning the mathematical procedural processes required to solve the problem, there are several decisions that students need to make, based on their science conceptual knowledge of average speed. The correct decisions and methods used to solve the problem depend on learners' schema construction and retrieval processes formed during prior instruction. Students with a good understanding of the concept of average speed would be expected to apply the three different values of average speed and time provided in the problem whereas those lacking understanding would not. Conceptual mistakes may include: (1) summing up all the average speeds in the table and dividing them by 3 or 2 depending on the interpretation of whether 0 km/h is to be considered as part of the average speed computation, and (2) dividing the total distance by the total time of 5 hours (instead of 6 hours) because they did not think that the one hour of rest (i.e., 0 km/h) should be considered as part of the average speed computation. For those students who made conceptual mistakes but used fewer operational lines to solve the problem, instruction should focus on developing their conceptual knowledge.

Students' conceptual and procedural knowledge depends on the schemas constructed during instruction. If instruction is sub-optimal, domain schemas will be poorly constructed, schema automation will be adversely affected, and students will struggle to solve problems with high element interactivity. However, if instruction is optimal, students will construct conceptually correct domain schemas, which will stabilize with practice over time, making schema automation possible during the problem-solving process (Sweller et al., 2011). For example, significant WM resources are required to manage the high element interactivity in simultaneously executing the three operations of multiplication, addition, and division involving nine magnitudes within a single operational line in step 1, Method 2: [(75 X 2) + (0 X 1) + (70 X 3)] / (2+1+3). Expert students would retrieve and automate their science and mathematical knowledge as schemas, thus reducing the element interactivity in the problem. This frees WM resources to deal with the new interacting elements in the problem, introducing germane cognitive load. If the element interactivity is within the capacity of WM, students' success rates in solving complex science problems are increased (Carlson et al., 2003).

CONCLUSION

Research in Cognitive Load Theory (CLT) tends to use element interactivity as a common explanatory mechanism for intrinsic cognitive load. Recent literature suggests that it should be central to CLT (Beckmann,

2010; Sweller, 2010), but little is known about how the conceptualization can be applied to all types of cognitive load. Researchers have also emphasized the need to reduce extraneous cognitive load to have more WM resources devoted to germane cognitive load, but the 'how' to do this effectively has been hampered by the absence of a well-articulated explanatory mechanism.

In this chapter, we have used element interactivity to explain all three forms of cognitive load experienced by learners when solving complex problems. This approach may also be used to focus instructors' attention on the level of complexity in problem-solving materials prior to administering them to students, enabling instructors to select appropriate teaching strategies to optimize learning opportunities. This is critical because on one hand, materials that are too complex are known to not only hinder learning and achievement in the short term, but have adverse long-term effects in terms of student motivation and their self-beliefs in their science ability (Kadir, 2006, 2018; Kadir et al., 2015; Kadir, Yeung, & Barker, 2012, 2013; Kadir & Yeung, 2016; Kadir, Yeung, & Diallo, 2017; Yeung, 1999; Yeung, Kuppan, Kadir, & Foong, 2010, Yeung & McInerney, 2005). On the other hand, materials that are too simple will result in the expertise reversal effect (Kalyuga et al., 2003), which could also lower student motivation. Expertise reversal effect comes about when instructional methods and materials aimed at novice learners become ineffective as learners gain expertise in the domain (Kalyuga, 2007).

Additional research is required to generalize the applicability of using element interactivity as a diagnostic tool in other science topics and curriculum domains. However, by examining students' work in a complex learning task through the lens of element interactivity, teachers would be able to:

1) gain insights about students' thought processes and estimate their level of expertise; and
2) evaluate the effectiveness of the instructional designs and materials.

REFERENCES

Ayres, P. (2013). Can the isolated-elements strategy be improved by targeting points of high cognitive load for additional practice? *Learning and Instruction, 23*(0), 115-124. doi: 10.1016/j.learninstruc.2012.08.002.

Baddeley, A. D. (1986). *Working memory.* Oxford, England: Oxford University Press.

Baddeley, A. D., & Hitch, G. J. (2000). Development of working memory: Should the Pascual-Leone and the Baddeley and Hitch models be merged? *Journal of Experimental Child Psychology, 77*(2), 128-137. doi: 10.1006/jecp.2000.2592.

Beckmann, J. (2010). Taming a beast of burden - On some issues with the conceptualisation and operationalisation of cognitive load. *Learning and Instruction, 20*(3), 250–264. doi: 10.1016/j.learninstruc.2009.02.024.

Carlson, R., Chandler, P., & Sweller, J. (2003). Learning and understanding science instructional material. *Journal of Educational Psychology, 95*(3), 629-640. doi: 10.1037/0022-0663.95.3.629.

Chi, M., Glaser, R., & Rees, E. (1982). Expertise in problem solving. In R. Sternberg (Ed.), *Advances in the psychology of human intelligence* (Vol. *1*, pp. 7–75). Hillsdale, NJ: Erlbaum.

Chinnappan, M., & Chandler, P. (2010). Managing cognitive load in the mathematics classroom. *Australian Mathematics Teacher, 66*(1), 5-11.

Ericsson, K. A. (2005). Recent advances in expertise research: A commentary on the contributions to the special issue. *Applied Cognitive Psychology, 19*(2), 233-241. doi: 10.1002/acp.1111.

Ericsson, K. A. (2006). An introduction to the Cambridge handbook of expertise and expert performance: Its development, organization, and content. In K. A. Ericsson, N. Charness, P. J. Feltovich & R. R. Hoffman (Eds.), *The Cambridge handbook of expertise and expert performance* (pp. 3-20). New York: Cambridge University press.

Kadir, M. S. (2006). *A study of students' perceptions and performance in a "Play-n-Learn" Physics workshop* (Master's thesis). Nanyang Technological University, Singapore.

Kadir, M. S. (2018). *Enlightening Science: Addressing the Cognitive and Non-Cognitive Aspects of Science Learning.* (Doctoral thesis). Australian Catholic University, Sydney, Australia.

Kadir, M. S., Foong, S.K., Wong, D., & Kuppan, L. (2011). PbI1@School: On secondary one students' understanding of speed. *Proceedings of the 4th Redesigning Pedagogy International Conference 2011, Singapore.* Paper retrieved from http://hdl.handle.net/10497/6822.

Kadir, M. S., Ngu, B. H., & Yeung, A. S. (2015). Element interactivity in secondary school mathematics and science education. In R. V. Nata (Ed.), *Progress in education* (Vol. 34, pp. 71-98). New York, NY: Nova.

Kadir, M. S., & Yeung, A. S. (2016). Academic self-concept. In V. Zeigler-Hill, & T. K. Shackelford (Eds.), *Encyclopedia of personality and individual differences* (pp. 1-8). New York, NY: Springer. Retrieved from http://link.springer.com/referenceworkentry/10.1007/978-3-319-2 8099-8_1118-1.

Kadir, M. S., Yeung, A. S., & Barker, K. L. (2012, December). *School achievement and attitudes towards physics: Findings from Singapore.* Poster session presented at the Joint Australian Association for Research in Education-Asia-Pacific Education Research Association Conference, Sydney, Australia.

Kadir, M. S., Yeung, A. S., & Barker, K. L. (2013). Relationships between self-concepts and achievements of high-ability students. In U. Tursini, D. Utian, S. Khongput, S. N. Chiangmai, H. Nguyen, & N. Setyorini (Eds.), *Postgraduate research in education: Proceedings of the second annual higher degree student-led conference, 9 November 2012* (pp. 75-92). New South Wales, Australia: The University of New South Wales. doi: 10.1.1.724.9991.

Kadir, M. S., Yeung, A. S., & Diallo, T. M. O. (2017). Simultaneous testing of four decades of academic self-concept models. *Contemporary Educational Psychology, 51,* 429-446. https://doi.org/10.1016/j.cedpsy ch.2017.09.008

Kalyuga, S. (2007). Expertise reversal effect and its implications for learner-tailored instruction. *Educational Psychology Review, 19*(4), 509-539. doi: 10.1007/s10648-007-9054-3.

Kalyuga, S., Ayres, P., Chandler, P., & Sweller, J. (2003). The expertise reversal effect. *Educational Psychologist, 38*(1), 23-31. doi: 10.1207/S15326985EP3801_4.

Kirschner, P. A., Sweller, J., & Clark, R. E. (2006). Why minimal guidance during instruction does not work: An analysis of the failure of constructivist, discovery, problem-based, experiential, and inquiry-based teaching. *Educational Psychologist, 41*(2), 75-86. doi: 10.1207/s15326985ep4102_1.

Landauer, T. K. (1986). How much do people remember? Some estimates of the quantity of learned information in long-term memory. *Cognitive Science: A Multidisciplinary Journal, 10*(4), 477 - 493. doi: 10.1207/s15516709cog1004_4.

Larkin, J., McDermott, J., Simon, D. P., & Simon, H. A. (1980). Expert and novice performance in solving physics problems. *Science, 208*, 1335-1342. doi: 10.2307/1684057.

Leahy, W., Hanham, J., & Sweller, J. (2015). High element interactivity information during problem solving may lead to failure to obtain the testing effect. *Educational Psychology Review, 27*(2), 291-304. doi: 10.1007/s10648-015-9296-4.

Miller, G. A. (1956). The magical number seven, plus or minus two: some limits on our capacity for processing information. *Psychological Review, 63*(2), 81-97. doi: 10.1037/h0043158.

Newell, A., & Simon, H. (1972). *Human problem solving.* New Jersey: Prentice-Hall.

Paas, F., Renkl, A., & Sweller, J. (2003). Cognitive load theory and instructional design: Recent developments. *Educational Psychologist, 38*(1), 1-4. doi: 10.1207/s15326985ep3801_1.

Reed, S. K. (1993). A schema-based theory of transfer. In D. K. Detterman & R. J. Sternberg (Eds.), *Transfer on trial: Intelligence, cognition, and instruction* (pp. 39–67). Norwood, NJ: Ablex.

Star, J., & Newton, K. (2009). The nature and development of experts' strategy flexibility for solving equations. *ZDM Mathematics Education, 41*(5), 557-567. doi: 10.1007/s11858-009-0185-5.

Sweller, J. (1988). Cognitive load during problem solving: Effects on learning. *Cognitive Science: A Multidisciplinary Journal, 12*(2), 257 - 285. doi: 10.1207/s15516709cog1202_4.

Sweller, J. (2010). Element interactivity and intrinsic, extraneous, and germane cognitive load. *Educational Psychology Review, 22*(2), 123-138. doi: 10.1007/s10648-010-9128-5.

Sweller, J., Ayres, P., & Kalyuga, S. (2011). *Cognitive load theory.* New York, NY: Springer.

Sweller, J., & Chandler, P. (1994). Why some material is difficult to learn. *Cognition and Instruction, 12*(3), 185–233. doi: 10.1207/s1532690xci 1203_1.

Tindall-Ford, S., Chandler, P., & Sweller, J. (1997). When two sensory modes are better than one. *Journal of Experimental Psychology: Applied, 3*(4), 257-287. doi: 10.1037/1076-898X.3.4.257.

Valcke, M. (2002). Cognitive load: Updating the theory? *Learning and Instruction, 12*(1), 147-154. doi: 10.1037/1076-898X.3.4.257.

Van Lehn, K. (1989) Problem solving and cognitive skill acquisition. In M. I. Posner (Ed.), *Foundations of cognitive science* (pp. 527–579). Cambridge, MA: MIT Press.

Yeung, A. S. (1999). Cognitive load and learner expertise: Split-attention and redundancy effects in reading comprehension tasks with vocabulary definitions. *Journal of Experimental Education, 67*(3), 197-217. doi:10.1080/00220979909598353.

Yeung, A. S., Kuppan, L., Kadir, M. S., Foong, S. K., (2010). Boys' and girls' self-beliefs, engagement, and aspirations in physics. *International Journal of Learning, 17*(10), 397-417.

Yeung, A. S., & McInerney, D. M. (2005). Students' school motivation and aspiration over high school years. *Educational Psychology, 25*(5), 537-554. doi: 10.1080/01443410500046804.

ABOUT THE AUTHORS

Munirah Shaik Kadir, PhD, is a physics teacher and educational researcher who has recently completed her PhD studies at the Australian Catholic University. Her research interests are cognitive and motivational aspects of learning in science education.

Alexander S. Yeung, PhD, is a professor and Deputy Director of the Institute for Positive Psychology and Education at the Australian Catholic University. His expertise includes cognition and instruction, educational and psychological studies, self-concept and learning motivation.

Anne Forbes, PhD, is a senior lecturer in STEM Education at Macquarie University. Her primary area of research is in ways to advance the teaching and learning of science education in schools, particularly the development of communities of science practice.

In: Progress in Education. Volume 55
Editor: Roberta V. Nata

ISBN: 978-1-53614-551-9
© 2019 Nova Science Publishers, Inc.

Chapter 8

OBJECTIVITY AND SUBJECTIVITY IN RESEARCH

Martin Spurin[1],, EdD and Paul Stansbie[2], PhD*
[1]University College Birmingham, Birmingham, England
[2]Grand Valley State University, Grand Rapids, MI, US

ABSTRACT

The quantitative and qualitative methods used in social science research are founded on different ontological and epistemological understandings and generally associate themselves with contrasting concepts and methods. Traditionally, quantitative approaches tend to focus on objective, statistical descriptions of reality whereas qualitative methods often reject the notion of non-subjective knowledge. This chapter considers these two methods through a critical consideration of the notions of objectivity and subjectivity involved in the research process with particular reference to educational research. Furthermore, it evaluates the value of both and questions whether objectivity is truly achievable leading to criticisms of both objective and subjective research and the debate of value-free and value-laden investigation. This chapter further posits that researchers cannot help but bring with them connections to their subject

* Corresponding Author Email: m.spurin@ucb.ac.uk.

and that this is part of the investigation process and an integral element of a researcher's understanding of the subject matter. It concludes by emphasising the need to recognise and be aware of the influences the researcher brings to their academic work in the pursuit of objectivity.

Keywords: objectivity, subjectivity, education research

INTRODUCTION

According to Gorard (2004), everyone is involved with research to some degree in their everyday lives (including infants), from planning journeys to solving problems and making decisions. For the most part, individuals rely heavily on the research and information shared by others and their findings are often accepted with few questions or challenges. For example, the existence, habitation, even the geographical location of Antarctica is something most seem happy to accept from our readings and media images instead of making our own investigations in an attempt to seek absolute confirmation. Gorard (2004) distinguishes personal everyday research from that research administered formally for academic purposes by the fact that it is carefully and rationally conducted and that the researcher should be prepared to bet on the results being true; what he calls the 'warrant'.

The debate about research and whether the results are true is "imprisoned" (Gorard, 2004, p10) in the concept of reality and is based on the question as to whether reality exists independently or through the interpretation of the mind (Crotty, 1998). Burgess et al. (2006) identify this as the concept of ontology and that researchers need to be aware of what they consider reality to be. If ontology is the study of the nature of being then questions are raised as to what things exist and what are their conditions of existence. According to Morrison (2009) while ontology tells us what there is to know, epistemology tells us how we might come to know it; in essence, the starting point of any formal research.

Coming to know reality through research requires rigour. This raises issues that need to be examined with any research; that of the degree of subjectivity that is involved in most social science research based on the notion that neither the subject nor the researcher can be completely objective. Positivists attempt to ensure that the conditions under which their research is conducted can be controlled and replicated; conversely in the social sciences it can be difficult to achieve such conditions if so desirable. There are inherent difficulties with research in social science based on the fact that the researcher(s) already share their world with those they are investigating and can only interpret, understand, and make sense of their findings from their own frame of reference (Capurro, 2000). The duplication/replication of a research study could possibly lead to different results if the principal researcher was repeating the same investigations using different categorisations or grading of variables. Furthermore, alternative results may be identified due to differing conditions, timing or interpretations. Therefore, researchers should be mindful that any investigation will have a degree of subjectivity that permeates their findings.

OBJECTIVITY AND SUBJECTIVITY

As objectivity and subjectivity are such a central theme in this chapter it is worth clarifying the definition of both. The Chambers dictionary (1994, p1164) in defining objectivity uses the phrase "exterior to the mind" while the Collins dictionary (1994, p1077) uses the term "independent of the attitudes of any individual". The Oxford Dictionary of English (2003) identifies it as "not influenced by personal feelings or opinions" (p1213) in considering or representing facts. However, it is the definition of subjectivity which highlights the potential problem when it comes to personal involvement. Chambers (p1717) defines subjectivity as "influenced by or derived from personal taste or opinion lacking impartiality"; Collins (p1536) relates the issue of values and how variable they are in the same way individual tastes differ. Therefore, it can be implied that subjectivity in research relates very closely to the person doing the research, their values, their tastes which they bring along with them into their chosen research process.

Objectivity, according to Hegelund (2005), is not influenced by personal feelings or opinions when considering facts and representing them, but he does acknowledge that we "cannot escape the knowledge we have in advance" (p656). In recognising this debate Phillips (1993) refers to Eisner (1986) who stresses that all methods and forms of representation are partial and that the concept of scientific research being 'objective' or 'value-free' is questionable. Phillips (1993) emphasises that objectivity, although more rational, should not be linked to certainty and concludes by saying that "neither subjectivity nor objectivity has an exclusive stranglehold on truth" (p61). May (2001) argues that the goal of scientific investigation has to be objectivity but this can only be above criticism if values are kept out. He questions, however, whether it is possible or desirable to suspend our sense of belonging as this is fundamental to social life.

PAST RESEARCH IN THE FIELD OF EDUCATION

Whether qualitative or quantitative methods are chosen in educational research, Gorard (2004, p. 2) simply states that there is no best method for social science research; "there is simply differential fitness for purpose". However, he does believe that much of the quantitative work currently being produced is often poor and continues unchecked (Gorard, 2003). One of the problems he identifies is that real teachers are too busy to concern themselves with what he calls "unintelligible partisan prose" (2004, p. 2). Hammersley (1993) concurs when he states that much published research is irrelevant because teachers do not read it and when they do, they find little interest in it. Although not discounting research in the field he does acknowledge that education is geared more toward reflection to improve practice. He goes onto state that:

> ... even if we research a problem we are by no means guaranteed a solution. Progress in research is often slow or non-existent, even in the natural sciences. There is no scientific method that guarantees results. Often a problem is investigated for a long time without much being achieved, and

discoveries that are made may owe as much to good fortune and to intuition as to method. (p. 216)

The word intuition stands out here indicating that knowledge and the interpretative nature of inquiry through qualitative methods is something not to be discounted in research. Phillips (1993) puts both quantitative and qualitative research in the same grouping in the sense that:

> ...bad work of either kind is equally to be deplored; and good work of either kind is still – at best – only tentative. But the good work in both cases will be objective, in the sense that it has been opened up to criticism, and the reasons and evidence offered in both cases will have withstood scrutiny. (p. 70)

The debate, as Phillips alludes to here, should be about the value and reliability of the research, what the research achieved and how transparent the process was, not whether qualitative or quantitative methods were adopted.

Educational research in the past has relied predominantly on the positivist approach (Anderson and Arsenault, 1998), but it has been argued that using this positivist approach it has not been able to examine human beings and their behaviour in a sufficiently in-depth way (Crossan, 2003). But education, like so many other disciplines, is not an easy subject to research. According to Freebody (2003), education is an intellectually and professionally challenging field; one he suggests more difficult than most other fields to research. Picciano (2004) meanwhile visualises education as a battlefield where 'paradigm' wars are being fought. The purpose of educational research according to Opie (2004) is to seek knowledge in the field to improve understanding, to explain it better, and with so many opinions around it helps "people decide which opinions are correct, or at least more correct" (Picciano, 2004, p. 3). The reason why there are so many opinions is that, according to Wallen et al. (2001), everyone has some sort of opinion about formal education because all have experienced it and it has had some sort of impact upon them. Therefore, we as researchers are not completely isolated as we are to some extent associated with the subject of our own investigations.

Capurro (2000, p. 79), although not talking specifically about educational research, reinforces the above point when he suggests that as a human being he is "not an isolated inquirer trying to reach the outside world from his ... encapsulated mind/brain"; it is a world shared with others. He goes on to mention the word 'pre-understanding' that is embedded within us. Gadamer (1975, p. 269) saw this as fore-meanings and therefore felt that the important issue was for the researcher to be aware of his or her own bias when approaching research. Although he was essentially referring to hermeneutics he relates to a fusion of horizons which are views and beliefs the researcher possesses and brings with him/her which are culturally and historically shaped through past and present traditions to form the starting point of the researchers' investigation (Crotty, 1998). Gadamer (1975) sees this as an essential element if the researcher wants a particular vantage point. He even feels that a person without horizons cannot see far enough and can therefore overvalue what is nearest to him, "whereas a person who has an horizon knows the relative significance of everything within this horizon" (p. 269).

This understanding and connection by the researcher to the subject being investigated is necessary in order to appreciate, acknowledge and analyse underlying meanings as it is meanings rather than phenomena that is significant (Cohen et al., 2003). For example, how something is said rather than what is said during an interview can convey much more meaning, and silence can indicate a reaction to something and speak louder than chosen words. Silverman (2006) acknowledges that without this connection and understanding the issue of reliability can be brought into question as the interpretation "may be gravely weakened by a failure to note apparently trivial, but often crucial, pauses, overlaps or body movements" (p. 46).

However, trying to interpret or read into things excessively can result in being too subjective in judging what is important and what is not relevant; what Hegelund (2005) calls "dangerous subjectivity" (p. 656). The problem, as Abbott (2003, p. 98) identifies, is that "the detection of significance is a subjective activity; significance does not occur ready made and labelled as such". This could be seen as a big disadvantage to the interpretivist perspective using qualitative research methods because the researcher can so easily misinterpret something based on their own assumptions and understanding.

The social researcher during his or her quest becomes a pioneer according to Shipman (1988); a term he uses because the researcher collects data on an area which is of particular interest to him or her. The researcher also makes sense of his or her observations using conceptual models with which they are familiar and have chosen, as well as drawing upon their own experience. Qualitative research suits this approach as it pays particular attention to humanistic factors as it is about exploring and making sense of the social world; an inherently subjective process.

CRITICISMS OF THE SUBJECTIVE AND OBJECTIVE APPROACH

Page & Stake (1979, p. 45) are quite dismissive of the argument to embrace subjectivity. He feels that it makes "evaluation, as a discipline, at times unable to discriminate between the effective and the trashy, between the facts of the educational world and the self-interest of the evaluator". Page & Stake refer to research conducted on behalf of administrators "who strongly desire certain outcomes" and so are not impartial. He condemns the weakness in research without established measurements which he sees as the "gold-core of good evaluation" (p. 45). Stevens et al. (1993, p. 37) advocate that "scientific knowledge must be free of metaphysics, that is it must be based on pure observation that is free of interests, values, purposes and psychological schemata of individuals". They do, however, concede to the idea that positivists in researching social science would "observe particular behaviours without taking into account the meaning that humans give to their actions" (p. 37). However, as Crotty (1998) points out, it is when meaning-making beings make sense of their finding that it contributes to this world of meaning. It is inescapable that behind all research, whether it be objective or positivist "there is a human being, or several human beings ... simply by being there we influence the research that is being created" (Etherington, 2006, p. 85).

Just as subjectivity is criticised, so too is the scientific, positivist approach. Crossan (2003) highlights the fact that the approach is limiting in examining human beings and their behaviours in an in-depth way. Crotty (1998, p. 42) mentions that western science has come under increasing attack and that "constructionism is very much part of the artillery brought against it". Skate (1979), writing with but in opposition to Page's 1979 article, mentions that the use of objective measures could be potentially irresponsible when it comes to evaluation in the social sciences because the measures become too restrictive. Gadamer (1975) relates to this irresponsibility when he refers to how statistics have been an excellent means of propaganda in the past. He states that "facts speak and hence simulate an objectivity that in reality depends on the legitimacy of the questions asked" (p. 268). Therefore, although the scientific positivist approach claims to be closer to objectivity it has not been above criticism, because at the centre of the debate is the issue as to whether research can be value-free or whether it is value-laden.

VALUE-FREE OR VALUE-LADEN?

Rokeach (1973, p. 30) recognises that man "is the only animal that can be meaningfully described as having values" and it is these values which are embedded within us and form our epistemological perspective.

> Values represent intrinsic beliefs we hold as people, organisations, societies and cultures. Values are held close to our hearts and impact decisions we make, the way we approach situations. (Anderson and Arsenault, 1998, p. 32)

Anderson and Arsenault continue to identify that it is these personal values that researchers bring with them and that they impact on the types of decision made as well as the direction the researcher takes. They influence rationality, which is essential to produce a critical account (Clough and Nutbrown, 2002). Even the choice of methodology and methods relates very closely to the assumptions one has about reality and these too are brought to our work (Crotty, 1998; Greenbank, 2003), particularly when inquiry involves a qualitative approach (Denzin and Lincoln, 2003).

The issue of whether a researcher can start from a position of being value-free is questioned by Greenbank (2003) who identifies (like Crotty, 1998) that the research methods adopted will be very much influenced by a person's ontological and epistemological position initially guided by their values. He uses the term value-neutral and value-free interchangeably but concludes by referring to Carr (1995) who said that anyone who believes they are value-neutral are just deluding themselves. This is because "no matter how well designed, research can never be value-free" as we are constantly "carrying a baggage of beliefs, assumptions, inclinations and approaches to reality (Anderson and Arsenault, 1998, p. 1). Greenbank (2003) in his article goes on to say that the chosen methods reflect the researcher's own values and that is why "value-neutral research is flawed" (p. 792); even though this is very much done at an unconscious level.

Popper (1976) sees these value judgments influencing even the positivist and scientific inquirers:

> We cannot rob the scientist of his partisanship without also robbing him of his humanity, and we cannot suppress or destroy his value judgements without destroying him as a human being and a scientist. Our motives and even our purely scientific ideals ... are deeply anchored in extra-scientific and, in part, in religious valuations. Thus the 'objective' or the 'value-free' scientist is hardly the ideal scientist. (Popper 1976, cited in Hammersley 1993, p. 70)

What the researcher cannot help but bring with them is their overall personal situation which includes (amongst other things) gender, ethnicity, economic circumstances, able-bodiedness and nationality. Abbott (2003) also recognises that the time in history we live in also shapes our views as each era has its own predominant concerns, beliefs, norms, vocabulary and understanding. Included within this category is culture, with its current fashions and preoccupations which influence our views even if some of them, as Abbott recognised, are media orchestrated. These all affect our perception of reality and therefore our ontological perspective. There is no culture-free reality to be sought.

> Every researcher speaks from within a distinct interpretive community that configures in its special way, the multicultural, gendered components of the research act.... Any gaze is always filtered through the lenses of language, gender, social class, race, and ethnicity. There are no objective observations, only observations socially situated in the worlds of – and between – the observer and the observed... The age of value-free inquiry for human disciplines is over. (Denzin and Lincoln 2003, p. 31)

We should not feel that by embracing our ontological perspective that our research is of any less significance as long as we can accept and acknowledge that it plays its part in our interpretations. The important thing is to be aware of the influence our values have over our observations. To maintain rigour, we should examine them carefully and explicitly as the legitimacy of these values within us help us to be more aware of our own bias (Gadamer, 1975). In fact, the fusion of horizons which Gadamer refers to helps with our range of vision within our research as "all methods and forms of representation are partial" (Eisner, 1986, cited in Hammersley, 1993, p. 58). It is therefore a starting point as "all research necessarily starts from a person's view of the world, which itself is shaped by the experience one brings to the research process" (Grix, 2002, p. 170). But Peshkin (1998) believes that researchers should go one step further and not just accept their own subjectivity.

> It is no more useful for researchers to acknowledge simply that subjectivity is an invariable component of their research than it is for them to assert that their ideal is to achieve objectivity .... When their subjectivity remains unconscious, they insinuate rather than knowingly clarify their personal stakes.... These qualities have the capacity to filter, skew, shape, block, transform, construe, and misconstrue what transpires from the outset

for a research project ... they can at least disclose to their readers where self and subject become joined (p. 17).

Peshkin does not dismiss subjectivity but recognises the need to disclose it. He concludes: "untamed subjectivity mutes the emic voice" (p. 21). Therefore, researchers need to be aware of their own selves as being central to their own research and to be aware of the effects influencing their journey; they cannot simply ignore the subjective perspective within their own research.

A RESEARCHER'S CONNECTION TO THE SUBJECT

Human thought through understanding cannot be something that can be dismissed because it starts from shared meanings and understanding through the process of rationalisation which is something that we use every day of our lives. When we hear a joke, we can take in the words with our senses, but we understand it or get the joke with our reason; in this context, it cannot be separated. This may be the real reason for natural scientists abandoning the quest for absolute objective knowledge, according to Douglas (1976), as it just cannot be achieved.

We cannot detach ourselves from ourselves. In fact, most educational research articles tend to be written in the first person using the pronoun 'I'. This, as Etherington (2006, p. 85) identifies, loses the anonymity, writing from inside our lives connecting with feelings, senses and therefore values. The question of our research is therefore within us. In fact, "all knowing, including methods, is acknowledged as a human construction and therefore value-laden" (Heshusius, 1989, p. 596) and that is why many social science researchers accept the influence of their own values (Greenbank, 2003). Values are so strong within us even though we may be unconscious of them, but they do shape the way we look at the world and how we make decisions. The important thing is to "attempt to understand and make explicit ... personal values while at the same time, seek to understand the values held by people, organisations or cultures being researched" (Anderson and Arsenault, 1998, p. 33). This relates very closely to Gadamer's (1975) fusion of horizons which the researcher possesses and needs to acknowledge from the start. So, whether quantitative or qualitative methods are being used, whether objectivity is at the foundation of the research, or whether subjectivity have been embraced and acknowledged the conclusion has to be that research accounts can only represent reality; they cannot reproduce it (Silverman 2006).

From the standpoint that objectivity is impossible to attain Etherington (2006) believes it essential that we develop an awareness of our own thoughts, feelings, culture and environment. We also need to consider our social and personal history which informs us as we design our research and gather data. By doing this it will help us to come close to the rigour that is required of good qualitative research. No research method or methodology is without criticism whatever the ontological, epistemological and methodological standpoints taken. All have their value, but essentially it is the final product which surely must be the important thing as long as the researcher, according to Gadamer (1975), is aware of their own bias from the start which Heshusius (1994) sees as the management of subjectivity. Whether it is research in education or any other field, the quest is to understand reality and thus it becomes a journey for the researcher. That journey does not end when the research project is completed, it continues along another path. It is always incomplete and ever-changing and by the time a piece of work is published the researcher may have reached another stage on their journey (Etherington, 2006). The process is, of course, important but the destination is even more so. As Clough and Nutbrown (2002, p12) state, "research which changes nothing – not even the researcher – is not research at all".

Conclusion

In summary, by considering the notions of objectivity and subjectivity in educational research, or any other research within the social sciences, it can be concluded that pure objectivity is not something that is achievable, although our research should aim to be as objective as possible. What we bring with us as researchers, the culture and traditions that shape our values which form our beliefs that influence our epistemological stance, are an important and integral part of research for it helps us to understand our subject. At the same time, it is important to be aware of, and acknowledge, the role it plays and how it can influence our work. Our research cannot help but contain subjectivity, and, why shouldn't it? After all, we exist in a "continually changing world of experience of which (we are) the centre" (Rogers 1951, p. 483).

REFERENCES

Abbott, R. (2003). Subjectivity as a Concern for Information Science: a Popperian Perspective. *Journal of Information Science.* 30 (2), 95-106.

Anderson, G. & Aresnault, N. (1998). *Fundamentals of Educational Research.* London, Falmer Press.

Burgess, H., Sieminski, S., and Arthur, L. (2006). *Achieving Your Doctorate in Education.* London, Sage.

Capurro, R. (2000). Hermeneutics and the Phenomenon of Information. In Mitcham, C. (ed) *Metaphysics, Epistemology, and Technology. Research in Philosophy and Technology.* Vol 19 pp. 79-85 Arizona, JAI/Elsevier.

Carr, W. (1995). *For Education: Towards Critical Educational Inquiry.* Buckingham, Open University Press.

The Chambers Dictionary. (1994). Edinburgh, Chambers Harrap Publishers.

Clough, P. & Nutbrown, C. (2002). *A Student's Guide to Methodology.* London, Sage.

Cohen, L., Manion, L., & Morrison, K. (2003). *Research Methods in Education.* 5th Edition. London, Routledge-Falmer.

Collins English Dictionary. (1994). 3rd Edition. Glasgow, Harper Collins.

Crossan, F. (2003). Research Philosophy: Towards an Understanding. *Nurse Researcher.* 11 (1) 46-55.

Crotty, M. (1998). *The foundations of Social Research.* London, Sage.

Denzin, N. K. & Lincoln, Y. S. (Ed.) (2003). *Strategies of qualitative Inquiry.* London, Sage.

Douglas, J. D. (1976). *Investigative Social Research.* London, Sage.

Eisner, E. (1986). The Primacy of Experience and the Politics of Method. In Hammersley, M. (Ed.) (1993) *Educational Research: Current Issues.* London, Open University Press.

Etherington, K. (2006). Reflexivity: Using our 'selves' in Narrative Research. In Trahar, S. (ed) *Narrative Research on Learning Comparative and International Perspectives.* London, Symposium Books.

Freebody, P. (2003). *Qualitative Research in Education: Introduction and Practice.* London, Sage.

Gadamer, H. G. (1975). *Truth and Method.* London, Sheed & Ward.

Gorard, S. (2003). Understanding Probabilities and Re-Considering Traditional Research Training. [online]. *Sociological Research Online,* Last accessed 11 November 2008 at http://www.socresonline.org.uk/8/1/gorard.html

Gorard, S. (2004). *Quantitative Methods in Social Science.* London, Continuum.

Greenbank, P. (2003). The Role of Values in Educational Research: the Case for Reflexivity. *British Educational Research Journal.* 29 (6), 791 – 801.

Grix, J. (2002). Introducing Students to the Generic Terminology of Social Research. *Politics* 22 (3), 175-186.

Hammersley, M. (Ed.) (1993). *Educational Research: Current Issues.* London, Open University Press.

Hegelund, A. (2005). Objectivity and Subjectivity in Ethnographic Method. *Qualitative Health Research.* 15 (5), 647-668.

Heshusius, L. (1989). Holistic Principles: Not Enhancing the Old but Seeing A-new. A Rejoinder. *Journal of Learning disabilities.* 22 (10), 595-602.

Heshusius, L. (1994). Freeing Ourselves From Objectivity: Managing Subjectivity or Turning Toward a Participatory Mode of Consciousness? *Educational Researcher.* 23 (3), 15-22.

May, T. (2001). *Social Research Issues, Methods and Process.* 3rd Edition. Maidenhead, Open University Press.

Morrison, A. (2009). Rumsfeld and the Known Knowns, *Praxis,* University College Birmingham.

Opie, C. (Ed.) (2004). *Doing Educational Research.* London, Sage.

Oxford Dictionary of English. (2003). 2nd Edition. Oxford, Oxford University Press.

Page, E. B. & Stake, R. E. (1979). Should Educational Evaluation Be More Objective or More Subjective? *Educational Evaluation and Policy Analysis.* 1 (1), 45-47.

Peshkin, A. (1998). In Search of subjectivity – One's Own. *Educational Researcher.* 17 (17), 17-21.

Phillips, D. C. (1993). Subjectivity and Objectivity: an objective Inquiry. In Hammersley, M. (Ed.) *Educational Research: Current Issues.* London, Open University Press.

Picciano, A.G. (2004). *Educational Research Primer.* London, Continuum.

Popper, K. R. (1976). The Logic of Social Sciences. In Hammersley, M. (Ed.) (1993) *Educational Research: Current Issues.* London, Open University Press.

Rogers, C. (1951). *Client-Centred Therapy.* Wilshire, Constable & Company.

Rokeach, M. (1973). *The Nature of Human Values.* London, Collier Macmillan.

Silverman, D. (2006). *Interpreting Qualitative Data.* 3rd Edition. London, Sage.

Shipman, M. (1988). *The Limitations of Social research.* 3rd Edition. London, Longman.

Stevens, P. J. M., Schade, A. L., Chalk, B., & Slevin, O. D'. A. (1993). *Understanding Research.* Oxford, Campion Press Limited.

Wallen, N. E. and Fraenkel, J. R. (2001). *Educational Research.* New Jersey, Lawrence Associates Inc.

CONTENTS OF EARLIER VOLUMES

Progress in Education. Volume 54.

Chapter 1	Diversity in Mathematics Teacher Preparation in the Era of Common Core: From Egyptian Papyrus Roll to Gestalt Psychology to Digital Computation *Sergei Abramovich*
Chapter 2	Strategies in Overcoming Teaching and Learning Challenges in Correctional Facilities in South Africa *Khulekani Collin Mbanjwa and Lineo Rose Johnson*
Chapter 3	Using Explicit Text Structure Instruction and Authentic Texts to Teach Children to Write Sequential Informational Text *Sarah K. Clark and Anne Clark Dallin*
Chapter 4	Learning Analytics for the Investigation of Learning Patterns and Improvement of Learning Design in a Blended Learning Environment *Andromachi Filippidi and Vassilis Komis*

Chapter 5	Comparison of Attitudes toward Inclusion in Primary School Students in Relation to the Contact with Physical Disability or Not in Physical Education Sessions *Iratxe López, Javier Yanci, Josune Rodríguez-Negro and Aitor Iturricastillo*
Chapter 6	Assessing Positive Education Using the PROSPER Framework *Rose Pennington, Anthony Dillon, Toni Noble and Alexander Seeshing Yeung*
Chapter 7	Furnishing Active Learning Classrooms for Blended Synchronous Learning *Peter Mozelius*
Chapter 8	The State of Readiness in the Implementation of Inclusive Education in Nzhelele West Circuit Secondary Schools *M. M. Serakalala, N. P. Mudzielwana and S. A. Mulovhedzi*

Progress in Education. Volume 53

Chapter 1	Flexible Study Options and Modes of Delivery in Higher Education: The Balance between Integrity and Commercialization *Mahmoud M. Bakr and Leanne C. Kenway*
Chapter 2	Introducing the Concept of 'Student Profiling': A Cross-Cultural Perspective for Understanding *Huy P. Phan, Bing H. Ngu, Hui-Wen Wang, Jen-Hwa Shih, Sheng-Ying Shi and Ruey-Yih Lin*

Chapter 3	The Educational Performance of Spanish Secondary Schools in PISA, 2003-2012
	Manuel Salas-Velasco
Chapter 4	Flipped Classrooms on University Students' Perceptions of Instructors' TPACK
	Syh-Jong Jang
Chapter 5	Types of Conclusions for Argumentative Discussions between Adults and Children
	Antonio Bova and Francesco Arcidiacono
Chapter 6	Student Perceptions of Fully Online Flipped Community Learning: A Case Study
	Wendy Barber and Todd Blayone
Chapter 7	Inverse Modeling Problems and Task Enrichment in Teacher Training Courses
	Victor Martinez-Luaces, Luis Rico, Juan Francisco Ruiz-Hidalgo and José Antonio Fernández-Plaza
Chapter 8	Conceptualization of Anti-Bullying Strategies: Key Aspects in Every Curriculum Area
	N. P. Mudzielwana

Progress in Education. Volume 52

Chapter 1	A Holistic Approach to Achieving Sustainable Mobility in the Alps
	Matej Ogrin, Tanja Vozelj, Katarina Žemlja and Tatjana Resnik Planinc
Chapter 2	The Central Functioning of Successful Schooling: The Relationship between Academic Engagement and Subjective Well-Being
	Huy P. Phan and Bing H. Ngu

Chapter 3	A Study of Teachers' Views on the Development of Values in Hong Kong's Music Education 20 Years after the Handover from the United Kingdom to China *Wai-Chung Ho*
Chapter 4	Mathematics Anxiety: Its Assessment, Determinants and Remedies *Donato Deieso and Barry J. Fraser*
Chapter 5	The Effect of Transformational Leadership on Educational Reform *Chanadra Whiting, Audrey P. Miller and Charles Whiting*
Chapter 6	A 'Diffractive' Exploration of Inclusive School Policy about Trans, Gender Variant and Intersex Students *Joanne Cassar*
Chapter 7	Metacognitive Awareness Outcomes Associated with Undergraduate Service Learning *Jennifer Katz and Dimitri Wing-Paul*
Chapter 8	Do Balance Intervention Programs Develop Aiming and Catching Skills in Primary Education Students? *Josune Rodríguez-Negro, Aitor Iturricastillo and Javier Yanci*

Progress in Education. Volume 51

Chapter 1	A Meta-Analysis of Internet Addiction Prevalence Among Iranian Youth from 2006-2016 *Ali Kheradmand, Bibi Eshrat Zamani and Nassim Hedayati*

Contents of Earlier Volumes

Chapter 2 Differences in On-Campus and Off-Campus Relationships between First-Time in College (FTIC) Community College Students: A National Investigation
Ericka Landry, John R. Slate, George W. Moore, Frederick C. Lunenburg and Wally Barnes

Chapter 3 Motivation and Anxiety in Foreign Language Acquisition
Krzysztof Polok and Iwona Szalbót

Chapter 4 Geology Teaching: A Practical Fieldwork Activity for High Education
Gina Pereira Correia

Chapter 5 "Premium" English: Internationalized and Diversified Qualifactions as Implied in Russian Higher Education
Hanzhou Pang

Chapter 6 Differences in Postsecondary Enrollment Rates by the Economic Status of Texas Public High School Graduates: A Statewide, Multiyear Analysis
Deshonta Holmes, John R. Slate, George W. Moore, Frederick C. Lunenburg and Wally Barnes

Chapter 7 Preservice Teachers' Reflections with Technology
Sarah Huisman and Natalie Kane

Chapter 8 Doing Interpersonal Assessment as a Way of Teaching Interpersonal Assessment
Matthew M. Yalch

Progress in Education. Volume 50

Chapter 1 The Universe of Learning:
Non-Equilibrium and Connectivity
Patricio Pacheco H.

Chapter 2 Special Needs and Inclusive Education from the
Perspective of Teachers: What Attitudinal Factors
Make up an Inclusive Mindset?
Henrike Kopmann and Horst Zeinz

Chapter 3 Learning Outside of the Classroom:
An Analysis of the Motivations and Benefits of
Older Adults' Cooperative Learning in Taiwan
Y. H. Lee and J. Y. Lu

Chapter 4 Evaluations of Resource Distribution Practices in
the Classroom: A Further Validation of Resource
Exchange Theory
Clara Sabbagh

Chapter 5 Mobile Learning: A New Step to
Engage Trainee Teachers
Sónia Cruz

Chapter 6 Postgraduate Supervision in the Recruitment of
Academics in a Sample of South African
Universities: Practices and Effects
Maura Mbunyuza-de Heer Menlah

Chapter 7	Psychology of Language Acquisition and Learning: Learning a Language across Engineering Matters at the University Level *Ruzan Galstyan-Sargsyan,* *Modesto Pérez-Sánchez* *and P. Amparo López-Jiménez*
Chapter 8	Problematic Texting and Self-Reported Executive Function in College Students *F. R. Ferraro, A. Hahn and D. Gulenchyn*

INDEX

A

academic freedom, 12, 14, 16, 17, 32
academic learning, x, 79, 84, 85, 93
academic performance, 85, 88, 109
academic settings, 82, 87
academic success, xii, 111, 144, 162
academic-vocational decisions, 136
acquired knowledge, x, 80, 82, 83, 87, 88, 93, 94, 96, 98, 101, 102
action planning, ix, 40, 51, 63, 64
adjunct faculty, 7, 10
administration, 3, 18, 19, 73
administrators, 18, 37, 171, 211
American Association of University Professors, 7, 16, 32, 33
Arizona State University, 15
attention, viii, xi, 10, 12, 16, 23, 24, 29, 69, 98, 120, 143, 149, 157, 162, 170, 171, 188, 198, 203, 211
autonomy, 86, 130, 147, 149

B

bachillerato, 117, 118, 130, 131, 132, 134
best practice, v, vii, x, 79, 80, 81, 82, 84, 85, 87, 88, 92, 93, 96, 98, 99, 101, 103, 108, 109
biology, 13, 19
blended-learning methodology (b-learning), 125
Bradley Foundation, 16

C

charter schools, 4, 5
children, 6, 30, 34, 54, 55, 57, 60, 66, 74, 75, 104, 145, 146, 158, 159, 161, 162, 170
classes, 44, 50, 108, 118, 135, 155, 158, 160, 168, 170
classification, 166
classroom, viii, xii, 2, 5, 11, 14, 15, 16, 18, 23, 24, 27, 28, 29, 30, 31, 41, 43, 46, 55, 58, 59, 63, 64, 65, 75, 84, 85, 88, 93, 106, 123, 126, 133, 167, 168, 169, 170,

Index

171, 172, 173, 174, 175, 176, 177, 178, 179, 180, 181, 183, 184, 200
cognition, viii, 1, 21, 24, 27, 107, 202, 203, 204
cognitive, v, vii, viii, x, xii, 1, 2, 20, 21, 22, 23, 24, 27, 28, 29, 30, 33, 36, 38, 54, 79, 80, 81, 83, 85, 86, 87, 88, 89, 90, 94, 102, 103, 104, 107, 109, 111, 185, 186, 187, 188, 189, 190, 191, 192, 193, 194, 195, 196, 197, 198, 199, 200, 202, 203
cognitive load, vii, viii, x, xii, 23, 80, 83, 86, 87, 88, 89, 94, 103, 107, 109, 111, 185, 186, 189, 191, 192, 193, 194, 195, 196, 197, 198, 199, 200, 202, 203
cognitive load imposition, vii, x, 80, 86, 87, 88, 94
cognitive load theory, xii, 23, 83, 88, 89, 103, 107, 109, 185, 186, 189, 198
cognitive myths, 24, 29
cognitive overload, viii, xiii, 27, 186
cognitive process, xiii, 27, 33, 186, 187, 188, 190
cognitive science, v, viii, 1, 2, 20, 21, 22, 23, 24, 28, 29, 30, 202, 203
cognitive theory, 27, 104
collaboration, 43, 44, 55, 59, 66, 116
collaborative action research, v, vii, ix, 39, 40, 41, 42, 43, 44, 46, 47, 52, 53, 66, 67, 68, 69, 70, 71, 73, 74, 76
collaborative class culture, 57, 67, 70
collectivism, 106, 111
college students, 139, 148
colleges, 3, 6, 10, 17, 18, 19, 20, 21, 36
colleges of education, 3, 17, 18, 19, 20, 21
collegial, 43, 44, 49, 53, 54, 55, 56, 60, 61, 64, 67, 68, 70
community building, ix, 40
content knowledge, 18, 24, 177
co-operative group, ix, 40, 59, 70
cooperative learning, 58, 116
creationism, 12, 13, 33, 35
crisis, v, 1, 2, 34

critical friends group discussions, ix, 40
critical thinking, x, 40, 124
cultural capital, vi, viii, xi, 143, 144, 145, 146, 147, 149, 150, 151, 155, 156, 157, 158, 159, 160, 161, 164, 165, 166
cultural knowledge, 144, 145, 159
culture, 29, 44, 57, 58, 59, 61, 63, 66, 67, 70, 72, 73, 138, 144, 145, 146, 148, 159, 163, 213, 216

D

debt, 6, 7, 32, 37
decision-making process, vii, xi, 113, 124, 125
deep learning, 22, 43, 81, 106, 110, 173
deVos, Betsy 4, 5, 34
digital study tools, x, 40
digital technologies, 177, 179, 180
drop-out, vi, xi, 113, 114, 125
dual coding, 27, 28, 33

E

economics, 6, 14
economy, 5, 6
education research, 111, 201, 206
education system, 5, 31, 114, 115, 118, 140, 146
educational administration, 18, 74
educational attainment, 13, 150, 151, 152, 155, 156
educational psychology, 18, 19, 36, 37, 75, 89, 105, 106, 107, 108, 109, 110, 111, 112, 115, 124, 131, 200, 201, 202, 203
educational research, viii, xiii, 2, 21, 28, 35, 36, 46, 70, 104, 106, 107, 110, 139, 166, 182, 183, 203, 205, 208, 209, 210, 215, 216, 217, 218, 219
educational system, 4, 31

element interactivity, viii, xii, 108, 111, 185, 186, 188, 189, 190, 191, 192, 193, 194, 195, 196, 198, 199, 201, 202
elementary school, 76, 170, 183
European higher education systems, 118
evolution, 11, 12, 13, 32, 35, 181
experiments, 5, 23
extraneous cognitive load, 186, 189, 193, 194, 195, 197, 198

F

faculty, 3, 7, 10, 15, 17, 21, 37, 52, 75
faith, 47, 48, 50
financial, 5, 15, 123, 158
flexibility, 168, 173, 175, 202
funding, vii, viii, 1, 3, 4, 5, 6, 7, 8, 9, 11, 14, 15, 16, 17, 30, 36, 48, 68, 115, 130

G

George Mason University, 14
germane cognitive load, 111, 186, 189, 191, 196, 197, 198, 202
Goldwater Institute, 16
groupthink, 18, 20

H

high school, 13, 120, 125, 130, 132, 133, 134, 203
higher education, 3, 6, 7, 9, 11, 14, 15, 17, 18, 20, 21, 32, 34, 35, 36, 37, 38, 104, 117, 118, 138, 141, 159, 181
Hong Kong, vi, viii, xi, 143, 144, 148, 149, 150, 151, 154, 157, 158, 159, 161, 162, 163, 164, 165

I

identification, 148, 163
identity, 21, 46, 73, 162
increase the motivation of students, xi, 113
indoctrination, 17, 18, 19, 20, 33
institution, 2, 9, 10, 38, 49, 68, 121, 123
intelligent design, 12, 13
internet, 16, 120, 126, 133, 138, 147, 152, 153, 156, 160, 162, 172, 180
intrinsic cognitive load, 186, 189, 191, 192, 193, 196, 198
intrinsic motivation, 89, 91

J

junior secondary school students, vi, viii, xi, 143, 144, 149, 164, 165

K

K-12, vii, viii, 1, 2, 3, 6, 11, 13, 14, 22, 29, 30, 31, 35, 73, 181
K-12 education, 3, 6, 11, 13
K-12 schools, 2, 30
Koch brothers, 14
Koch family foundations, 16
Koch Foundation, 15, 34
Koch Institute, 17, 37

L

learning environment, 58, 62, 77, 138, 171, 175, 178, 181, 182
learning outcomes, x, 20, 22, 29, 40, 46, 52, 67, 68, 110
learning process, 23, 59, 114, 116, 123, 168
learning styles, 21, 22, 23, 27, 33, 34, 35, 36, 120, 127

learning task, viii, xii, 88, 98, 185, 186, 187, 191, 196, 199
linguistic, 27, 28, 162, 163
long term memory, 23, 27, 189, 194, 202

M

manipulatives, 28, 38
mathematical knowledge, 198
mathematical procedures, 195, 196
mathematics, vii, x, 34, 80, 82, 84, 85, 86, 88, 92, 93, 94, 95, 98, 103, 106, 109, 182, 200, 201
mathematics learning, v, vii, x, 80, 82, 86, 88, 93, 95, 98, 103
memory, 23, 24, 25, 26, 27, 28, 33, 34, 187, 188, 189, 194, 199, 200, 202
mentoring, 40, 47, 51, 54, 64, 65, 67, 68, 70, 73, 121
Michigan, 4, 5, 8, 34, 110
Milton Friedman, 4
Moodle platform students, 125
motivation, xi, 16, 67, 70, 82, 91, 98, 103, 104, 107, 108, 113, 116, 199, 203, 204
music, xi, 144, 145, 147, 149, 152, 153, 154, 156, 157, 158, 159, 160, 162, 163, 164, 165
musical preferences, vi, viii, xi, 143, 144, 145, 147, 149, 150, 153, 157, 158, 159, 160, 162
myths, viii, 1, 21, 22, 24, 29, 30

N

non-technicist, 43, 70

O

objectivity, vi, viii, xiii, 205, 206, 207, 208, 212, 214, 216, 218, 219

obligatory secondary education, 116, 117, 128, 129
operational lines, 194, 195, 197
operations, 26, 47, 194, 198
oposiciones, 119
optimal achievement best, x, 80, 90, 92, 93, 94, 95, 97, 99, 100, 102
optimal functioning, 80, 81, 82, 85, 89, 90, 91, 93, 101
Organization for Economic Co-Operation and Development (OCDE), 115, 124, 125, 140

P

parental support, 158, 164, 165
parents, xi, 4, 6, 12, 32, 63, 132, 143, 145, 146, 147, 151, 155, 156, 157, 159, 161
pedagogical approaches, xii, 167, 170
pedagogy, x, 40, 50, 52, 68, 70, 74, 184
peer feedback, ix, 40, 56
peer relationship, 67, 85, 106
personal development, 114, 136
personal experience, x, 80, 82, 84, 85, 87, 89, 93, 94, 96, 98, 101, 102
personal functioning, x, 80, 82, 85, 86, 87, 93, 95, 96, 98, 100, 101, 102
personal values, 212, 215
personality, 58, 63, 67, 201
per-student funding, 6, 7
physical education, 18, 74, 175
physics, 201, 202, 203
positive psychology, x, 79, 80, 105, 106, 108, 110
primary school, 73, 149, 181
private schools, 4, 33, 130
problem solving, xii, 25, 89, 109, 185, 186, 187, 189, 190, 194, 196, 197 198, 199, 200, 202
professional development, ix, 39, 40, 43, 45, 68, 69, 71, 74, 75, 76, 77

psychology, x, 19, 79, 80, 104, 105, 106, 108, 110, 124, 131, 135, 136, 183, 200
public education, 3, 5, 31, 36
public schools, 3, 4, 5, 11, 12, 33, 35, 36

R

race, 4, 21, 165, 214
reading, 18, 27, 28, 54, 58, 70, 166, 193, 203
realistic achievement best, x, 80, 90, 92, 93, 94, 95, 97, 99
release, ix, 40, 46, 47, 48, 50, 51, 54, 60, 65, 67, 68, 70
research-based, 4, 19, 81

S

salaries, 3, 15, 30
scaffolding, 22, 28, 60
schema, 84, 88, 94, , 189, 190, 191, 194, 195, 196, 197, 198, 202
schemata, 211
school choice, 4, 5, 35
school performance, xii, 49, 144
schooling, 31, 81, 84, 100, 105
science, iv, vi, viii, xii, xiii, 1, 2, 11, 12, 13, 18, 20, 21, 22, 23, 24, 28, 29, 30, 32, 33, 35, 36, 49, 59, 66, 67, 74, 105, 107, 108, 109, 130, 140, 165, 175, 181, 185, 186, 187, 189, 190, 191, 192, 197, 198, 199, 200, 201, 202, 203, 204, 205, 206, 208, 211,212, 215, 217, 218
scope, x, 11, 80, 84, 85, 116
secondary education, 108, 116, 117, 118, 119, 120, 121, 124, 128, 135, 169
secondary school students, vii, viii, xi, 104, 113, 124, 143, 144, 149, 164, 165
secondary schools, xi, 111, 120, 124, 144, 148, 150, 151, 165, 182
secondary students, 122, 163, 169, 191

Secretary of Education, 4
social class, 145, 146, 214
social environment, 114, 122
social inequality, 145, 146
social influence, 108, 149
social media, viii, 1, 15, 16, 19, 20, 22, 147, 181
social relationships, 84, 85
social sciences, 75, 117, 130, 134, 207, 212, 216
social status, xii, 144, 145, 147, 157, 158, 159, 161, 162
socio-cultural, 21, 29, 41, 68
socio-economic status, 20, 104, 145
standards, 4, 12, 32, 34, 57, 170
strike, 30, 157
student achievement, x, 33, 40, 43, 70, 76, 106
student debt, 6, 7, 32
student motivation, 66, 199
student relationships, ix, 40, 104, 109
student well-being., x, 40
student-centred learning, 172
student-led inquiry, 67, 70
subjective well-being, 85, 89
subjectivity, vi, viii, xiii, 205, 206, 207, 208, 210, 211, 212, 214, 215, 216, 217, 218, 219
success criteria, ix, 40, 55, 56, 66, 67, 70
support materials, 122

T

teacher education, 29, 35, 74, 77
teacher inquiry, ix, 39, 40, 41
teacher preparation, 18, 27
teacher strikes, 3, 34
teacher training, xi, 113
teacher-educators, v, vii, ix, 39, 40, 47, 50, 59, 66, 68, 69, 71
teacher-student relationship, 91, 104, 109

technology, xii, 22, 28, 110, 116, 121, 139, 141, 144, 147, 157, 160, 162, 165, 167, 169, 174, 175, 176, 180, 181, 183, 217
tenure, 7, 10, 14
testing, 4, 13, 26, 34, 172, 180, 182, 201, 202
thought processes, 28, 194, 199
threats, v, vii, viii, 1, 2, 11, 14, 16, 29, 30, 139
to practice, xi, 70, 113
transformational, ix, 39, 59, 63, 67, 82
tuition, 6, 7, 8, 9, 37, 38
Turning Point USA, 16, 17
tutoring, 115, 121, 125, 132
types of cognitive load, viii, xii, 185, 186, 189, 198

U

university, vi, vii, viii, xi, 1, 2, 3, 6, 7, 10, 11, 12, 14, 15, 16, 17, 18, 19, 20, 22, 29, 30, 31, 71, 73, 76, 77, 79, 104, 108, 110, 112, 113, 114, 116, 117, 118, 120, 121, 122, 123, 124, 125, 131, 133, 136, 137, 138, 139, 140, 141, 143, 149, 162, 164, 165, 167, 168, 175, 184, 185, 199, 200, 201, 203, 204, 205, 217, 218, 219
university presidents, 15, 17

V

virtual education, vi, 113, 114
virtues, x, 40, 44, 63, 64, 65, 66, 67, 70
visual, 27, 28, 33, 45, 77, 163
vocabulary, 203, 213
vocational training, 117, 118, 119, 121, 122, 124, 125, 138, 139
voucher systems, 4, 35

Playing to Learn: Experiences in Virtual Biology Environments

Authors: Johnnie Wycliffe and Frank Muwanga-Zake (University of New England, Australia)

Series: Education in a Competitive and Globalizing World

Book Description: This book outlines theoretical frameworks that apply in playing to learn and characteristics of games that are important in encouraging learning. Regrettably however, abstract and boring systems, as well as watching television, replace such enjoyment in learning. Fortunately, robust virtual environments and realities ease the rigour in designing and in executing educational play.

Softcover ISBN: 978-1-60876-862-2
Retail Price: $69

Education of Children in Nursing Homes: Characteristics and Challenges

Editor: Monica Huxley

Series: Progress in Education

Book Description: This book examines the characteristics of children in nursing homes; how such children are referred for and receive education; the challenges in delivering services to these children; and monitoring of the education of children in nursing homes.

Hardcover ISBN: 978-1-63463-268-3
Retail Price: $140

Progress in Education. Volume 54

Editor: Roberta V. Nata

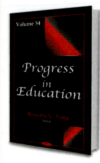

Series: Progress in Education

Book Description: In this collection, the authors open with the proposition that all teachers must ensure students develop their metacognitive skills, reflect deeply about thinking, and learn how to apply concepts, while continually encouraging students to question their understanding and ask questions to gain clarity.

Hardcover ISBN: 978-1-53614-425-3
Retail Price: $250

Progress in Education. Volume 56

Editors: Roberta V. Nata

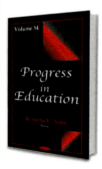

Series: Progress in Education

Book Description: In the opening chapter of *Progress in Education. Volume 56*, the authors set out to stimulate thought on teaching practices, also on how these can be innovated by using (but not only) current technologies, and on the conditions necessary for their effective delivering.

Hardcover ISBN: 978-1-53614-553-3
Retail Price: $250